Study Guide

Introduction to
Logic

Study Guide

Packard ■ Faulconer

Introduction to

Logic

Larry W. Draper

Brigham Young University

D. VAN NOSTRAND COMPANY
New York Cincinnati Toronto London Melbourne

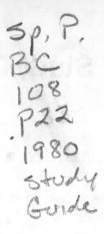

D. Van Nostrand Company Regional Offices:
New York   Cincinnati

D. Van Nostrand Company International Offices:
London   Toronto   Melbourne

Copyright © 1980 by Litton Educational Publishing, Inc.

ISBN: 0-442-25706-6

Published by D. Van Nostrand Company
135 West 50th Street, New York, N.Y. 10020

10 9 8 7 6 5 4 3 2 1

Preface

This Study Guide supplements Packard/Faulconer's Introduction to Logic by providing: (1) restatements of text materials in language familiar to the student; (2) additional comments on some materials covered in the text, and (3) exercises with solutions. The Guide is most effective when used in close conjunction with the textbook.

In logic, as in other disciplines, restating a difficult principle in simpler terms serves to make the concept clearer. This procedure is used throughout the Study Guide. We suggest that students first read a section of the textbook and then its counterpart section in the Study Guide and that they do the exercises and solutions, which comprise a useful self-testing device. Answers are of little value when the student does not understand how they are reached. The solutions and final answers show how the answers were obtained.

The Guide offers additional comments on areas that are covered briefly in the text. Students who find these explanations unnecessary and simplistic should move on to the next section.

Reading the text and Study Guide should help students in a number of ways: (1) to refine intuitions about whether an argument is good or bad: a skill useful in dealing with complex arguments and issues; (2) to develop a number of reasoning skills: recognizing, analyzing, and criticizing arguments in academic papers, political speeches, newspapers, and elsewhere; (3) to become better able to analyze and discuss issues and to present views reasonably and convincingly, and (4) to be exposed to philosophical thinking.

I wish to express sincere thanks to Dennis J. Packard and James E. Faulconer for their excellent suggestions and criticisms of the manuscript. I also wish to thank Jan Chambers and Laurie Bonner for clerical assistance.

L.W.D.

Contents

Study Guide

Introduction to
Logic

Introduction

The four types of logic we shall examine deal with different kinds of sentences. Consider, for example, the following four sentences:

If Mary wins then John celebrates.
Either all things have order or some don't.
If John hunts, then someone eats something.
The father of any boy is the father of a male.

The first of these sentences is relatively simple. If we wish to analyze it, we simply need to know the meaning of the connector words <u>if</u> and <u>then</u> and we can determine the truth or falsity of the entire sentence, given the truth or falsity of the smaller sentences, <u>Mary wins</u> and <u>John celebrates</u>. The logic in which we deal with these connector words, such as <u>if . . . then</u>, <u>and</u> and <u>or</u>, and the relationships they establish between sentences which they connect is called truth-functional logic.

In sentences of the second type, we must deal not only with connector words, but with words such as <u>all</u> and <u>some</u> which establish quantities. This type of logic is called monadic logic.

In the third sentence we deal not only with truth-functional connector words and quantities, but with names, like <u>John</u>, and verbs, like <u>hunts</u> and <u>eats</u>. This type of logic we call quantificational logic.

The fourth type of logic, quantificational logic with identity and operations, employs what are called operations, such as <u>the father of</u>, and the notion of identity ("="), or <u>is</u>. Without the tools for analyzing sentences containing operations, such as <u>Jan is my wife</u>, we are unable to deal with many natural kinds of arguments. We cannot even deal with simple claims such as <u>The holder of any ticket will be admitted</u> if we cannot analyze the phrase <u>the holder of</u>. Thus, without adding operations and identity to our repertoire, we would be too limited to give an analysis of many simple arguments.

1 Informal Logic

KEY TERMS

The following are definitions of the most important terms or concepts used in this chapter. Each of the key terms is also discussed in the chapter. Refer to these definitions often until their meanings are completely clear.

Argument A series of statements in which the conclusion is said to follow from the assumptions.

Assumption One of the components of an argument, assumptions are sentences that when true are said to support the conclusion.

Conclusion One of the components of an argument, a conclusion is the sentence that follows the assumptions.

Validity An argument is valid if and only if there is no argument of its form (called a counterexample) that has true assumptions and a false conclusion.

Counterexample An argument that has true assumptions and a false conclusion is a counterexample of itself or of some argument of the same form.

Implicit Assumption An assumption which is intended as part of an argument but is not stated in the argument.

Fallacy A bad argument. Fallacies are bad arguments because either they are invalid or they require the use of false implicit assumptions.

ARGUMENTS

Arguments are made up of assumptions and a conclusion. Sometimes arguments have only one assumption or they may have no assumptions but only a conclusion. Arguments come in many forms. Several different forms of argument are illustrated in the text. For example, 'A', 'B' so, 'C' in which 'A', 'B', and 'C' are sentences. If 'Smith is a Democrat' stands for 'A', 'All Democrats are honest' stands for 'B', and

1

'Smith is honest' stands for 'C', then we can state this simple argument in many different ways. One example would be as follows: 'A'. Hence, since 'B', 'C'. Or in English: Smith is a Democrat. Hence, since all Democrats are honest, Smith is honest. Another form for this argument could be the following: Because 'A' and 'B', 'C'. Or: Because Smith is a Democrat and all Democrats are honest, Smith is honest.

So you see that although an argument can be stated in many different ways, each form is basically the same, usually having one or more assumption and a conclusion. Pick up any newspaper or magazine and try to pick out arguments by identifying the assumptions and the conclusion.

CHARACTERIZING VALIDITY

How often do we hear people agreeing with an argument say: "That's true." But in logic, statements and not arguments are true or false. When most people say that an argument is true they mean either that the conclusion follows from the assumptions or that the argument is valid. But in everyday language the word valid usually has a different meaning than in logic. Valid has a very precise meaning in logic, since arguments and not statements are considered valid or invalid. The text discusses what valid means and arrives at a definition of valid that is applicable to any argument regardless of its complexity.

What do we mean by the "form" of an argument? Take for example the argument: If Richard Nixon is the president of the United States, then Pat Nixon is the first lady. Richard Nixon is not the president of the United States, so Pat Nixon is not the first lady. What is the form of this argument? This argument has the same form as: If Billy paints, then Kathryn cries. Billy does not paint, so Kathryn does not cry. Do you see how the form is the same? If we change Richard Nixon is the president of the United States to Billy paints and Pat Nixon is the first lady to Kathryn cries then you should see that the forms are the same. Some students find that by using boxes, circles, and other geometric figures they can visualize the form of an argument better. Here is an example:

If [Billy paints,] then (Kathryn cries.)

[Billy paints.]

So, (Kathryn cries.)

We can use boxes and circles to help us visualize any argument that has this form as well as many other arguments having different forms. Can you think of another argument which has the same form as the one above? All you need to do is fill in the boxes and circles with any statement.

If [＿＿＿＿＿＿＿＿] then (＿＿＿＿＿＿)

[＿＿＿＿＿＿＿＿＿＿＿]

So (＿＿＿＿＿＿)

2

Let us use the argument about Richard and Pat Nixon mentioned earlier. Does this argument have the same form as the previous one?

If [Richard Nixon is the president of the United States,] then (Pat Nixon is the first lady.)

[Richard Nixon is not the president of the United States.]

So, (Pat Nixon is not the first lady.)

Are the forms the same? Not quite! In the second box we have Richard Nixon is not the president of the United States. In the first box we have Richard Nixon is the president of the United States. This is a minor but significant difference. If we adopt the method of using geometric shapes to represent statements, we must be consistent. Whatever statement appears in the first box must also appear unchanged in the second box. The contents of the circle must also conform to this basic guideline. Is the statement in the first circle the same as the statement in the second circle? Again, not quite. So again we must be consistent or the method will be of no use. What can we do to remedy this situation? Can we change the statements in the boxes and circles so that they are consistent without at the same time also changing the meaning of the argument? Since the contents of the first box says that Richard Nixon is the president of the United States and the contents of the second box says that he is not the president, we simply need to change the second box to match the first. We can do this by placing it is not the case that in front of the second box, as follows:

It is not the case that [Richard Nixon is the president of the United States.]

Does this mean the same as Richard Nixon is not the president of the United States? Yes, it does. We can do the same for the statement about Pat Nixon. Instead of Pat Nixon is not the first lady we can write:

It is not the case that (Pat Nixon is the first lady.)

Now the contents of the circle is the same in both cases. So we can rewrite the argument as follows:

If [Richard Nixon is the president of the United States,] then (Pat Nixon is the first lady.)

3

It is not the case that | Richard Nixon is the president of the United States. |

So, it is not the case that (Pat Nixon is the first lady.)

Is the statement which appears in the first box the same as the statement in the second box? Are the statements in both circles also consistent?

Now can we construct an argument about Billy and Kathryn having the same form? Fill in the boxes and circles with the appropriate statements.

If | Billy paints, | then (Kathryn cries.)

It is not the case that | Billy paints. |

So, it is not the case that (Kathryn cries.)

Let's try this method using an exercise from the text. In Exercises 1.3.1 of the text we are given the argument: If Lincoln helped solve the slave problem, then Lincoln was a great humanitarian. Lincoln was a great humanitarian. Therefore, Lincoln helped solve the slave problem. Can you put circles and boxes around the appropriate statements so that the form of the argument is apparent?

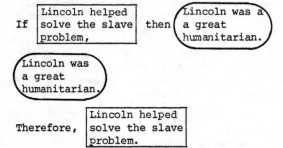

If | Lincoln helped solve the slave problem, | then (Lincoln was a a great humanitarian.)

(Lincoln was a great humanitarian.)

Therefore, | Lincoln helped solve the slave problem. |

The next argument in Exercise 1.3.1 has this form:

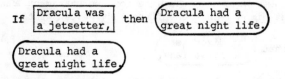

If | Dracula was a jetsetter, | then (Dracula had a great night life.)

(Dracula had a great night life.)

Therefore, _____ .

In the text the conclusion is left blank. How should we fill in the blank? If this argument has the same form as the preceding one, then the conclusion should be the same as the statement in the first box. The statement in the box was <u>Dracula was a jetsetter</u>. The conclusion, therefore, should be as follows:

4

Therefore, | Dracula was a jetsetter. |

Hopefully, you will recognize that all four arguments in Exercises 1.3.1 have the same form.

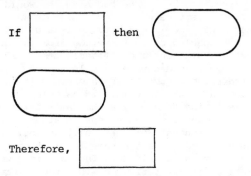

If [ ] then ( )

( )

Therefore, [ ]

Only the statements in the boxes and circles are different. The form is the same. As you work through Exercises 1.3 you should realize by placing boxes and circles around the appropriate statements the form of the argument becomes easier to visualize. This method will also help you to determine which statements in the arguments should be used to fill in the blanks.

COUNTEREXAMPLES

Since the purpose of Exercises 1.3 is to give you practice in determining validity, the first argument in each exercise will probably be the most difficult to judge correctly. The subsequent arguments in each series, however, should become progressively easier as you become more familiar with this method for determining validity. Consider, for example, the last argument of Exercise 1.3.1: If _____, then Lincoln was married. _____. Therefore, Lincoln was a polygamist. If we use boxes and circles we obtain the following form:

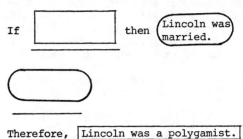

If [ ] then (Lincoln was married.)
_____

( )
_____

Therefore, | Lincoln was a polygamist. |

First we fill in the blanks at the same time filling in the empty box and circle. Now we have:

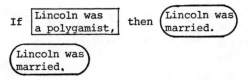

If [Lincoln was a polygamist,] then (Lincoln was married.)
(Lincoln was married.)

5

Therefore, | Lincoln was a polygamist.

This argument obviously has true assumptions. That is, the statement If Lincoln was a polygamist then Lincoln was married is true. We know that Lincoln was not a polygamist, but if he had been, he would have been married. So the statement is true even though Lincoln was not a polygamist. Also the statement Lincoln was married is true. So the assumptions are true. But the conclusion is false. So from the definition of validity we know that this argument about Lincoln's marital status is invalid. Thus this argument is a counterexample to the arguments that precede it. Since the three arguments which preceed it have the exact same form, we know that all three are invalid as well.

Essentially, Exercise 1.3 is trying to show you that an intuition about an argument is often faulty. Many times we accept an argument as valid, although if we examined the argument more carefully we could construct a counterexample—an argument that has the same form but obviously has true assumptions and a false conclusion. Thus at times we accept the validity of arguments before we really consider their form. Although all the statements (the two assumptions and the conclusion in the first argument of Exercises 1.3.1 are true, the argument is still invalid because the form of the argument is such that the assumptions could be true and the conclusion false. Indeed, the argument involving Lincoln and polygamy represents this type of argument.

The text contains enough practice exrecises to help you become familiar with a variety of different forms. You will encounter arguments which contain assumptions and conclusions of the following forms:

If □ then ○ ; If □ , ○ ; □ if ○ ; Either □ or ○ ;

□ or ○ ; Both □ and ○ ; □ and ○ ; Neither □ nor ○ ;

and It is not the case that □ . Just as before the boxes and circles

can be filled in with simple phrases or sentences.

Exercises 1.4 in the text illustrate arguments having a different form than those in Exercises 1.3. In these exercises you will attempt to determine the validity or invalidity of arguments composed of sentences that contain quantifiers. The words all and some are quantifiers. Although these arguments have a form different from those we discussed previously, we can still use the same principles to determine their validity. We can also apply the method of using geometric shapes to determine the form of these arguments.

In these exercises you will encounter arguments made up of sentences of the following forms:

All □ are ○ ; All □ ○ ; No □ are ○ ; No □ ○ ;

Some □ are ○ ; Some □ ○ ; Some □ are not ○ ; Some □ do

not ○ . As before, the boxes and circles should be filled in with noun,

adjective, or verb phrases. These arguments are frequently called syllogisms. In Chapter 3, we refer to them as monadic arguments.

Let us try to answer one exercise—Exercise 1.4.30:

6

All [Communists] are (Socialists)

Some /liberals\ are not (Socialists.)

Therefore, some /liberals\ are not [Communists.]

Here we need a third geometric figure to differentiate the noun
liberals from the others. In this example we have chosen a triangle but
any figure which can be drawn around the word or phrase other than a box
or circle would do just as well. Remember we only use these geometric
figures to make the form more obvious. So our form in this exercise is:

All ☐ are ◯ . Some △ are not ◯ . Therefore, some △ are not

☐ . Can you complete the other two arguments in this exercise? It is

not difficult; just put the correct words in the correct box, circle,
or triangle.

All [marines] are (courageous.) Some /soldiers\ are not (courageous.)

Therefore, some /soldiers\ are not [marines.] Can you determine whether
the argument is valid or not? Finish the exercise and check to see if
the assumptions are true and the conclusion is false.

Exercises 1.5 take us a step further in complexity. These type of
arguments are called quantificational arguments and quantificational
arguments with identity. Although these arguments have forms which are
more difficult to recognize at first, we can still employ the method of
using geometric shapes to make the form more apparent. Let us try Exercise 1.5.70:

For every individual, if that individual is [a Nazi,] then

/Patton attacks\ that individual. Therefore, if

(the best friend of Hitler) is [a Nazi,] then /Patton attacks\

(the best friend of Hitler.)

Now that we can visualize the form of the argument, it should be
easy to complete the next argument and check for validity. We do this
just as we did before, checking to see if the assumptions are true and
the conclusion is false.

For every individual, if that individual is [part of the world,]

then /God created\ that individual. Therefore, if

(the misery in the world) is [part of the world,] then /God created\

(the misery in the world.)

Is this argument valid? Unfortunately, the truth or falsity of the
assumptions and conclusion are not obvious. Indeed, much philosophizing
has been done on this very question. Actually, the argument is valid.
It means the same as saying that all

7

$\square$'s are $\triangle$'s. So, if $\bigcirc$ is a $\square$, then $\bigcirc$ is a $\triangle$. But if you doubt the validity of the argument, the burden is on you to provide a counterexample.

IMPLICIT ASSUMPTIONS

Consider the following argument: If a solar generator is turning, then the sun is shining. So, if a solar generator is turning, then it is not midnight. Is this argument valid? It is not, but it could easily be made valid if we added the absurdly obvious statement: If the sun is shining, then it is not midnight. Many times in everyday life we state or hear arguments of this type. It is certainly not always necessary to include obvious statements in your arguments to convince others of the validity of your claims. These statements are called implicit assumptions and are used more often than we realize.

We can use implicit assumptions to criticize some arguments that we do not accept. Consider the following argument: If Jimmy Carter runs for president, then I will vote Republican. If Ted Kennedy runs for president, then I will vote Republican. So, I will vote Republican.

Is the argument a good one? The answer may partly depend on your political persuasion, but the argument has a missing assumption which must be included to make it valid. Without the missing assumption the argument could have true assumptions and a false conclusion. Suppose for example that neither Carter nor Kennedy runs for president but instead J. Edgar Hoover's son runs on the Democratic ticket. Also suppose I had worked for the FBI for twenty years and had become good friends with Hoover's son. So I vote for Hoover on the Democratic ticket. I did not vote Republican; therefore the conclusion is false. The assumptions can still be true, however, because if Carter runs on the Democratic ticket, then Hoover cannot. Hoover is my only choice for the Democratic party, so I vote Republican. If Kennedy runs on the Democratic ticket, then again Hoover, my only choice among Democrats, cannot run, so I vote Republican. Since the assumptions can be true and the conclusion false, the argument is invalid. What implicit assumption will make this argument valid? Consider the following statement:

Either Jimmy Carter will run for president
or Ted Kennedy will run for president.

If we add this implicit assumption to the argument, then it becomes valid. But is this assumption necessarily true? Although it may be possible for either Carter or Kennedy to run for president, it does not have to be so. If J. Edgar Hoover's son ran for president on the Democratic ticket, then obviously the implicit assumption would be false. Thus, we have used an implicit assumption to criticize the argument.

Exercises 1.5 in the text will give you practice in finding implicit assumptions. Let us do Exercise 1.5.2:

Capital punishment is unjust because it is irreversible punishment.

What implicit assumption must be added to make the argument valid? Could we add the statement: Irreversible punishment is unjust? Now the argument reads:

8

Capital punishment is irreversible punishment. Irreversible punishment is unjust. So capital punishment is unjust.

Now the argument is valid, but is the added implicit assumption plausible? Is it true? Is irreversible punishment unjust? Can a twenty-year sentence served in the federal penitentiary be reversed? Can the twenty years be given back? No. So a twenty-year sentence in prison cannot be reversed. But is a twenty-year sentence considered unjust? No. Judges hand down decisions like this every day and few opponents of capital punishment complain. The point is that our added implicit assumption is not plausible. Most punishment is irreversible. So if we accept the implicit assumption, we must also accept the fact that most punishment is unjust. Few if any would accept this position, so we have shown that by adding an implausible implicit assumption, the original argument is fallacious. In other words, in order for the original argument to be valid, we must accept an assumption which is obviously not true.

Many arguments can be criticized in this way. In fact, in the text you are asked to criticize several philosophical papers by adding an implausible implicit assumption to those arguments that you think are fallacious.

FALLACIES

In the text you are shown examples of the most common fallacies and the names which are commonly used in reference to them. These fallacies are bad arguments because they require implausible implicit assumptions to make them valid. Among the fallacies discussed in the text, there are also several other fallacies which are caused by ambiguity.

AMBIGUITY

As the text points out there are three kinds of ambiguity which cause fallacies.

1. Structural Ambiguity
2. Word Ambiguity
3. Functional Ambiguity

Structural ambituity is caused when a phrase is constructed in such a way that it could be interpreted to mean two different things. Consider Exercise 1.9.3: John wore the coat out. So, John went out.

The assumption is ambiguous because its construction allows us to interpret its meaning in two ways:

1. John wore out the coat.

Here wore out means that the coat was worn for such a long time that it began to have holes in it. Hence, it wore out.

2. John wore the coat out.

In this case the coat was put on before going out to eat or out on the town.

If we interpret the sentence the second way, the argument in the exercise is valid. But if we interpret the sentence in the first way, a fallacy is committed. This fallacy is called amphiboly. When a sentence or phrase is structurally ambiguous, then the fallacy of amphiboly is likely to result.

Another kind of fallacy that occurs because of ambiguity is called equivocation. Equivocation is caused by word ambiguity. Consider Exercise 1.9.7: He works in an aluminum plant. Therefore, some plants are aluminum. In this argument we have the problem of word ambiguity. The word plant can mean either a factory where things are manufactured or it can mean a green garden plant. Some might contend that it is not ambiguous given the context of the sentence. What about the following sentence? Lyle took pictures of the rubber plant. The context of this sentence gives you no clue as to whether Lyle took pictures of a factory where they make car tires or the greenery in my mother's living room. Exercise 1.9.7 commits a fallacy of equivocation because in the assumption the word plant means factory, but in the conclusion plant means an oxygen-producing green foliage. Any time a word is used to mean one thing in the assumption(s) and a different thing in the conclusion, a fallacy of equivocation is committed.

There is another kind of ambiguity which causes equivocation. This third kind of ambiguity is sometimes called functional ambiguity. Consider the following sentence: Dr. Seuss is a baby doctor. In this sentence Dr. Seuss could be either a pediatrician or he could be an exceptionally bright baby who made it through medical school. Another example might be: Butch Cassidy was a cat burglar. Cat burglar is functionally ambiguous. We know what a cat is and we know what a burglar is, but when we put them together we are not sure what the combination means. Does it mean a burglar who steals cats or a burglar who sneaks around at night climbing tall buildings like a cat? Fortunately, the meaning of most functionally ambiguous phrases is clear from the context of the sentence or by convention. Some functionally ambiguous phrases, however, such as the phrase 'Chinese spy' used in the text, are not clear from the context. Thus we cannot know if the conclusion follows from the assumptions because we do not know what is intended by the assumption. As before, fallacy of equivocation occurs when the meaning of the phrase in the assumption(s) is different from the meaning of the phrase in the conclusion.

CONVINCINGNESS

In philosophy most discussion is either for or against a previously stated position or opinion. For example, one philosopher may argue his opinion that men are free to choose all their actions. Another philosopher may disagree, stating that men are victims of their enrivonment and cannot freely choose but only react to stimuli. In this case the second philosopher might try to convince us that the first philosopher's conclusion—that men are free agents—is faulty.

In the text we learn that there are four different things of which arguments can try to convince us:

1. Arguments for the conclusion.
2. Arguments for the assumption.
3. Arguments against the assumption.
4. Arguments against the conclusion.

10

These kinds of arguments were carefully explained in the text and several principles of convincingness were subsequently formulated.

Principle 1: An argument is not convincing for the conclusion if the assumptions are not plausible.

Principle 2: An argument is not convincing for the assumptions if the conclusion is not plausible.

Principle 3: An argument is not convincing against the assumptions if the conclusion is plausible.

Principle 4: An argument is not convincing against the conclusion if the assumptions are plausible.

These principles can help you to construct arguments which will support your viewpoint as you critique those views which you do not agree with. For example, if you hear an argument which agrees with your opinions on some matter and you wish to convince your friend of the argument's validity, then according to Principle 1 the assumptions must be plausible if you are to give a convincing argument for the conclusion.

To have a convincing argument for the assumptions (Principle 2) you must have a plausible conclusion. And to convincingly argue against the assumptions (Principle 3) you must have an implausible conclusion. So whatever you agree with or disagree with, to successfully convince your fellow philosophers of your point of view you will have to use arguments. The arguments you use will be of these four types and to argue convincingly you will need to use the appropriate principle of convincingness. These principles of convincingness are very useful and should be referred to repeatedly in criticizing the philosophical papers in the text.

DEFINITIONS

At the beginning of Chapter 1 the text goes through a long process of trying to determine a good definition of validity. Why was this process so difficult? To be adequate, a good definition must encompass two general principles:

1. A definition should agree with the cases we are certain about.
2. A definition should help us decide the cases we are not certain about.

Suppose we had a definition of an armadillo. Suppose also we were shown a cage that contained one thousand animals and were asked to pick out the armadillos. Using our definition, we can be sure that 571 of the animals in the pen are armadillos, but we are not certain that the other 429 animals in the pen are not armadillos. Would we then say that our definition was a good one? Probably not, since 42 percent of the cases could not be determined from our definition. The definition does not help us decide the cases we are not certain about. We need to find a better definition to help us determine which animals among those we are uncertain about could be legitimately classified as armadillos.

Thus, every definition can be scrutinized from two points of view. If it stands up to our scrutiny, then it is a good definition. A better definition may be needed, however, if a case not previously considered is brought to our attention. Although the current definition does not help us deal with this case, it may be possible to adjust the definition in such a way that will enable us to consider new cases of this sort.

Truth-Functional Logic

KEY TERMS

Syntax The rules that tell us how to make meaningful expressions. Syntax is much like English grammar. It gives us rules for taking single words and putting them together to construct sentences that make sense.

Symbolic Notation A system which allows us to make long complicated English sentences into short, less complex expressions so they can be handled quickly and with ease.

Semantics A set of rules that tell us the truth value of a formula if we are given the truth values of the atomic formulae, that is, the formulae which make up the formula.

Formulae Sentences or expressions that have been formed according to the rules of syntax. Sometimes they are called schema or WFF (Well-Formed Formula).

Argument A set of formulae in which the conclusion is said to follow from the assumption(s). There must be one conclusion and usually there are at least two and often many more than two assumptions. For some arguments there are no assumptions.

Assumptions One of the components of an argument. The conclusion follows from the assumptions. Assumptions are frequently called premises. The words can be interchanged. Temporary assumptions are special kinds of assumptions and are handled differently.

Conclusion One of the components of an argument. There is only one conclusion for every argument. The conclusion is said to "follow" from the assumption(s). The conclusion is said to be true if it follows from the assumption(s) and the assumptions are true.

Validity An argument is valid if we cannot (according to the rules of semantics) have a situation in which the assumptions (all the assumptions) are true and the conclusion is false.

Counterexample A possible situation in which the assumptions are true and the conclusion is false. If such a possible situation exists for

12

a particular argument, then that argument is valid. Thus, if a counterexample can be given, that is proof that the argument is invalid.

Intuitive An intuitive understanding is an understanding that comes from commonsense, everyday experiences or instincts.

Formal A formal method is one that proceeds by a set of established rules. For example, constructing formulae by using the F rules is a formal approach. Also, constructing proofs by the P rules is a formal approach.

Proof A formal procedure which "shows" that one formula follows from a set of other formulae. This is demonstrated by a series of numbered lines.

SYNTAX

ENGLISH SYNTAX

The first notion we will discuss is syntax. Syntax is that part of logic which tells us what counts as a meaningful expression. Grammar does the same thing in English. Without grammar we might have sentences like "fur the brown has dog" rather than "the dog has brown fur." Similarly, the rules of syntax tell us how to make sentences or formulae in the language of logic.

The text begins its discussion of syntax by giving you a set of sentences and a set of connecting words. From these and the rules of syntax other sentences were constructed. For example, it is not the case that Good is pleasant or evil exists is constructed from the sentences evil exists and Good is pleasant. We will discuss syntax in much the same way If you feel you understand the text and its explanation, you might want to skip this section of the Study Guide.

Consider a set of sentences different from those in the text: Cows moo; Dogs bark; Birds sing; Fish breathe; Lions meow. We will call these sentences atomic formulae and from these formulae we will construct other formulae. We also need the following connecting words: and; or; if-then; if and only if; it is not the case that. With these and the rules of syntax we can construct formulae. So let us state the rules as they appear in the text.

Rules of Syntax

An expression is an atomic formulae or a formula if and only if it is so according to the following rules:

F Rule 1. The following are atomic formula and, hence, formulae:
Cows moo; Dogs bark; Fish breathe; Lions meow.
F Rule 2. If U and W are formulae, then so are the following: U and W; It is not the case that U; U or W, If U then W; U if and only if W.

(Note that in F Rule 2 U and W can stand for any formulae, whether atomic or not.)

13

These rules of syntax are identical to those in the text except for two small changes. First, the atomic formulae are different. Second, these rules are called F rules. They are called F rules to differentiate them from S rules, P rules, and T rules. The F stands for formula. The F should help you remember that it is a rule of syntax rather than some other rule. The reason to differentiate between rules should become clear when we get to the rules of semantics, the rules of proof, and the rules of translation. So, F Rule 1 means Rule of Syntax 1.

As was shown in the text, we can construct many formulae or sentences using this new set of atomic formulae and the rules of syntax. For instance: It is not the case that fish breathe. Birds sing and dogs bark. Cows moo or lions meow. These are all formulae by the rules of syntax. The important thing is not whether fish breathe or evil exists but how the atomic formulae are constructed using the connecting words and the rules of syntax. We could make up another set of atomic formulae from which sentences or formulae could be constructed in the same way. Syntax is concerned with how sentences are put together, not what the sentences mean or whether they are true or not.

You should also notice that F Rule 2 designates where the connecting word must appear in the sentence. For example, and fish breathe dogs bark is not a formula because the connecting word and appears at the beginning of the sentence instead of between the two atomic formulae. If birds sing also is not considered a formulae because the If-then connecting words have not been used properly according to F Rule 2.

EXERCISES 2.1

For each of the following sentences, determine which are formulae and which are not. Provide a formal construction for those sentences that are formulae. For those that are not formulae, explain why they are not and what changes could be made to make them formulae. For example:

If it is not the case that fish breathe, then cows moo if and only if lions meow.

This example is a formula, so we must construct it formally as follows:

1. fish breathe is a formulae by F Rule 1.
2. it is not the case that fish breathe is a formula by line 1 and F Rule 2.
3. cows moo is a formula by F Rule 1.
4. lions meow is a formula by F Rule 1.
5. If it is not the case that fish breathe, then cows moo is a formula by lines 2 and 3 and F Rule 2.
6. If it is not the case that fish breathe, then cows moo if and only if lions meow is a formula by lines 4 and 5 and F Rule 2.

This constitutes a formal construction in which each line is justified by one of the two F rules. Let us try another example:

Dogs bark if and only if lions don't meow.

This example is not a formula and thus we must explain why it is not and how to make it a formula. Dogs bark if and only if lions don't meow is

14

not a formula because <u>lions don't meow</u> is not a formula, nor is it an atomic formula, so the whole sentence is not a formula. We need to change <u>lions don't meow</u> to <u>it is not the case that lions meow</u>. Having changed this sentence into a formula, we could construct it formally.

1. Dogs bark and fish breathe if and only if birds sing.
2. The lions meow or birds sing.
3. Cows moo and fish sing.
4. If fish breathe or dogs bark, then it is not the case that lions meow.
5. It is not the case that it is not the case that cows moo.
6. No fish breathe.
7. Cows moo if and only if fish don't breathe.
8. If and only if cows moo and lions meow.
9. Fish breathe or it is not the case that dogs bark if and only if lions meow, then it is not the case that birds sing.
10. Birds sing or cows moo if and only if lions don't meow and dogs bark.

SYMBOLIC NOTATION

Symbolic notation is intended to shorten the sentences (formulae) we use so that they can be handled more quickly, helping us to get more done. As was pointed out in the text, mathematics would be next to impossible if we did not use symbols. Likewise, without musical notes on a bass clef it would be hard to learn the tuba. The notes on the page symbolize the pitch or sound of the instrument.

We represent each atomic formula in English with a lower case English letter. For formulae (complex formulae) we use upper case English letters. Again, this is done to shorten or abbreviate the English formulae (sentences) in order to make them easier to work with. For example, if <u>dogs bark</u> is designated <u>d</u> and <u>lions meow</u> is designed <u>m</u>, then the sentence <u>dogs bark</u> or <u>lions meow</u> can be symbolized <u>d</u> or <u>m</u>.

The connecting words are also symbolized as follows: A dot $(S \cdot U)$ for <u>and</u>. A hyphen $(- S)$ for <u>it is not the case that</u>. A "hook" $(S \supset U)$ for <u>if-then</u>. A small v $(S \lor U)$ for <u>or</u>. Three parallel lines $(S \equiv U)$ for <u>if and only if</u>. So <u>d</u> or <u>m</u> becomes <u>d v m</u>.

Now let us restate the rules of syntax for symbolic notation.

Rules of Syntax

An expression is an <u>atomic formula</u> or a <u>formula</u> if and only if it is so according to the following rules:

F Rule 1. The following are atomic formulae and, hence, formulae.
    p, q, r, s, t, ...
F Rule 2. If <u>U</u> and <u>W</u> are formulae, then so are the following:
    $(U \cdot W)$, $- U$, $(U \lor W)$, $(U \supset W)$, $(U \equiv W)$.

The following exercises are similar to those given in the text for this section.

EXERCISES 2.2

Determine which of the following are formulae according to the rules of syntax for symbolic notation. For those that are not formulae explain why not and what is needed to make them formulae. Provide a formal construction for those sentences that are formulae. For example: $(p \lor \cdot q)$.

This is not a formula. Two connecting symbols placed together are not allowed by the rules of syntax for symbolic notation. To make it a formula we only need to remove one of the connecting symbols.

1. $\lor q \equiv s$
2. $(p \supset q) \lor r$
3. $(s \supset t) \equiv -p$
4. $(q \cdot r) \equiv \lor$
5. $(p \lor q) \supset$
6. $-(\equiv t \cdot r)$
7. $-p((p \supset r)(s \lor t))$
8. $s \lor t$
9. $p \equiv (q r \lor t)$
10. $-(((p \supset r) \cdot (t \lor q)) \equiv (-s \lor -p)$

AMBIGUITY AND PARENTHESES

"Baked potato or fries and steak for $2.95." This sentence taken from the text shows how certain sentences are ambiguous. Does it mean baked potato for $2.95 or fries and steak for $2.95? If it means the former, then we would all stop ordering baked potatoes at our favorite restaurant. Obviously, it means either baked potato and steak for $2.95 or fries and steak for $2.95. The meaning of many sentences like this one are clear only because of the context of the sentence. The context in this case tells us that the sentence does not mean baked potato for $2.95. But the meaning of many sentences is not clear simply given their contexts. In logic we cannot afford ambiguity of this type. We must be more precise and not depend on the context of the sentence to supply an unambiguous meaning. This is particularly true when we are working with formulae in symbolic notation. So we need a method of eliminating the ambiguities that might arise when working with symbols.

We will use parentheses to eliminate problems of this sort. This means that the formula $p \cdot q \lor r$ is not correctly written because we have no way of knowing precisely what is meant. This formula should be written $(p \cdot q) \lor r$ or $p \cdot (q \lor r)$ whichever meaning is intended. The text also mentions another method of eliminating ambiguity that is equally precise but does not require excessive use of parentheses. In the text we are given the following hierarchy of inclusiveness for connecting words:

1. if and only if;
2. if-then;
3. and and or;
4. it is not the case that.

So if you see a formula like the following: $p \equiv r \supset s \cdot t$, it means $p \equiv (r \supset (s \cdot t))$. Without these conventions $p \equiv r \supset s \cdot t$ could mean $(p \equiv r \supset (s \cdot t))$ or $p \equiv (r \supset s) \cdot t$ or $p \equiv r \supset (s \cdot t)$ or any number of possible arrangements of parentheses. Notice that the third level of inclusiveness has two connectors <u>and</u> and <u>or</u>. This is because they carry equal force and, consequently, parentheses are absolutely necessary in formulae that contain these two connectors alone.

SEMANTICS

TRUTH AND FALSITY

One of the things we are concerned with in logic is the truth or falsity of formulae. Is a formula true or is it false? Arguments consist of a series of formulae. The truth or falsity of these formulae in various possible situations determines whether an argument is valid or not. Since we ultimately want to know if an argument is valid or not, we must first determine whether the formulae in the argument are true or false in various possible situations.

A word on atomic and complex formulae may be appropriate at this point. There are two kinds of formulae:

1. atomic formulae.
2. formulae.

The second kind (formulae) could be called complex formulae because complex formulae are always made up of atomic formulae. We use the word formulae to designate either atomic formulae or complex formulae but atomic formulae do not designate both kinds.

Since few arguments consist of only atomic formulae, we need to be able to determine the truth or falsity of complex formulae. Even if there were many arguments which consisted of entirely atomic formulae, they would be of little interest because they would not require rules of semantics to determine their truth value. The following is an example of an argument of this type:

1. Dogs bark.
2. Lions meow.
So, fish breathe.

To determine the validity of this argument, we do not need rules of semantics. We only need to know the truth value of each of the three formulae in various possible situations. This is because all three formulae are atomic formulae and we can designate the truth values of these atomic formulae so as to determine validity. But consider another argument:

1. If dogs bark, then birds sing.
2. Dogs bark.
So, birds sing.

The same reasoning as before would apply to this argument except for the first formula. Formula 1 is not an atomic formula and if we simply designate the truth values of the atomic formulae, we will still not know the truth value of Formula 1. If we say that <u>Birds sing</u> is false and that <u>Dogs bark</u> is true, then we know the truth value of Formula 2 and the truth value of the conclusion formula, but we still do not know the truth value of Formula 1. Formula 1 gives us problems.

What do we do with Formula 1? Up to this point we had no way of determining the truth value of a complex formula.

This is where we need the rules of semantics. They provide us with rules that allow us to determine the truth values of complex formulae if we have the truth values of the constituent atomic formulae. The text has given you an intuitive explanation for the <u>and</u> and <u>or</u> connecting words. The <u>not</u> connector is too simple to need extensive explanation. This leaves the <u>if-then</u> and the <u>if and only if</u> connectors which we will not explain. An intuitive explanation has been given in the text for the <u>if-then</u> connector. This should be sufficient. If you understand the <u>if-then</u> connector, then the <u>if and only if</u> should give you no problems. <u>If and only if</u> (that is, $(S \equiv U)$), is equivalent to two <u>if-then</u> formulae connected with an <u>and</u> (that is, $(S \supset U) \cdot (U \supset S)$). If you do not intuitively understand these explanations, then just accept them for now and use them. The intuitive understanding will come with time.

It is absolutely necessary that you memorize these rules. Every student I have known who did poorly in logic did so because he or she had failed to memorize these rules.

Rules of Semantics

According to any possible situation and for any formulae $\underline{U}$ and $\underline{W}$:

S Rule 1. $\underline{(U \cdot W)}$ is true if both $\underline{U}$ and $\underline{W}$ are true. In the other cases, it is false.

S Rule 2. $\underline{-U}$ is true if $\underline{U}$ is false and false if $\underline{U}$ is true.

S Rule 3. $\underline{(U \vee W)}$ is false if both $\underline{U}$ and $\underline{W}$ are false. In the other cases, it is true.

S Rule 4. $\underline{(U \supset W)}$ is false if $\underline{U}$ is true and $\underline{W}$ is false. In the other cases, it is true.

S Rule 5. $\underline{(U \equiv W)}$ is true if $\underline{U}$ and $\underline{W}$ have the same truth value (in other words, if either both are true or both are false). In other cases, it is false.

These rules have been stated exactly as in the text except for the addition of the letter S in front of each rule. The S stands for <u>semantics</u> and is intended to help you remember that these are rules of semantics and not rules of syntax or any other rules. So, S Rule 1 stands for Rule of Semantics 1.

In order to help you to remember these rules, consider what we call truth tables. Truth tables are like math tables. They show every possible situation a formula can have. A possible situation is a case in which a formula has a truth value. For example, suppose we are given the formula <u>fish breathe</u>. <u>Fish breathe</u> is true or it is false. There are only two possible situations. The more atomic formula or formulae there are in an argument the greater the number of situations that are possible. <u>Fish breathe and lions meow</u> is constructed from two atomic formulae and so there are four possible cases or situations of true and false. Let us look at each possible situation.

Situation 1. Both <u>fish breathe</u> and <u>lions meow</u> can be true.
Situation 2. <u>Fish breathe</u> can be true and <u>lions meow</u> can be false.
Situation 3. <u>Fish breathe</u> can be false and <u>lions meow</u> can be true.
Situation 4. Both <u>fish breathe</u> and <u>lions meow</u> can be false.

So there are four possible situations of true and false for this formula. Let us symbolize the formula to make our discussion shorter. Suppose that _fish breathe_ is symbolized p and _lions meow_ is symbolized q. From the above information we can construct a table like this:

	p · q
Situation 1.	T T
Situation 2.	T F
Situation 3.	F T
Situation 4.	F F

Now, according to S Rule 1, Situation 1 is true and all other situations are false. So to complete the table we add a T for Situation 1 **and** an F for all others. Now the table is complete and looks like this:

	p · q
Situation 1.	T T T
Situation 2.	T F F
Situation 3.	F F T
Situation 4.	F F F

By studying the table we notice only one case or situation that has a T under the connector symbol. In this case (that is, (p · q)) the T appears under the dot. This tells us that (p · q) is only true in one case, Situation 1, and that (p · q) is false in all other cases. Given this information we could write a rule of semantics for the _and_ connecting word. So you see from a truth table we could devise a rule of semantics. You will remember, however, that the truth table was obtained from the rule of semantics. So, if we have one we can obtain or construct the other and if we have the other, then we can obtain the first. Therefore, you should learn one or the other or both. Can you give rules of semantics for the other truth tables?

EXERCISES 2.3

From the following truth tables give a rule of semantics which will encompass the information contained in them. Do not refer to the already stated S rules. Afterwards, compare your rule with the S rules as previously stated (that is, S Rule 2 through 5).

1. - p
   F T
   T F

2. p v q
   T T T
   T T F
   F T T
   F F F

3. p ⊃ q
   F T T
   T F F
   F T T
   F T F

4. p ≡ q
   T T T
   T F T
   F F T
   T F T

Suppose we had the complex formula r ≡ ((s v t) ⊃ (p · q)). If r was true, s was true, t was true, p was true, and q was false, then what would be the truth value of the whole formula? First put the T's and F's in the appropriate places as follows:

19

$r \equiv ((s \lor t) \supset (p \cdot q)$

$\underline{T} \quad \underline{T} \quad \underline{T} \quad \quad \underline{T} \quad \underline{F}$

This formula could be looked at as an <u>if and only if</u> formula with
<u>r</u> on the left side of the <u>if and only if</u> and the $((s \lor t) \supset (p \supset q))$
on the right side of the <u>if and only if</u>. We could look at it like a
$(\underline{S} \equiv \underline{U})$ formula with the <u>r</u> substituted for <u>S</u> and $((s \lor t) \supset (p \supset q)$ substituted for <u>U</u>.

We know the truth value of the left side; it is true. So, in order
to find the truth value of the whole formula, we have to find the truth
value of $((s \lor t) \supset (p \supset q))$. But $((s \lor t) \supset (p \supset q)$ is just like an
<u>if-then</u> formula. If we substitute $(s \lor t)$ for <u>S</u> and $(p \supset q)$ for <u>U</u>, then
we have a simple $\underline{S} \supset \underline{U}$ formula.

$$(\underbrace{s \lor t}_{S}) \underset{\supset}{\supset} (\underbrace{p \supset q}_{U})$$

So we need to find out what the truth value of $(s \lor t)$ is and then treat
it as if it were <u>S</u> in the <u>if-then</u> formula $(\underline{S} \supset \underline{U})$. Then we need to find
the truth value of $(p \supset q)$ and treat it as if it were <u>U</u> in the $(\underline{S} \supset \underline{U})$
formula.

Therefore, we first need to know the truth values of $(s \lor t)$ and
$(p \supset q)$. We know what the atomic formulae are, so we find that $p \supset q$
is false because <u>p</u> is true and <u>q</u> is false. We can illustrate the solution to this problem by placing a line below each atomic formula and
each connector as follows:

p ⊃ q

— — —

Next we place a <u>T</u> on the line beneath the <u>p</u> and an <u>F</u> on the line beneath
the <u>q</u>.

p ⊃ q

<u>T</u> _ <u>F</u>

S Rule 4 tells us that $p \supset q$ is false, so we place an <u>F</u> on the line beneath the "hook" symbol.

p ⊃ q

<u>T</u> <u>F</u> <u>F</u>

Lastly, we check off the formulae which were used to obtain the final
truth value.

p ⊃ q

<u>T</u> <u>F</u> <u>F</u>

We will not need to consider the formulae that are checked off. Only
the truth values that are not checked off are considered in determining
further truth values. Next we need to determine a truth value for
$(s \lor t)$. <u>s</u> is true and <u>t</u> is false. So $s \lor t$ is true by S Rule 3.

(s ∨ t)

<u>T</u> <u>T</u> <u>F</u>

Now we consider both these formulae together:

$$((s \lor t) \supset (p \supset q))$$
$$\underline{T}\ \underline{T}\ \underline{F} \qquad \underline{T}\ \underline{F}\ \underline{F}$$
$$\checkmark \quad \checkmark \qquad \checkmark \quad \checkmark$$

We consider only those underlined truth values that do not have check marks. The result is shown as follows:

$$((s \lor t) \supset (p \supset q))$$
$$\underline{T} \qquad\qquad \underline{F}$$

If we consider this formula as if it were an $\underline{S \supset U}$ formula, then we would find it to have the truth value false by S Rule 4. This could be represented as follows:

$$((s \lor t) \supset (p \supset q))$$
$$\underline{T} \quad F \quad F$$
$$\checkmark \qquad \checkmark$$

Since we know the right side of the formula is false and the left side was said to be true, our formula would look like this:

$$r \equiv ((s \lor t) \supset (p \supset q))$$
$$\underline{T} - \quad \underline{T}\ \underline{T}\ \underline{F} \quad F \quad \underline{T}\ \underline{F}\ \underline{F}$$
$$\checkmark \quad \checkmark\ \checkmark\ \checkmark \quad \checkmark\ \checkmark\ \checkmark$$

By S Rule 5 we know the whole formula is false. Our final step looks like this:

$$r \equiv ((s \lor t) \supset (p \supset q)$$
$$\underline{T}\ F \quad \underline{T}\ \underline{T}\ \underline{F} \quad F \quad \underline{T}\ \underline{F}\ \underline{F}$$
$$\checkmark \quad \checkmark\ \checkmark\ \checkmark \quad \checkmark \quad \checkmark\ \checkmark\ \checkmark$$

The final truth value can be circled if you like. You will notice that all the atomic formulae and all the connecting symbols have a truth value below them and they are all checked off except for one. The one that is not checked off is the truth value of the entire formula.

Let us look at a few more examples and then try some exercises.

EXERCISES 2.4

Given the possible situation—p:F, q:T, r:F, s:T—find the truth value of the following:

Example: $(p \supset r) \equiv - s$
$$F\ T\ F \quad \textcircled{F}\ F\ T$$
$$\checkmark\ \checkmark\ \checkmark \qquad - \checkmark$$

Example: $- ((r \equiv s) \cdot - (p \supset q))$
$$\textcircled{T} \quad F\ F\ T \quad F\ F \quad F\ T\ T$$
$$\checkmark\ \checkmark\ \checkmark \quad \checkmark\ \checkmark \quad \checkmark\ \checkmark\ \checkmark$$

1. $- - (p \supset s) \supset (r \cdot t)$
2. $(((s \supset t) \supset r) \supset p) \supset q)$

21

3. $(q \supset (r \supset (s \supset (t \supset r))))$
4. $(p \cdot r) \lor (s \supset t) \equiv (- q \lor - s)$
5. $((p \equiv q) \lor (s \equiv r)) \supset (t \equiv r)$
6. $((s \supset t) \supset (q \supset p)) \supset (- r \supset - t)$
7. $((t \equiv s) \supset (s \equiv v)) \supset (t \equiv r)$
8. $(p \supset (q \supset (p \supset q))) \equiv (((s \supset t) \supset s) \supset t)$
9. $(r \equiv - s) \equiv ((- p \equiv - q) \lor - t)$
10. $- - - (p \lor - - q) \equiv (- - s \cdot - t)$

VALIDITY

What is a valid argument? You have been given the definition of a valid argument in the text. It may be easier, however, to understand validity by first talking about invalidity. The definition says an argument is valid if and only if there is no possible situation, called a counterexample, according to which the assumptions are true and the conclusion is false. If we can show a counterexample (that is, a possible situation in which the assumptions are true and the conclusion is false), then we have shown the argument to be invalid. If a counterexample cannot be given, then the argument is valid.

Consider the following common argument:

If it is raining outside, then the streets are wet.
It is raining outside.
_____

So, the streets are wet.

To make the discussion easier, let us translate the argument into symbolic notation:

r: it is raining outside.
w: the streets are wet.

Using the above key, the argument looks like this:

$r \supset w$
r
_____

So, w

To check validity, we need to determine whether there is a possible situation in which the assumptions are true and the conclusion is false. $r \supset w$ and r are the assumptions and w is the conclusion. This argument has only four possible situations:

Situation A: 1. $r \supset w$
$$\frac{T}{\nearrow} \frac{T}{=} \frac{T}{\nearrow}$$

2. r
$$\frac{T}{=}$$

So, w
$$\frac{T}{=}$$

Situation B: 1. $r \supset w$
$$\frac{T}{\nearrow} \frac{F}{=} \frac{F}{\nearrow}$$

2. r
$\underline{T}$

So, w
$\underline{\underline{F}}$

Situation C: 1. r ⊃ w

$$\underset{\sqrt{}}{F} \underset{=}{T} \underset{\sqrt{}}{F}$$

2. r
$\underline{\underline{F}}$

So, w
$\underline{\underline{T}}$

Situation D: 1. r ⊃ w

$$\underset{\sqrt{}}{F} \underset{=}{T} \underset{\sqrt{}}{F}$$

2. r
$\underline{\underline{F}}$

So, w
$\underline{\underline{F}}$

Do any of the situations have true assumptions and a false conclusion? Situations A and C have true conclusions, so we will ignore them for now. Remember we are looking for a situation that has true assumptions and a false conclusion. Situations B and D are the only ones left to consider. They both have false conclusions, so we will examine them further. Do they have true assumptions? In Situation B assumption 2 is true but assumption 1 is false. So, since both assumptions are not true (that is, one is true and the other is false) Situation B does not satisfy our criterion. We will ignore Situation B for now and continue our search. Again, do you remember what we are looking for? We need to find a situation in which the assumptions are true and the conclusion is false. If we find this situation, then the argument is not valid (that is, invalid). If we do not find such a situation, then the argument is valid.

You must understand that if a situation can be found for which you have true assumptions and a false conclusion, then the argument is invalid. Suppose for a moment that Situation B satisfied the criterion for an invalid argument (that is, it was found to give true assumptions and a false conclusion). Suppose also that Situations A, C, and D did not fit the criterion (that is, they did not have true assumptions and a false conclusion). In this case you may be inclined to think that Situations A, C, and D make the argument valid and Situation B does not. But this is not so. If one situation is found which satisfies the criterion, then it does not matter what the other situations are like. Suppose we had a complex argument consisting of sixty-four possible situations. If only one of those sixty-four situations gave true assumptions and a false conclusion, then the argument would be invalid. Even though there were sixty-three situations in which the criterion was not met, the argument would still be invalid just because of the one situation in which the criterion was met. Situations are not valid or invalid. Only arguments are valid or invalid. Now let us return to our example. We have considered Situations A, B, and C. Only D is left to consider. Situation D gives a false conclusion. But does D give true assumptions? Assumption 1 is true but assumption 2 is false. So Situation

D like the others does not satisfy the criterion for an invalid argument. Of the four possible situations, none gave true assumptions and a false conclusion. So we conclude that the argument:

r ⊃ w
r
_____

So, w

is a valid argument. Now let us look at another argument that is slightly different:

1. If it is raining outside, then the streets are wet.
2. The streets are wet.
_____

So, it is raining outside.

In symbolic notation we have:

1. r ⊃ w
2. w
_____

So, r

This argument also has only four possible situations. Let us consider all of them as before:

Situation A: 1. r ⊃ w
                      T T T
                      √ = √

           2. w
                    T
_____

           So, r
                      T

Situation B: 1. r ⊃ w
                      T F F
                      √ = √

           2. w
                    F
_____

           So, r
                      T

Situation C: 1. r ⊃ w
                      F T T
                      √ = √

            2. w
                    T
_____

           So, r
                      F

Situation D:　　1. $r \supset w$
$$\frac{F}{7} \overset{T}{=} \frac{F}{7}$$

2. w
$$\underset{=}{F}$$

So, r
$$\underset{=}{F}$$

Now, Situations A and B both have a true conclusion, so we need not consider them. Situations C and D both have a false conclusion, so we need
to consider these situations. Let us look at Situation D first. Assumption 1 and assumption 2 are true. Thus, there is a situation in which
the assumptions are true and the conclusion is false. Therefore, the
argument:

r $\supset$ w
w

So, r

is invalid. Note that we need not have all four situations fulfill the
criterion. To make the argument invalid only one situation is required
to give true assumptions and a false conclusion. If we had a more complex argument (one that is made up of several atomic formulae rather
than just the two atomic formulae of the previous two examples) there
would be six, eight, sixteen or even more situations possible. No matter how many possible situations an argument can have, it still only
requires one situation with true assumptions and a false conclusion to
make the argument invalid. Could there be another explanation for the
streets being wet? Yes. The street sweeper might have caused the streets
to be wet instead of the rain.

Remember it does not really matter whether or not it is raining or
whether or not the streets are wet. The important thing to remember is
the form of the argument. If the argument or any argument with the same
form could have true assumptions and a false conclusion, then the argument is invalid.

PROOFS

Because we will use examples of proofs in our explanation of how
proofs are done, we first need to know what a proof is and the rules
which govern the construction of proofs.

A proof is a series of statements (formulae) which show the validity of an argument and the statements in the proof must all be justified either by a given assumption or one of the rules of proof.

Rules of Proof

P Rule 1. A line is justified if it, together with preceding lines
in force, constitutes one of the valid arguments listed.
P Rule 2. A line is justified (as a temporary assumption, abbre-
viated TAS) if we indent it.
P Rule 3. A line, U $\supset$ S, is justified (by If-then introduction) if
U is the temporary assumption beginning an indentation
and S is the last line of the indentation.

25

The P in P Rule stands for <u>proof</u>. P Rule 1 stands for Rule of Proof
The use of these rules will become clear as you encounter examples of
proofs done in the text as well as in the Study Guide.

When we first discussed validity it was in the context of counterexamples and invalidity. We adopted a negative approach in our discussion. Rather than demonstrate the validity of an argument, we showed
that the argument was not invalid. There is another approach to the
concept of validity that we will not develop—proofs. Proofs show validity without the use of counterexamples. This is very important because in the more advanced stages of logic, counterexamples become
much more difficult to find. You might search for hours for a possible
situation to show a counterexample when one does not exist. If a counterexample does not exist, then the argument is valid. This is where
proofs are useful.

VALID ARGUMENTS USED FOR PROOFS

To do proofs you were given several valid arguments called "Basic
Valid Arguments." Each connector has an introduction instance and an
elimination instance. Let us look at these arguments intuitively.

The 'And' Arguments

<u>And Introduction (&I)</u>

S, U; so, S·U

If <u>S</u> is true and <u>U</u> is true, then putting <u>S</u> and <u>U</u> together with an
'and' connector gives us:

S · U
<u>T</u>   <u>T</u>

By S Rule 1 we know that the only case in which an <u>and</u> formula is
true (that is, <u>S · U</u>) is the case in which both formulae that make
up the <u>and</u> formula are true. In our cases both <u>S</u> and <u>U</u> are true;
so, <u>S · U</u> is also true.

S · U
<u>T T T</u>
√ = √

Therefore, given the following:

Assumption 1.   S
Assumption 2.   U
                   ⎯⎯⎯⎯
So, the conclusion. S · U

then there is no possible situation in which the premises could be
true and the conclusion false. In a sense we have added or "introduced" an <u>and</u> connector. Thus, this argument is called And Introduction.

And Elimination (&E)

    S · U; so, S
    S · U; so, U

If (S · U) is a true statement, then we know from S Rule 1 that there is only one situation that makes an and formula true. This is the situation in which both S and U are true. If they were both not true, then (S · U) would not be true. But since (S · U) is true, then the formula S is also true. And since (S · U) is true, then the formula U is also true. Therefore, if we have the following argument:

Assumption 1.   (S · U)
                          ──────────

So, the conclusion.   S

then there is no possible situation in which the assumptions are true and the conclusion false. Therefore, the argument is valid and we have gone from a (S · U) formula to an S formula. In a sense we have eliminated the and in (S · U). Thus, this argument is called And Elimination.

The 'Or' Arguments

Or Introduction (OrI)

    S
    ──────────
    so, S v U

If we know S is true then we can "introduce" an or without changing the truth of S. Remember that S Rule 3 tells us that only one side of an or statement need be true for the whole formula to be true. If we know S is true, then it does not matter whether the other side of the or statement is true or false. U can be true or false and the whole formula (S v U) is still true.

    S v U   S v U
    T T T   T T F
    $\overline{7} = \overline{7}$ $\overline{7} = \overline{7}$

We have introduced an or to something we know is true. Thus, we call this argument Or Introduction.

Or Elimination (OrE)

This argument requires three assumptions:

Assumption 1.   P v R
Assumption 2.   P ⊃ Q
Assumption 3.   R ⊃ Q

So, the conclusion.   Q

Stated in English this formula has the form:

Either you will have cake or ice cream for dessert.
If you have cake, then you will get a stomachache.
If you have ice cream, then you will get a stomachache.

So, you will get a stomachache.

Regardless of what you choose for dessert, you will get a stomachache.
If (P v R) is true, then either P is true or R is true or both are true. And since P is true, then Q is true. If R is true, then Q is true. So, regardless of which is true, P or R, the conclusion Q is still obtained. In a sense we have eliminated the or formula. Thus, we call this argument Or Elimination.

The 'Not' Arguments

Not Introduction (NI)

S ⊃ (U · - U)
so, - S

Remember, for an argument to be valid, it cannot be the case that the conclusion is false and the assumptions are true. In the case of Not Introduction there is only one assumption, namely S ⊃ (U · - U). Now, we know from previous examples that (U · - U) is always false. If you do not believe so, then try all the possible situations. If U is true then we have:

U · - U
T F F T
7 = 7 7

If U is false, then we have:

U · - U
F F T F
7 = 7 7

So regardless of whether U is true or false, U · - U is always false.
Now, if a counterexample is possible we first need to determine whether the argument has true premises. In this argument we only need to be concerned with one premise because there are no others, namely, S ⊃ (U · - U). But (U · - U) is always false. Since the only way for S ⊃ (U · - U) to be true is for S to be false, we have:

S ⊃ (U · - U)
F T   F
√ =   7

If S were true, then S ⊃ (U · - U) would be false. So S must be false. But if S is false, then we know that - S has to be true. Hence, we conclude - S is true.
Stated another way, if we know S ⊃ (U · - U) is true, then S must be false. And is S is false, then we can conclude that - S is true. In a sense we "introduce" a not. Thus this argument is called Not Introduction.

28

Not Elimination (NE)

A demonstration of Not Elimination proceeds in much the same way as Not Introduction:

-S ⊃ (U · -U)

If we know that -S ⊃ (U · -U) is true, then -S must be false because (U · -U) is always false. So if -S is false, then S must be true, and hence we can conclude S from -S ⊃ (U · -U). In a sense we have eliminated a not. Thus, this argument is called Not Elimination.

It may be helpful to remind you here that S and U stand for any formula. This means that q ⊃ (w · -w), so, -q is a valid argument if q and w are formulae. As another example consider:

(p ⊃ q) ⊃ ((s v t) · -(s v t)) so, -(p ⊃ q)

This is a valid argument (according to Not Introduction) as long as (p ⊃ q) and (s v t) are formulae. When we substitute (p ⊃ q) for S and (s v t) for U we have S ⊃ (U · -U); so, -S which is an instance of Not Introduction. It is very important to remember S and U can represent any formula.

The 'If and Only If' Arguments

If and only if Introduction (IffI)

If we know that ((S ⊃ U) · (U ⊃ S)) is true, then we know that both (S ⊃ U) is true and (U ⊃ S) is true by S Rule 1. If S is true, then U cannot be false because if U were false then (S ⊃ U) would be false by S Rule 4. And since we know that (S ⊃ U) is true, we also know that U is true. Thus, if S is true, U must also be true. Now, what if S is false? If S is false, then U can be either true or false. Suppose we choose U to be true.

S ⊃ U
F T T
V = V

So, S ⊃ U is true.

But what about U ⊃ S? If we choose S to be false, it does not matter whether U is true or false. I hope you can recognize that if S is true, then U must also be true for both (S ⊃ U) and (U ⊃ S) to be true. And if S is false, then U must also be false for both S ⊃ U and U ⊃ S to be true. So, if S is true, U must be true; and if S is false, U must be false. Note that this is essentially how the rule of semantics for the if and only if connector is stated. Therefore, for the argument ((S ⊃ U) · (U ⊃ S)); so, (S ≡ U), we can show that there is no possible situation in which the assumptions are true and the conclusion is false. So the argument is valid. From (S ⊃ U) and (U ⊃ S) we can derive (S ≡ U). Thus, in a sense, we have introduced an if and only if formula. Consequently, we arrive at the Basic Valid Argument called If and only if Introduction.

If and only if Elimination (IffE)

If and only if Elimination is the exact reverse of **if and only if Introduction** and so no explanation is necessary.

The 'If-Then' Arguments

In our discussion of all the previous Basic Valid Arguments, we began with the introduction instance of each connecting word and followed with a discussion of the elimination instance. For the if-then arguments we reverse the order of discussion. We do so because the If-then Introduction argument is the most difficult to explain and so we leave it for last. This will also allow us to use all the other Basic Valid Arguments, if necessary, in our explanation of If-then Introduction.

If-then Elimination (IfE)

The argument If-then Elimination is probably used more than any other argument (that is, except for invalid arguments which are used all the time and are the reason we study logic in the first place). The If-then Elimination argument has the form:

1. $S \supset U$
2. S

So U

The argument is valid, so we know that there is no possible situation in which the premises are true and the conclusion is false. Consequently, we can use If-then Elimination in constructing proofs. Whenever we have two premises of the form $S \supset U$, S, we can then conclude U. In a sense we eliminate the if-then formula. Thus, we call this argument If-then Elimination. This argument has several other different names, such as modus ponens, affirm the antecedent, and so on. Many of the other Basic Valid Arguments are also known by other names but we choose to use the introduction and elimination names because they bring a sense of consistency or continuity to the subject. Actually the term elimination is somewhat misleading. We do not eliminate formulae. Whenever an elimination is used, the formulae that made up the argument still exist. Many times these same formulae are used in other steps of a proof. We will give examples of this shortly. There is an exception, however, which we will discuss later when we explain If-then Introduction.

Consider the following proof:

1. $p \supset (q \cdot r)$ As
2. $w \supset p$ As
3. $p \supset s$ As
4. w As
Show $r \cdot s$
(Show s)
5. p (IfE, 2, 4)
6. s (IfE, 3, 5)
(Show r)
7. $q \cdot r$ (IfE, 1, 5)
8. r (&E, 7)
9. $r \cdot s$ (&I, 6, 8)

30

As you can see in line 5 we use If-then Elimination to obtain p from lines 2 and 4. We do not use lines 2 or 4 again, but they could be used if we needed them. Consider the next step. We use lines 3 and 5 to derive line 6. Then we use line 5 again along with line 1 to derive line 7. So even though we used line 5 (as well as line 3) to derive line 6 and even though we call the argument If-then "Elimination," line 5 is not eliminated because we use line 5 again to derive line 7. The word "elimination" is simply an expression. It refers to the method of taking an If-then formula and combining it with another formula to obtain a different formula—one that is not an If-then formula. Thus, the If-then formula has been "eliminated." This is the rationale behind the name of the argument.

If-then Introduction (IfI)

The If-then Introduction argument is one of the more difficult to understand, but it is nevertheless one of the more important because it is used a great deal. Careful reading of both this section of the Study Guide along with the text is essential. Let us begin with an example:

1. w ⊃ (g ⊃ r)
2. r ⊃ s
3. q
Show w ⊃ s

In this proof we notice something striking even before we get started. The show statement is a conditional formula (an If-then formula). In trying to show an If-then formula, we assume for the time being (that is, temporarily) the formula on the left side of the "hook."

The formula on the left side of the "hook" in an If-then formula is called the antecedent because it occurs before the rest of the formula. The formula on the right side of the If-then formula is called the consequent. In this example our show statement is w ⊃ s. So w is the antecedent and s is the consequent. Also, in this proof assumptions 1 and 2 are both If-then formulae. Can you determine which formulae are the antecedents and which are the consequents? In assumption 1, w is the antecedent. In assumption 2, r is the antecedent. In assumption 2, s is the consequent. But what is the consequent in assumption 1? Some (and I suspect most) will say r. Others will say q. Who is right? Neither! The consequent of assumption 1 is (q ⊃ r). Now back to our discussion of If-then Introduction.

We need to assume for the time being the antecedent of our show statement. In this case we assume (temporarily assume) w. But because it is a temporary assumption, we need to designate it in some unique way because temporary assumptions must be handled differently than regular assumptions. We could adopt any one of several different conventions to differentiate between the two types of assumptions. Indeed, many conventions have been tried. But the one that seems best is the indention method.

When we temporarily assume any formula we indent to the right. For example in our proof we would indent the temporary assumption w as follows:

1. w ⊃ (q ⊃ r)   As
2. r ⊃ s   As
3. q   As
Show w ⊃ s
    4. w   Tas

31

Line 4 has been indented to the right and we have stated that line 4 is a temporary assumption by the letters Tas. This will remind us that w has only been assumed on a temporary basis and that the proof cannot be completed until we somehow return to our original position. This is accomplished by the use of the If-then Introduction argument. Let us complete the proof and then we will discuss the details.

After line 4 we state what we are trying to show from our temporary assumption:

```
1. w ⊃ (q ⊃ r)    As
2. r ⊃ s          As
3. q              As
Show (w ⊃ s)
    4. w          Tas
    [Show s]
```

This show statement is simply to help us remember what we need to show next in order to arrive at the end of the proof. So, we must work toward showing s. From lines 1 and 4 we can derive (q ⊃ r) by If-then Elimination. Then, with lines 5 and 3, we derive r, again by If-then Elimination. Finally, by using If-then Elimination and lines 2 and 6, we derive s which is what we were trying to show. The proof now looks like this:

```
1. w ⊃ (q ⊃ s)    As
2. r ⊃ s          As
3. q              As
Show (w ⊃ s)
    4. w          Tas
    [Show s]
    5. q ⊃ r      (IfE, 1, 4)
    6. r          (IfE, 3, 5)
    7. s          (IfE, 2, 6)
```

We have arrived at s which means we have shown what we intended to show and are ready to complete the proof.

It is at this point in the proof that we use the If-then Introduction argument. The argument allows us to combine (with a "hook") the line that was temporarily assumed and the line that was derived through a sequence of steps from all the previous lines in the proof. All of this simply means that lines 4 and 7 can be put together using the "hook" connector. Line 4 is the antecedent and line 7 is the consequent. When we use this rule we can eliminate the indention caused by the temporary assumption in line 4. Thus, we write line 8 even with and below line 3. The proof now looks like this:

```
1. w ⊃ (q ⊃ r)    As
2. r ⊃ s          As
3. q              As
Show (w ⊃ s)
    4. w          Tas
    [Show s]
    5. q ⊃ r      (IfE, 1, 4)
    6. r          (IfE, 3, 5)
    7. s          (IfE, 2, 6)
8. w ⊃ s          (IfI, 4, 7)
```

32

From lines 4 and 7 neither of which are If-then formulae, we have in a sense constructed an If-then formula. Thus we "introduce" an If-then formula and, therefore, we call this argument If-then Introduction. We have arrived at w ⊃ s which is what we were trying to show. So we are finished with the proof.

We must be careful to use If-then Introduction exactly as it has been stated. In the above example, only lines 4 and 7 could be used for If-then Introduction. Many students will make the error of thinking that it is alright to use any lines at all to connect two formulae by If-then Introduction. Some students, for example, will try to derive r ⊃ s in line 8 by using If-then Introduction. But this is not correct. Deriving r ⊃ s would require the use of lines 6 and 7 but only lines 4 and 7 can be used in an If-then Introduction step. Consider the following proof which is an example of this type of error.

```
1. p ⊃ (q ⊃ w)      As
2. w ⊃ (t ⊃ s)      As
3. t ⊃ w            As
4. q · t            As
Show (w ⊃ s)
    5. p            Tas
    [Show s]
    6. q ⊃ w        (IfE, 1, 5)
    7. q            (&E, 4)
    8. w            (IfE, 6, 7)
    9. t ⊃ s        (IfE, 2, 8)
   10. t            (&E, 4)
   11. s            (IfE, 9, 10)
12. w ⊃ s           (IfI, 8, 11)
```

This proof is not valid because line 12 uses If-then Introduction incorrectly. But this does not mean that the proof cannot be done correctly. At line 5 the person doing this proof noticed that if he temporarily assumed p, he could obtain s, which is what he proceeded to do. But what he failed to realize (and failed to realize this because he did not understand the If-then Introduction argument) was that in order to show w ⊃ s you must first temporarily assume w. Many students believe they only need to show s any way they can.

It may be well to note here that it was not wrong in the previous proof to assume p temporarily in line 5. You can assume anything you want at any time. But you must use that temporary assumption in an If-then Introduction step somewhere later in the proof.

Now, let us finish the proof the correct way.

```
1. p ⊃ (q ⊃ w)      As
2. w ⊃ (t ⊃ s)      As
3. t ⊃ w
4. q · t
Show (w ⊃ s)
    5. w            Tas
    [Show s]
    6. t            (&E, 4)
    7. t ⊃ s        (IfE, 2, 5)
    8. s            (IfE, 6, 7)
9. w ⊃ s            (IfI, 5, 8)
```

33

Here is a small trick that has helped some students remember which
lines you can use when doing an If-then Introduction step in a proof.
Draw a line alongside the column of line numbers in the proof. If you
had a proof with no temporary assumptions, then you would simply have
a straight vertical line. But this trick was not intended for use in
proofs with no temporary assumptions. If a temporary assumption is required, the line should move to the right where the indention is made
and should then proceed vertically until another indention is made or
the If-then Introduction step eliminates the indention. Wherever it is
appropriate, move the line to follow the column of line numbers.
How would this line be drawn for the proof we just finished?

```
 1. p ⊃ (q ⊃ w)      As
 2. w ⊃ (t ⊃ s)      As
 3. t ⊃ w            As
 4. g · t            As
Show (w ⊃ s)
    5. w             Tas
   [Show s]
    6. t ⊃ s         (IfE, 2, 5)
    7. t             (&E, 4)
    8. s             (IfE, 6, 7)
 9. w ⊃ s            (IfI, 5, 8)
```

Keep in mind this line is not part of the proof but is only there
to help you remember which lines are to be used in the If-then Introduction step. The line follows the column of line numbers down from 1
to 5. Then it moves over (to show the indented temporary assumption)
and follows the column of numbers from lines 5 to 8 where it then
shifts back to the original column of numbers at line 9. This trick
may come in handy when you do proofs which require more than one temporary assumption. Consider this proof:

```
1. q ⊃ r             As
2. r ⊃ t             As
3. t ⊃ s             As
Show q ⊃ (r ⊃ s)
    4. q             Tas
   [Show (r ⊃ s)]
    5. r             Tas
   [Show s]
    6. t             (IfE, 2, 5)
    7. s             (IfE, 3, 6)
 8. (r ⊃ s)          (IfI, 5, 7)
9. q ⊃ (r ⊃ s)       (IfI, 4, 8)
```

Each time a temporary assumption was made the vertical line followed the indention by moving to the right. In line 8 only lines 5
and 7 can be used for that If-then Introduction step. The vertical line
should help remind us that line 5 was the last temporary assumption made
because that is where the vertical line last moved to the right to follow the indention. Thus, line 8 uses If-then Introduction, and r from
line 5 must be the antecedent of the If-then formula that is "introduced." The consequent of the If-then formula must be s in line 7. Because of the If-then Introduction step, line 8 moves back to the left
and essentially does away with the indention caused by the temporary

34

assumption in line 5. Now line 8 is directly below line 4. Again, the vertical line helps to highlight these moves to the left and the right so that we know which lines are available for use in the If-then Introduction steps. In line 9 q̲ must be the antecedent of the If-then formula which was made by using If-then Introduction. q̲ was temporarily assumed in line 4 and our vertical line should help us see that fact. Line 4 is where our vertical line shifted and thus line 4 must become the antecedent in an If-then formula. The consequent must be $(r \supset s)$ from line 8 because line 8 is the only line in the proof which is in the same column as line 4. Again, the vertical line should help to point out this fact to us. Obviously practice at doing proofs of this kind will be more useful than any amount of explanation so take advantage of the exercises given in both the text and the Study Guide.

As the text points out, once an If-then Introduction step is taken, then those steps which preceded it (the indented steps) are no longer in force. This means that those steps cannot be used in the proof any longer. Consider one of our previous examples:

```
1. p ⊃ (q ⊃ w)      As
2. 2 ⊃ (t ⊃ s)      As
3. t ⊃ w            As
4. q · t            As
Show (w    s)
   5. w             Tas
   [Show s]
   6. t ⊃ s         (IE, 2, 5)
   7. t             (&E, 4)
   8. s             (IfE, 6, 7)
9. w ⊃ s            (IfI, 5, 8)
```

When we arrive at line 9, lines 5 through 8 are no longer in force and therefore we can ignore them. It is as if those lines were never part of the proof. We can say this because, in a sense, line 9 states what was done in lines 5 through 8. In the future there will be proofs which will require several temporary assymptions and we need to remember which lines are in force and which are not. Consider another of our previous examples:

```
1. q ⊃ r    As       As
2. r ⊃ t    As       As
3. t ⊃ s    As       As
Show (q ⊃ (r ⊃ s))
   4. q              Tas
   [Show (r ⊃ s)]
      5. r           Tas
      [Show s]
      6. t           (IfE, 2, 5)
      7. s           (IfE, 3, 6)
   8. r ⊃ s          (IfI, 5, 7)
9. q ⊃ (r ⊃ s)       (IfI, 4, 8)
```

When we arrive at line 8, lines 5 through 7 are no longer in force. We can ignore them and in fact must not use them in any subsequent part of the proof. Lines 1 through 4 are in force and can be used if necessary. When we arrive at line 9, lines 4 and 8 are dropped. They are no longer in force and consequently could not be used if the proof were to proceed further. At this point only lines 1, 2, 3, and 9 are in force.

Along with the Basic Valid Arguments just discussed, there is also a set of Derived Valid Arguments which will save you time in doing proofs, so learn them all.

PROOF STRATEGIES

Before we practice these concepts by doing proofs it will be helpful to discuss proof strategies. For convenience let us restate the proof strategies:

Strategy 1. Whenever the elimination form of one of the Basic Valid Arguments can be applied, apply it.

Strategy 2. To show S ⊃ U, assume S as a temporary assumption. Then, show U and use If-then Introduction.

Strategy 3. To show S · U, show S and U and use And Introduction.

Strategy 4. To show S v U, show either S or U and use Or Introduction.

Strategy 5. To show -S, show S ⊃ U · -U for some U (by assuming S, showing U · -U, and then using If-then Introduction), and then use Not Introduction.

Strategy 6. To show S, when you seem to be getting nowhere, show -S ⊃ U · -U (by assuming -S, showing U · -U, and using If-then Introduction) and use Not Elimination.

Strategy 7. To show R, when you still have S v U in force, show U ⊃ R and show S ⊃ R, and then use Or Elimination. In other words, assume S and show R and use If-then Introduction. Then assume U and show R and use If-then Introduction. Once you have done this, since you have S v U, S ⊃ R, and U ⊃ R, you can show R by Or Elimination.

Strategy 8. To show S ≡ U, show S ⊃ U and U ⊃ S and use If and only if Introduction. In other words, assume S and show U and use If-then Introduction. Then assume U and show S and use If-then Introduction. Finally use If and only if Introduction.

In the text you were told that proof strategies are like the strategy one would use when playing chess and that rules of proof were like the rules of the game (for example, a pawn can move one space per move except on the first move when it can move two spaces).

Strategy 1

The proof strategies are intended to get you started. They will help you understand what you need to do. Take Strategy 1 for example: "Whenever the elimination form of one of the Basic Valid Arguments can be applied, apply it." This means that if you have an argument like the following:

1. p ⊃ q   As
2. q ⊃ (r · s)   As
3. p   As
Show s

you should begin by applying any elimination argument (from the list of Basic Valid Arguments). This will require that you know the Basic Valid Arguments well. Are there any basic elimination arguments that can be applied? Yes, but only one. So Strategy 1 tells us to apply it. Thus, add to the proof as follows:

```
| 1. p ⊃ q          As
| 2. q ⊃ (r · s)    As
| 3. p              As
| Show s
| 4. q              (IfE, 1, 3)
```

We have applied Strategy 1 and made some progress. What next? It worked once so let us try Strategy 1 again. Are there any basic elimination arguments that can be applied? Yes, but again just one. So apply it.

```
| 1. p ⊃ q          As
| 2. q ⊃ (r · s)    As
| 3. p              As
| Show s
| 4. q              (IfE, 1, 3)
| 5. (r · s)        (IfE, 2, 4)
```

Again we have made progress. What now? There is no reason to change strategies as long as we have one that works well. So try to use Strategy 1 again. Are there any basic elimination arguments that can be applied? Yes! So apply them. Again, in this case there is only one:

```
| 1. p ⊃ q          As
| 2. q ⊃ (r · s)    As
| 3. p              As
| Show s
| 4. q              (IfE, 1, 3)
| 5. r · s          (IfE, 2, 4)
| 6. s              (&E, 5)
```

Now we are done. You will notice that for this proof, only elimination arguments were necessary so that we only needed Strategy 1. Sometimes you will find that Strategy 1 will not help. It is then that you want to go on to the other strategies. Let us look at another example:

```
| 1. p ⊃ (w · z)    As
| 2. t ⊃ (q · p)    As
| 3. x ⊃ (r · t)    As
| 4. x              As
| Show w · p
| 5. (r · t)        (IfE, 3, 4) Strategy 1
| 6. r              (&E, 5) Strategy 1
| 7. t              (&E, 5) Strategy 1
| 8. (q · p)        (IfE, 2, 7) Strategy 1
| 9. q              (&8) Strategy 1
| 10. p             (&8, Strategy 1
| 11. w · z         (IfE, 1, 10) Strategy 1
| 12. w             (&E, 11) Strategy 1
| 13. z             (&E, 11) Strategy 1
| 14. w · p         (&I, 10, 12) Strategy 3
```

You will notice that in lines 6, 9, and 13 we made And Elimination steps which were not used to obtain the conclusion and so these steps were not necessary. In other words the proof could have looked like this:

```
1. p ⊃ (w · z)        As
2. t ⊃ (q · p)        As
3. x ⊃ (r · t)        As
4. x                  As
Show w · p
5. (r · t)            (IfE, 3, 4)
6. t                  (&E, 5)
7. q · p              (IfE, 2, 6)
8. p                  (&E, 7)
9. w · z              (IfE, 1, 8)
10. w                 (&E, 9)
11. w · p             (&I, 8, 10)
```

This proof is three steps shorter, which does not mean that the previous proof is wrong. The reason there were extra steps in the previous proof was that we followed Proof Strategy 1, which advises us to use elimination arguments wherever possible. Many times this will involve using extra steps. But until you become proficient at doing proofs, it is best simply to follow this strategy even though your proofs are a few steps longer than necessary. After you have done proofs for a while, you will be able to eliminate the extra steps without difficulty.

Strategy 2

Strategy 2 is a formal statement of how If-then Introduction works. We have already discussed how you use If-then Introduction so we will not review the method here. You cannot use If-then Introduction without adopting Strategy 2. So, if you have read this far, you should already have mastered the If-then Introduction argument. Just remember that if you need to show an If-then statement like (q · r) ⊃ -w, then you should use Strategy 2 by temporarily assuming the antecedent (q · r) and indenting and then working to show -w. After you have done so, you are ready to use the If-then Introduction argument. This will give you (q · r) ⊃ -w, which is what you are trying to show.

Strategy 3

If you want to show an and statement like p · q, you should first show p then q and then use And Introduction. Let us look at an example. Suppose we have two assumptions ((p · q) · (r · s)) and (-t · w) and we want to show (r · -t). We set up the proof like this:

```
1. (p · q) · (r · s)     As
2. (-t · w)              As
Show (r · -t)
```

Our statement is in the form (S · U) and so this proof will require use of Strategy 3. To do this proof we will also need to use Strategy 1 several times. Strategy 3 says we start by showing S. In our case S is represented by r. So we need first to show r. We can state this in the proof as follows:

```
1. (p · q) · (r · s)      As
2. (-t · w)               As
Show (r · -t)
[Show r]
```

Now, to derive _r_, we use Strategy 1 and eliminate where possible.

```
1. (p · q) · (r · s)      As
2. (-t · w)               As
Show (r · -t)
[Show r]
3. (p · q)                (&E, 1)
4. (r · s)                (&E, 1)
```

Lines 3 and 4 are eliminated from line 1. We can also use And Elimination on both lines 3 and 4 to obtain:

```
1. (p · q) · (r · s)      As
2. (-t · w)               As
Show (r · -t)
[Show r]
3. (p · q)                (&E, 1)
4. (r · s)                (&E, 1)
5. p                      (&E, 3)
6. q                      (&E, 3)
7. r                      (&E, 4)
```

Now we have shown _r_ in line 7, so we are half done. Next we need to show -_t_. Therefore, after line 7 we state that we are trying to show -_t_.

```
1. (p · q) · (r · s)      As
2. (-t · w)               As
Show (r · -t)
[Show r]
3. (p · q)                (&E, 1)
4. (r · s)                (&E, 1)
5. p                      (&E, 3)
6. q                      (&E, 3)
7. r                      (&E, 4)
[Show -t]
```

Now we can go back to eliminating wherever possible (Strategy 1). At this point we can still use And Elimination on line 2. This will give us:

```
1. (p · q) · (r · s)      As
2. (-t · w)               As
Show (r · -t)
[Show r]
3. (p · q)                (&E, 1)
4. (r · s)                (&E, 1)
5. p                      (&E, 3)
6. q                      (&E, 3)
7. r                      (&E, 4)
[Show -t]
8. -t                     (&E, 2)
```

Now we have shown -t and we are ready to use And Introduction (recommended in Strategy 3). So the proof is completed as follows:

```
| 1. (p · q) · (r · s)    As
| 2. (-t · w)             As
| Show (r · -t)
| [Show r]
| 3. (p · q)              (&E, 1)
| 4. (r · s)              (&E, 1)
| 5. p                    (&E, 3)
| 6. q                    (&E, 3)
| 7. r                    (&E, 4)
| [Show -t]
| 8. -t                   (&E, 2)
| 9. (r · -t)             (&E, 7, 8)
```

Strategy 4

Strategy 4 is used whenever we need to show an <u>or</u> statement. Simply find one side of the <u>or</u> statement and use Or Introduction. Consider the following proof:

```
| 1. t ⊃ w        As
| 2. q · t        As
| Show w v p
| [Show w]
| 3. q            (&E, 2)
| 4. t            (&E, 2)
| 5. w            (IfE, 1, 4)
```

So, we have shown <u>w</u>. Now, Strategy 4 says we should use Or Introduction. Thus, we obtain the following:

```
| 1. t ⊃ w        As
| 2. q · t        As
| Show w v p
| [Show w]
| 3. q            (&E, 2)
| 4. t            (&E, 2)
| 5. w            (IfE, 1, 4)
| 6. w v p        (OrI, 5)
```

Let us try a proof that is a little harder:

```
| 1. s ⊃ (q ⊃ r)        As
| 2. p ⊃ t              As
| 3. w                  As
| 4. (w v u) ⊃ (p · s)  As
| Show t v (q ⊃ r)
```

We know by Strategy 4 that we need to show <u>t</u> or we need to show (q ⊃ r). Let us look for <u>t</u>.

```
| 1. s ⊃ (q ⊃ r)        As
| 2. p ⊃ t              As
```

40

```
 3. w                     As
 4. (w v u) ⊃ (p · s)     As
Show t v (q ⊃ r)
[Show t]
 5. w v u                 (OrI, 3)
 6. p · s                 (IfE, 4, 5)
 7. p                     (&E, 6)
 8. s                     (&E, 6)
 9. t                     (IfE, 2, 7)
```

We have shown <u>t</u>, so now we use Or Introduction to finish:

```
 1. s ⊃ (q ⊃ r)           As
 2. p ⊃ t                 As
 3. w                     As
 4. (w v u) ⊃ (p · s)     As
Show t v (q ⊃ r)
[Show t]
 5. w v u                 (OrI, 3)
 6. p · s                 (IfE, 4, 5)
 7. p                     (&E, 6)
 8. s                     (&E, 6)
 9. t                     (IfE, 2, 7)
10. t v (q ⊃ r)           (OrI, 9)
```

We could also have done this proof by trying to find <u>(q ⊃ r)</u> instead of <u>t</u> (same strategy). It would look like this:

```
 1. s ⊃ (q ⊃ r)           As
 2. p ⊃ t                 As
 3. w                     As
 4. (w v u) ⊃ (p · s)     As
Show t v (q ⊃ r)
[Show q ⊃ r]
 5. w v u                 (OrI, 3)
 6. p · s                 (IfE, 4, 5)
 7. p                     (&E, 6)
 8. s                     (&E, 6)
 9. q ⊃ r                 (IfE, 1, 8)
10. t v (q ⊃ r)           (OrI, 9)
```

Strategies 5 and 6

These strategies are instances of <u>proof by contradiction</u>. They can be used effectively whenever nothing else seems to work. Suppose you are trying to show <u>-q</u>. This strategy advises you to assume <u>q</u> temporarily and then try to find a contradiction. Then you use If-then Introduction followed by Not Introduction, giving you <u>-q</u>, which is what you want to show. Here is an example of Strategy 5:

```
 1. -p                    As
 2. t ⊃ p                 As
Show -t
[Show t ⊃ (U · -U)]
 3. t                     Tas
[Show (U · -U)]
```

41

```
 |4. p                   (IfE, 2, 3)
 |5. (p · -p)            (&I, 1, 4)
┌─6. t ⊃ (p · -p)        (IfI, 3, 5)
 |7. -t                  (NI, 6)
```

You will notice that Strategy 2 was required to show the if-then state-
ment -t ⊃ (p · -p). Strategies 5 and 6 will always entail the use of
If-then Introduction argument (that is, Strategy 2). Also, when using
Strategies 5 and 6, you will always be looking for a contradiction
(U · -U).

    Here is an example of Strategy 6. It is the same as Strategy 5 ex-
cept that you are trying to show a formula that has no not connector.
In Strategy 5 you are trying to show a not formula (a formula which
has a not connector).

```
 |1. (r · s)              As
 |2. -p ⊃ -s             As
 |Show p
 |[Show -p ⊃ U · -U]
 └─3. -p                 Tas
 |[Show U · -U]
 |4. -s                  (IfE, 2, 3)
 |5. s                   (&E, 1)
┌─6. s · -s              (&I, 4, 5)
 |7. -p ⊃ (s · -s)       (IfI, 3, 6)
 |8. p                   (NE, 7)
```

    The key idea to keep in mind when using these two strategies (Stra-
tegies 5 and 6) is to assume temporarily the negation of what you are
trying to show and then work for a contradiction. If you are trying to
show q and you do not seem to be getting anywhere, then temporarily
assume -q and work toward showing a contradiction (U · -U). If you want
to show (u · t) and you are not making much progress, then assume
(u · t), which is the negation of what you want to show. Then work toward showing a contradiction (U · -U). Once you reach the contradiction, use If-then Introduction and then either Not Introduction or Not
Elimination depending on the specific proof.

    Here is one way of looking at these strategies: If you have an ar-
gument that you know is valid but you cannot seem to show the conclusion (that is, you cannot give a proof), then assume the negation of
the conclusion, which is the same as saying you assume the negation of
what you are trying to show. From this assumption you eventually obtain
a contradiction (that is, U · -U). Then use If-then Introduction. Now,
we know that (U · -U) must always be false. And since we have arrived
at each of our steps along the way by correct use of the Basic Valid
Arguments, we know that S ⊃ (U · -U) must be a true formula. But if
(U · -U) is false, then S must be false. Otherwise S would be true and,
if S were true, then S ⊃(U · -U) would be false. S ⊃ (U · -U) cannot
be false because it was derived correctly by the use of the Basic Valid
Arguments. All this means that S must be false. And if S is false, its
negation is true. So we derive -S by Not Introduction or Not Elimination, whichever applies.

This strategy is used when the Or Elimination argument is adopted. You begin with an <u>or</u> statement that is in force and then try to show that either side of the <u>or</u> statement will give you the desired conclusion. This strategy teaches us how to do a "proof by cases." Let us look at an example.

```
1. t ⊃ s            As
2. s ⊃ (t ⊃ w)      As
3. q v t            As
4. r ⊃ (s · t)      As
5. q ⊃ r            As
Show w
```

First we temporarily assume the left side of the <u>or</u> statement (that is, q v t) in line 3. Starting with the assumption q we then work toward showing <u>w</u>.

```
1. t ⊃ s            As
2. s ⊃ (t ⊃ w)      As
3. q v t            As
4. r ⊃ (s · t)      As
5. q ⊃ r            As
Show w
[Show q ⊃ w]
   6. q             Tas
   [Show w]
   7. r             (IfE, 5, 6)
   8. s · t         (IfE, 4, 7)
   9. s             (&E, 8)
  10. t ⊃ w         (IfE, 2, 9)
  11. t             (&E, 8)
  12. w             (IfE, 10, 11)
```

So, we have arrived at <u>w</u>. We are halfway there. (Notice that lines 6 through 12 are all obtained from elimination arguments by following the good advice of Strategy 1.) Now, we use If-then Introduction on lines 6 and 12 to obtain q ⊃ w. Then we temporarily assume the other side of the <u>or</u> statement in line 3 (the right side), which is <u>t</u>. Next, we try to show <u>w</u> again. After we show <u>w</u>, we use If-then Introduction. Finally, Or Elimination completes the strategy.

```
1. t ⊃ s            As
2. s ⊃ (t ⊃ w)      As
3. q v t            As
4. r ⊃ (s · t)      As
5. q ⊃ r            As
Show w
[Show q ⊃ w]
   6. q             Tas
   [Show w]
   7. r             (IfE, 5, 6)
   8. s · t         (IfE, 4, 7)
   9. s             (&E, 8)
  10. t ⊃ w         (IfE, 2, 9)
```

43

```
    11. t                    (&E, 8)
    12. w                    (IfE, 10, 11)
 13. q ⊃ w                   (IfI, 6, 12)
 [Show t ⊃ w]
    14. t                    Tas
    [Show w]
    15. s                    (IfE, 1, 14)
    16. t ⊃ w                (IfE, 2, 15)
    17. w                    (IfE, 14, 16)
 18. t ⊃ w                   (IfI, 14, 17)
 19. w                       (OrE, 3, 13, 18)
```

Notice that the use of the Or Elimination argument is unique in that it requires three lines and that all the other Basic Arguments require only one or two lines.

Strategy 8

This is simply Strategy 2 and Strategy 3 taken together at the same time. If you have to show (p ≡ q), then show (p ⊃ q) · (q ⊃ p), which requires the use of Strategy 3. But to show (p ⊃ q) · (q ⊃ p), first you have to show (p ⊃ q), which requires the use of Strategy 2 and then (q ⊃ p), which also requires the use of Strategy 2. Strategy 8 is used a great deal in the later chapters in showing equivalence and equality.

You should now have a feel for the proof strategies and be able to construct proofs. So, let us do some exercises.

EXERCISES 2.5

Construct proofs for the following arguments:

Example: q ⊃ r; so -r ⊃ -q

```
 1. q ⊃ r                    As
 Show -r ⊃ -q
```

Because the conclusion of this argument is an If-then formula (that is, it has the form (S⊃U) we use Strategy 2. Then, we temporarily assume -r and show -q:

```
 1. q ⊃ r                    As
 Show -r ⊃ -q
    2. -r                    Tas
    [Show -q]
```

At this point we seem to be getting nowhere. We have considered Proof Strategies 1 through 4 and none of them apply. So let us try Strategy 5:

```
 1. q ⊃ r                    As
 Show -r ⊃ -q
    2. -r                    Tas
    [Show -q]
    [Show q ⊃ (U · -U)]
       3. q                  Tas
```

44

```
    [Show (U · -U)]
    4. r                    (IfE, 1, 3)
    5. r · -r               (&I, 2, 4)
    6. q ⊃ (r · -r)         (IFI, 3, 5)
    7. -q                   (NI, 6)
 8. -r ⊃ -q                 (IFI, 2, 7)
```

Notice that this is a proof of one of the Derived Valid Arguments given in the text. q ⊃ r; so, -r ⊃ -q is an instance of the Derived Valid Argument.

Contraposition (C)

1. p ⊃ q, -r ⊃ p; so, -r ⊃ q
2. (p · q), (r · s); so, (q · s)
3. (q · s), (t · p); so, (t · q) v r
4. (r v s), (-r · -t); so, s (Hint: use Disjunctive Syllogism)
5. (s · t) · p, q ⊃ r, p ⊃ q; so, w v r
6. (p · s), q ≡ s; so, q
7. -(p v q), -q ⊃ r; so, (r v s) (Hint: use Demorgans Law)
8. -r ⊃ (s ⊃ t), -(r v t); so, -s
9. (p ⊃ q), p · (q ⊃ -p); so, s
10. (p ⊃ q), -s ⊃ -(q · r); so, r ⊃ (p ⊃ s)

TRANSLATION

In order for logic to be of use to us we need to be able to apply it to everyday life. But most arguments do not come to us like r ⊃ w, r; so w. They come to us like this: If it is raining outside, then the streets are wet. The streets are not wet, so it is not raining outside. Arguments come to us in English sentences, not in symbolic formulae.

Consequently, we need a set of rules that will help us translate English sentences into symbols so that we can easily determine whether an argument is valid or not. The text points out that these rules of translation will not always give accurate results. Like the proof strategies, they only provide guidelines. Practice will benefit you most. So let us state the rules and try our hand at some exercises.

Rules of Translation

T Rule 1. Both S and U, S and U, S, but U translate as (S · U).
T Rule 2. Either S or U, S or U, unless S, U, S unless U translate as S v U.
T Rule 3. It is not the case that S translates as -S.
T Rule 4. Neither S nor U translates as (S · -U).
T Rule 5. S just in case U, just in case U, S, S if and only if U translate as (S ≡ U).
T Rule 6. If S then U, U if S, S only if U, only if U, S, U provided that S, provided that S, U translate as (S ⊃ U).
T Rule 7. An atomic sentence with an underlined letter translates as that letter.

The T in T rule stands for translation, so T Rule 6 means Rule of Translation 6.

Now, let us try some simple translations.

45

EXERCISES 2.6

Translate the following sentences according to the rules of translation.

Example: Dogs bark, but unless birds sing, lions meow.
1. Dogs bark, but unless birds sing, lions meow.
2. d̄ but unless b l by T Rule 7.
3. d but (b v l) by T Rule 2.
4. d · (b v l) by T Rule 1.

1. Lions meow provided that fish breathe or cows moo.
2. Trees bloom if and only if spring is here unless temperatures rise.
3. If a dog barks, then it makes a noise unless Mary Jean is not there to hear it.
4. Either birds sing or the Mormon Tabernacle Choir sings, but if birds sing, then Larry is happy.
5. The sky is blue provided the sun is shinning but unless the sun is shining, the sky is black.
6. Picasso paints and Beethoven composes but provided that Lyle has a bat and ball, baseball is in season.
7. Just in case the weather is nice Aaron will plan a picnic unless Tom is in town. If Tom is in town then they will go golfing.
8. If Dean and Marva have money, then they will buy a Mercedes only if a BMW is more expensive.
9. Ellen will sew, if Jeff will mow provided that Simon does not cry or Jeremy does not sigh.
10. David is an engineer just in case Julie is a fair teacher but only if Trudy plants tomato vines will Eric have spaghetti at dinner time.

 ## Monadic
Logic

Quantifiers Quantifiers are the connecting words 'for some' and 'for every'. They are special connecting words that allow us to handle formulae that describe quantities.

Boundness When a formula is preceded by a quantifier, the formula is said to be bound. For several reasons we must always be aware of which formulae are bound and which are not.

Universe of Discourse A set that contains at least one element. The elements are called objects and they are usually just numbers. Atomic formulae are true or false for the elements (objects) in the universe of discourse.

Monadic Monadic refers to formulae that contain one indefinite pronoun.

Denotation When we assign an object in the universe of discourse to be true of a formula, it is said that the formula is denoted to be true of that object. P:1 means that P is denoted to be true of 1.

Subscription This is a method of placing a number (representing the objects in the universe of discourse) slightly below and alongside an atomic formula. This is done to show all the possible situations in a universe of discourse that a formula can have.

One of the valuable things about the text is that when we begin a new logic we do not have to start from scratch. We simply add on to what we already have and continue. So, let us do just that, continue.

SYNTAX

ENGLISH SYNTAX

The syntax for monadic logic is the same as that for truth-functional logic except that we add two new connectors. The text also introduces a new set of atomic formulae. These formulae are much the

47

same as those in truth-functional logic except that they begin with the word _it_. _It has order_ or _it is the universe_. The word _it_ is an indefinite pronoun and the use of the indefinite pronoun is what essentially distinguishes this new set (the monadic set) of atomic formulae from the other sets. These formulae can be used just like the others; that is, we can make more complex formulae from them. Some examples might include the following: _It is not the case that it is the universe_; _if it is the universe, then it has order and it has a designer_; and so on ad infinitum. Along with these new atomic formulae we have two new connectors. These new connectors are called quantifiers because they quantify the formulae to which they are connected. The quantifiers are _for everything_ and _for something_. They are also referred to as universal and existential quantifiers, respectively.

It makes sense to say _for everything it has a designer_ or _for something it has order_. But it seems awkward to say _for everything cows moo_ or _for something fish breathe_. Do you see the difference? The new connectors (quantifiers) work well with the new set of atomic formulae (that is, the atomic formulae which contain the indefinite pronoun _it_) but do not work well with the truth-functional atomic formulae. The truth-functional atomic formulae do not contain any indefinite pronouns.

Suppose we had another set of atomic formulae (monadic atomic formulae) that consisted of the following: _It is red_. _It is blue_. _It has aesthetic beauty_. _It is heavy_. With these new atomic formulae and the rules of syntax we can determine whether a sentence is a formula or not Let us state the rules of syntax and then do some exercises.

Rules of Syntax

An expression is an atomic formula or a formula if and only if it is so according to the following rules:

F Rule 1. The following are atomic formulae, hence formulae: It is red; it is blue; it has aesthetic beauty; it is heavy.

F Rule 2. If _U_ and _W_ are formulae, then so are the following: _U_ and _W_; it is not the case that _U_; _U_ or _W_; if _U_ then _W_; _U_ if and only if _W_.

F Rule 3. If _U_ is a formula, then so are the following: For everything, _U_ (or we could say: Everything is such that _U_); for something, _U_ (or we could say: Something is such that _U_).

EXERCISES 3.1

Determine which of the following sentences are formulae according to the rules of syntax. For those that are formulae, provide a formal construction. For those that are not formulae, explain why not and what changes would be necessary to make them formulae.

Example. If it is red, then it has aesthetic beauty or it is heavy.

1. _It is red_ is a formula by F Rule 1.
2. _It is heavy_ is a formula by F Rule 1.
3. _It has aesthetic beauty_ is a formula by F Rule 1.
4. _It has aesthetic beauty or it is heavy_ is a formula by lines 2 and 3 and F Rule 2.

5. <u>If it is red, then it has aesthetic beauty or it is heavy</u> is a formula by lines 1 and 4 and F Rule 2.

Remember F Rule stands for Rule of Syntax.
   Let us try a more difficult exercise.

   Example: For something, it has aesthetic beauty if and only if for everything, it is red and it is blue.

   1. <u>It has aesthetic beauty</u> is a formula by F Rule 1.
   2. <u>For something it has aesthetic beauty</u> is a formula by line 1 F Rule 3.
   3. <u>It is red</u> is a formula by F Rule 1.
   4. <u>It is blue</u> is a formula by F Rule 1.
   5. <u>It is red and it is blue</u> is a formula by lines 3 and 4 and F Rule 2.
   6. <u>For everything it is red and it is blue</u> is a formula by line 5 and F Rule 3.
   7. <u>For something it has aesthetic beauty if and only if for everything it is red and it is blue</u> is a formula by lines 2 and 6 and F Rule 2.

So, the person who made this statement likes only paintings that have a lot of reds and blues. Try the following exercises on your own:

   1. It is blue, or it is red and it has aesthetic beauty.
   2. It is not the case that it has aesthetic beauty if and only if it is heavy or it is red.
   3. If it is red, then it is not the case that for something it has aesthetic beauty.
   4. If the apple is red, then it is not the case that it is blue.
   5. It is heavy or it is aesthetically beautiful if and only if it isn't the case that it is blue.
   6. For everything if it is not the case that it is blue, then for something it is red.
   7. It's not red, so it's not beautiful.
   8. If it is heavy, then it is not red or it is not blue.
   9. If for everything it is not the case that it is heavy, then it is red and it has aesthetic beauty.
   10. It is heavy if and only if for something it is red or for everything it is blue or it is not the case that it has aesthetic beauty.

SYMBOLIC NOTATION

   The rules of syntax for symbolic notation in monadic logic are the same as those in truth-functional logic except that we add two new symbols for the quantifiers.

Rules of Syntax

   An expression is an atomic formula or formula if and only if it is so according to the following rules:

F Rule 1. The following are atomic formulae and hence, formulae:
p, q, r, s, t, ...
F Rule 2. If U and W are formulae, then so are the following:
(U · W), -U, (U v W), (U ⊃ W), (U ≡ W).
F Rule 3. If U is a formula, then so are the following: ∀U, ∃U.

Now let us do some more exercises using the symbolic notation.

EXERCISES 3.2

Determine which of the following are formulae according to the rules of syntax for symbolic notation (the F rules). For those that are formulae, provide a formal construction. For those that are not formulae, explain why not and what changes would be necessary to make them formulae.

Example: ∃p ⊃ (r ⊃ ∀t).

1. p is a formula by F Rule 1.
2. r is a formula by F Rule 1.
3. t is a formula by F Rule 1.
4. ∃p is a formula by line 1 and F Rule 3.
5. ∀t is a formula by line 3 and F Rule 3.
6. r ⊃ ∀t is a formula by lines 2 and 5 and F Rule 2.
7. ∃p ⊃ (r ⊃ ∀t) is a formula by lines 4, 6, and F Rule 2.

Example: ((∀ · ∃p) ⊃ ∃r).

This is not a formula because there is a for everything (universal) quantifier by itself. It is not quantifying any formula, so it cannot be a formula by F Rule 3. To make it one, we need to put a formula after the quantifier like this: ∀q. So, ((∀q ·∃ p) ⊃ ∃r) would be a formula.

1. ∀(p ⊃ q) ≡ (∃r · t)
2. ∃ ∀p ⊃ (q v t)
3. ∃(p · q) ⊃ ∀(s ≡ (r · t))
4. ∀(∃p ⊃ q) v s
5. t ≡ ∃ v (p · q)
6. ∀ ⊃ q
7. (q ⊃ r) ⊃ ∀(∃p ⊃ r)
8. (r ≡ -s) v ∃
9. ∀ v ∃q
10. -(p ⊃ q) ≡ ((∃s v -t) · ∀(q ⊃ r))

BOUNDNESS

The next notion that we need to discuss is boundness. This is a difficult concept for many and careful study of the text is important. First, let us state the idea as it was given in the text.

An occurrence of an atomic formula in a given formula is bound if and only if it occurs in a part of the formula that begins with a quantifier, ∀ or ∃. Otherwise it is free.

Atomic formulae are bound if they follow a quantifier. For example,

in the formula $\exists p$, the p is an occurrence of an atomic formula and p
is a formula that begins with a quantifier, namely $\exists$. So, in this case
p is bound. But there are formulae that may have more than one occurrence of an atomic formula. What then? Suppose we have a formula
$\exists p \supset p$. This formula has two occurrences of the atomic formula p. So,
which is bound? The atomic formula p occurs in the formula $\exists p$ which
is part of another more complex formula $\exists p \supset p$. $\exists p$ is the antecedent
of the If-then formula $\exists p \supset p$ and p is the consequent of the formula
$\exists p \supset p$. So once again, which occurrence of p if any is bound? The occurrence of p in the antecedent begins with a quantifier, namely $\exists$.
So, the occurrence of p in the antecedent is bound. Now, how about the
occurrence of p in the consequent? The consequent does not begin with
a quantifier, so the occurrence of p in the consequent is not bound.
What would it take to make the occurrence of p bound in both cases
(that is, bound in the consequent also)? Placing a set of parentheses
around the formula $p \supset p$, giving the formula $\exists (p \supset p)$, would make both
occurrences of p bound. Can you explain the difference? In the latter
case we must consider the whole formula $(p \supset p)$. The whole formula
$(p \supset p)$ now begins with a quantifier, whereas before only the antecedent of the formula began with a quantifier.

Let us look at some more examples. In the text we are told that
for the formula $p \supset \exists p$, the first occurrence is not bound but the
second occurrence is. Do you see why? The first occurrence of p does
not begin with a quantifier but the second occurrence of p does begin
with a quantifier. So, the first occurrence of p is free, and the second
occurrence is bound. The same is true for $(p \cdot r) \supset \forall(q \supset p)$ because
the first occurrence of p (that is, $(p \cdot r)$) does not begin with a
quantifier but the second occurrence of p (that is, $\forall(q \supset p)$) does begin with a quantifier, namely $\forall$.

EXERCISES 3.3

Part A

Rewrite the following formula by adding a quantifier that will
bind the first occurrence of q but not the second. (Note that there
may be more than one correct solution.)

Example: $(p \cdot q) \supset (s \vee q)$.
Solution: $\forall(p \cdot q) \supset (s \vee q)$.

1. $s \equiv (p \vee q) \cdot (q \supset p)$
2. $q \cdot (s \vee r) \equiv -q$
3. $(p \supset -s) \vee (-q \cdot q)$
4. $(t \cdot -q) \equiv ((s \supset q) \vee p)$
5. $(r \supset s) \vee ((t \supset (p \cdot q)) \vee (-q \cdot s)))$

Part B

Now, using the same exercises above, rewrite the formulae adding a
quantifier that will bind both occurrences of q's but as little else
as possible. In other words, bind both q's but in doing so, bind as
few occurrences of other atomic formulae as possible. This will require
one quantifier and one set of parentheses only.

51

SEMANTICS

UNIVERSE OF DISCOURSE

The only really new concept in semantics for monadic logic is the universe of discourse. Because the atomic formulae in monadic logic begin with the word it, we have to designate what it can refer to. Are we going to let it refer to anything in the universe or are we going to specify what it can refer to? As stated in the text, a universe of discourse is a set of objects that contains at least one element in it. The set containing one apple is a universe of discourse. Also, the set containing one apple and one bar of gold is a universe of discourse.

In order to be able to find truth values for monadic formulae, we will need rules of semantics (S rules which tell us the truth value of quantified formulae). For example, when is ∀p a true statement? ∀p is true when every case of p is true. Every case? Yes! Does that mean every case in the whole universe? No. It means every case in the universe of discourse.

Suppose p stands for it is red. And suppose that our universe of discourse contains the following objects: an apple, a bar of gold, and a bluebird. Now is ∀p true? To find out we must check the universe of discourse. The first object in the universe of discourse is an apple. An apple is red, so p is true for that object in the universe of discourse. So, is ∀p true? We have not checked all the objects in the universe as yet. Let us look at the other objects. The next object is a bar of gold. It is red is not true of a bar of gold, so p is false for that object in the universe of discourse. Our last object is a bluebird. It is red is also not true of a bluebird. So out of the three objects in the universe of discourse, two made p false and one made p true. So is ∀p true? p is true of one object but it is false for two objects, so p is not true for all objects in the universe of discourse. Therefore, ∀p is false. How about ∃p? Is p true of something in the universe of discourse? Yes, It is true for the apple. p is true for one object in the universe of discourse, so ∃p is true. Let us try an exercise that is a little harder. But first let us state the rules of semantics for monadic logic.

Rules of Semantics

According to any possible situation and for any U and W, S Rule 1, S Rule 2, S Rule 3, S Rule 4, and S Rule 5 (the rules for and, not, or, if-then, and if and only if) are the same as the corresponding S rules of truth-functional logic.

> S Rule 6. ∀U is true if U is true for all objects in the universe of discourse, but false if U is false for some object in the universe of discourse.
>
> S Rule 7. ∃U is true if U is true of some object in the universe of discourse, but false if U is false for all objects in the universe of discourse.

Suppose we have the formula ∃(p · q) in which p is the statement it is red and q is the statement it is blue. Is ∃(p · q) a true statement? Let us find out. ∃(p · q) will be true or false given some possible situation. So, we first need to state what a possible situation is in monadic logic. In truth-functional logic, a possible situation was simply the combinations of true and false that a formula could have. In monadic logic it is more. A possible situation in monadic logic is (1) a universe of discourse and (2) an assignment of objects in the universe of discourse to the atomic formulae in the formula being considered.

This means that if we assign an object in the universe of discourse (say, an apple) to the atomic formula it is red and an object (say, a bluebird) to the atomic formula it is blue, then we say that an apple is true of it is red and a bluebird is true of it is blue. But this also means that a bluebird would be false of it is red, not because bluebirds are not red but because we only assigned the object apple to it is red. Any object in the universe of discourse that is not assigned to it is red is said to be false of it is red.

POSSIBLE SITUATIONS AND TRUTH

There is one more thing we must consider before we can determine the truth value of the formula $\exists(p \cdot q)$. In truth-functional logic a formula was true or false according to a given possible situation. The atomic formulae were either true or false. But in monadic logic the atomic formulae are true or false for the objects in the universe of discourse. So, an atomic formula in monadic logic could be true of one object in the universe of discourse but false of another object in the universe of discourse. Thus, each object in the universe of discourse must be considered. One device that enables us to find the truth value of a formula (that is, by considering each object in the universe of discourse) is called expansion. When we expand a monadic formula we write it in such a way as to consider each object in the universe of discourse. Expansion is done by taking the monadic formula (the formula that has a quantifier), dropping the quantifier, and rewriting the remaining formula twice. For instance, $\exists(p \cdot q)$ is expanded in this way: $(p \cdot q) \vee (p \cdot q)$.

The two $(p \cdot q)$ formulae are connected by an or connector. Then, the atomic formulae are subscripted by the names of the objects in the universe of discourse. The first $(p \cdot q)$ is subscripted by the name of the first object in the universe of discourse, that is, apple. So, we have:

$$((p_{apple} \cdot q_{apple}) \vee (p \cdot q)$$

The second $(p \cdot q)$ is subscripted by the second object in the universe of discourse, that is, bluebird. So, we have:

$$((p_{apple} \cdot q_{apple}) \vee (p_{bluebird} \cdot q_{bluebird}))$$

Now we can say that $\exists(p \cdot q)$ is true if and only if $((p_{apple} \cdot q_{apple}) \vee (p_{bluebird} \cdot q_{bluebird}))$ is true because $((p_{apple} \cdot q_{apple}) \vee p_{bluebird} \cdot q_{bluebird}))$ states the truth value of $(p \cdot q)$ for every object in the universe of discourse. Since $(p \cdot q)$ must be true of only one object in the universe of discourse to make $\exists(p \cdot q)$ true, then $(p \cdot q)$ must be true of the first object in the universe of discourse or $(p \cdot q)$ must be true of the second object in the universe of discourse. Determining the truth value of $((p_{apple} \cdot q_{apple})$

v $(p_{bluebird} \cdot q_{bluebird}))$ is the best approach to the problem, for if $(p_{apple} \cdot q_{apple})$ is true, then $((p_{apple} \cdot q_{apple}) \vee (p_{bluebird} \cdot q_{bluebird}))$ will also be true by S Rule 3.

Suppose we define the possible situation as follows:

Universe of Discourse; {apple, bluebird}; p: apple; q, bluebird

Now, is $((p_{apple} \cdot q_{apple}) \vee (p_{bluebird} \cdot q_{bluebird}))$ true or false? According to the possible situation, p is true of apple but is true of nothing else. So, p is true of apple but false of bluebird.

$$(p_{apple} \cdot q_{apple}) \vee (p_{bluebird} \cdot q_{bluebird}))$$
$$\underline{T} \quad - \quad - \quad \underline{F} \quad -$$

Also, according to the possible situation, q is true of bluebird but true of nothing else. So, q is true of bluebird but false of apple.

$$(p_{apple} \cdot q_{apple}) \vee (p_{bluebird} \cdot q_{bluebird})$$
$$\underline{T} \quad \underline{F} \quad - \quad \underline{F} \quad \underline{T}$$

By S Rule 1 we know that $(p_{apple} \cdot q_{apple})$ is false and also by S Rule 1 we know that $(p_{bluebird} \cdot q_{bluebird})$ is false as well.

$$(p_{apple} \cdot q_{apple}) \vee (p_{bluebird} \cdot q_{bluebird})$$
$$\underline{\frac{T}{\vee}} \quad \underline{\frac{F}{\vee}} \underline{\frac{F}{\vee}} \quad \textcircled{\frac{F}{\vee}} \underline{\frac{F}{\vee}} \quad \underline{\frac{F}{\vee}} \underline{\frac{T}{\vee}}$$

Since the expansion is false, then (p · q) is not true of any object in the universe of discourse and, thus, (p . q) is not true for some object in the universe of discourse. Therefore, $\exists (p \cdot q)$ is false. Like anything else in logic, this method of finding the truth value of quantified formulae may take some practice, so let us examine another problem. Before we start we will abbreviate our universe of discourse to include numbers instead of apples and bluebirds. 0 will stand for apple and 1 will stand for bluebird. Now our possible situation looks like this:

Universe of Discourse: {0, 1}; p: 0, q: 1

Let us change the formula slightly and determine the truth value according to the given possible situation. Suppose instead of $\exists (p \cdot q)$ we had $\exists (p \vee q)$. The first step is expansion of the formula. This time, rather than subscripting with apple and bluebird, we subscript with 0 and 1.

$$(p_0 \vee q_0) \vee (p_1 \vee q_1)$$

Now, p is true of 0 but false of 1. So we have:

$$(p_0 \vee q_0) \vee (p_1 \vee q_1)$$
$$\underline{T} \quad - \quad - \quad = \quad \underline{F} \quad - \quad -$$

54

q is true of 1 but false of 0. This gives us:

$$(p_0 \lor q_0) \lor (p_1 \lor q_1)$$
$$\underline{T} \; \underline{F} \; = \; \underline{F} \; \underline{T}$$

And by S Rule 3 we have:

$$(p_0 \lor q_0) \lor (p_1 \lor q_1)$$

$$\frac{T}{\sqrt{}} \; \frac{T \; T}{\sqrt{}} \; = \; \frac{F}{\sqrt{}} \; \frac{T \; T}{\sqrt{}}$$

Finally, by S Rule 3 again we obtain:

$$(p_0 \lor q_0) \lor (p_1 \lor q_1)$$

$$\frac{T}{\sqrt{}} \; \frac{T \; F}{\sqrt{}} \; \boxed{T} \; \frac{F}{\sqrt{}} \; \frac{T \; T}{\sqrt{}}$$

So, since (p_0 \lor q_0) \lor (p_1 \lor q_1)$ is true, $\exists(p \lor q)$ is also true because $(p \lor q)$ is true for some object in the universe of discourse, namely 0 and 1.

Consider one more example. Suppose our possible situation is still the same:

Universe of Discourse: {0, 1}; p: 0; q: 1

Suppose also that the formula in question is $\exists(p \equiv q)$. We begin by expansion. $\exists(p \equiv q)$ becomes:

$$(p \equiv q) \lor (p \equiv q)$$

Next we subscript the atomic formulae on the left side of the <u>or</u> with the first object in the universe of discourse—in this case 0. So we have:

$$((p_0 \equiv q_0) \lor (p \equiv q))$$

Now we subscript the right side of the <u>or</u> with the only other object in the universe of discourse remaining and the expansion is finished. This gives us the following:

$$((p_0 \equiv q_0) \lor (p_1 \equiv q_1))$$

In reality what we have done is to state that $(p \equiv q)$ is true if and only if $((p_0 \equiv q_0) \lor (p_1 \equiv q_1))$ is true. So all we have to do now is determine the truth value of $((p_0 \equiv q_0) \lor (p_1 \equiv q_1))$.

We know from our possible situation that p is true of 0 but false of 1. Therefore:

$$((p_0 \equiv q_0) \lor (p_1 \equiv q_1))$$
$$\quad \underline{T} \qquad\qquad \underline{F}$$

Also, our possible situation informs us that q is true of 1 but false of 0. So, we obtain:

$$((p_0 \equiv q_0) \lor (p_1 \equiv q_1))$$
$$\quad \underline{T} \; \underline{F} \qquad \underline{F} \; \underline{T}$$

By S Rule 5 we obtain:

$$((p_0 \equiv q_0) \lor (p_1 \equiv q_1)$$
$$\underset{\sqrt{}}{T} \; \underset{\sqrt{}}{F} \; \underset{\sqrt{}}{F} \qquad \underset{\sqrt{}}{F} \; \underset{\sqrt{}}{F} \; \underset{\sqrt{}}{T}$$

And by S Rule 3 we obtain:

$$((p_0 \equiv q_0) \lor (p_1 \equiv q_1)$$
$$\underset{\sqrt{}}{T} \; \underset{\sqrt{}}{F} \; \underset{\sqrt{}}{F} \; \boxed{F} \; \underset{\sqrt{}}{F} \; \underset{\sqrt{}}{F} \; \underset{\sqrt{}}{T}$$

So, the expansion is false and, consequently, $\exists(p \equiv q)$ is also false. We have considered everything in the universe of discourse (that is, 1 and 0) and the formula is false.

Let us consider a slightly more complex formula:

$$\forall((p \supset q) \lor s)$$

What is the truth value of this formula given the following possible situation?

Universe of Discourse: {1, 0}; p: 1; q: 0; s: 0

As before, we need to expand the formula. To do this, we must first rewrite the formula twice because there are two objects in the universe of discourse. Then, we need to connect both formulae with an <u>and</u> as follows:

$$(((p \supset q) \lor s) \cdot ((p \supset q) \lor s))$$

You are probably asking why we used an <u>and</u> to connect the expanded formulae in this case when before we used an <u>or</u>. In this case we need to connect the formulae with an <u>and</u> because in order for the formula to be true it must be true for every object in the universe of discourse. Remember that an <u>and</u> formula is false if one side is false. So for every object in the universe of discourse, the formula must be true. If the formula (<u>(p ⊃ q) ∨ s)</u> were false for some object in the universe of discourse, then this would make the whole expanded formula false, which is what we want it to accomplish. The previous examples was a <u>for some</u> formula (that is, <u>∃(p ≡ q))</u>, which need only be true for one object in the universe of discourse in order to be true. So whenever you are expanding a <u>for every</u> formula, you should connect the expanded formulae with an <u>and</u> and whenever you are expanding a <u>for some</u> formula you connect the expanded formulae with an <u>or</u>.

Now, let us return to our example. Our next step is to subscript each atomic formula in the expanded formula with 0 and 1. The reason we subscript with 0 and 1 is that they are the only two objects in the universe of discourse.

$$(((p_0 \supset q_0) \lor s_0) \cdot ((p_1 \supset q_1) \lor s_1))$$

Next, we find the truth value of each atomic formula by looking at our possible situation. <u>p</u> is false of 0 but true of 1.

$$(((p_0 \supset q_0) \lor s_0) \cdot ((p_1 \supset q_1) \lor s_1))$$
$$\underset{}{F} \; -- \quad -- \quad = \quad \underset{}{T} \; -- \quad --$$

$\underline{q}$ is true of 0 but false of 1:

$$(((p_0 \supset q_0) \lor s_0) \cdot ((p_1 \supset q_1) \lor s_1)$$
$$\underline{F}\;\_\;\underline{T}\;\;\_\_\;\;=\;\;\underline{T}\;\_\underline{F}\;\;\_\_$$

$\underline{s}$ is true of 0 but false of 1:

$$(((p_0 \supset q_0) \lor s_0) \cdot ((p_1 \supset q_1) \lor s_1))$$
$$\underline{F}\;\_\;\underline{T}\;\;\_\underline{T}\;\;=\;\;\underline{T}\;\_\underline{F}\;\;\_\underline{F}$$

Now, we simply use the S rules to determine the truth value of the whole expanded formula:

$$(((p_0 \supset q_0) \lor s_0) \cdot ((p_1 \supset q_1) \lor s_1))$$
$$\underset{\diagup}{F}\;\underset{\diagup}{TT}\;\;\underset{\diagup}{TT}\;\;\underset{}{\textcircled{F}}\;\;\underset{\diagup}{T}\;\underset{\diagup}{FF}\;\;\underset{\diagup}{FF}$$

Thus, since this formula is false, then $\forall((p \supset q) \lor s)$ is also false.

Now let us try another example which will give us different problems:

$$\exists(q \supset r) \lor \forall(s \lor t)$$

First let us state a possible situation:

Universe of Discourse: {0, 1, 2}; q: 0; r: 1; s: 2; t: 0

The first step is to expand our formula. But which part of the formula should we do first? In this case it does not matter. The best approach will probably be to expand $\exists(q \supset r)$ first, then expand $\forall(s \supset t)$ and then connect them together as follows:

$$((q_0 \supset r_0) \lor (q_1 \supset r_1) \lor (q_2 \supset r_2))$$

Wait a minute! Why did I rewrite the formula three times? Those of you who ask this question have forgotten the rule mentioned earlier. When expanding a formula, you rewrite the formula as many times as there are objects in the universe of discourse. This possible situation has a universe of discourse that contains three objects. Now we expand $\forall(s \lor t)$ as follows:

$$((s_0 \lor t_0) \cdot (s_1 \lor t_1) \cdot (s_2 \lor t_2)$$

Next we need to put both expansions back together. So, our formula looks like this:

$$((q_0 \supset r_0) \lor (q_1 \supset r_1) \lor (q_2 \supset r_2)) \lor ((s_0 \lor t_0) \cdot (s_1 \lor t_1) \cdot (s_2 \lor t_2))$$

The next step is simply to assign truth values to the invididual atomic formula according to the possible situation and then figure out the truth value of the whole formula, according to the S rules (rules of semantics).

$$((q_0 \supset r_0) \lor (q_1 \supset r_1) \lor (q_2 \supset r_2)) \lor ((s_0 \lor t_0) \cdot (s_1 \lor t_1) \cdot (s_2 \lor t_2))$$
$$\underline{T}\;\_\underline{F}\;\;\_\;\underline{F}\;\underline{T}\;\;\_\;\underline{F}\;\underline{F}\;\;=\;\;\underline{F}\;\_\underline{T}\;\;\_\;\underline{F}\;\underline{F}\;\;\_\;\underline{T}\;\underline{F}$$

Now, one final step using the S rules:

$$((q_0 \supset r_0) \lor (q_1 \supset r_1) \lor (q_2 \supset r_2)) \lor ((s_0 \lor t_0) \cdot (s_1 \lor t_1) \cdot (s_2 \lor t_2)$$

$$\begin{array}{ccc} T & FF \\ \diagup & \diagup\diagup \end{array} \quad \begin{array}{ccc} T & F & TT \\ \diagup & \diagup & \diagup\diagup \end{array} \quad \begin{array}{ccc} T & F & TF \\ \diagup & \diagup & \diagup\diagup \end{array} \quad \textcircled{$\underset{=}{T}$} \quad \begin{array}{ccc} F & TT \\ \diagup & \diagup\diagup \end{array} \quad \begin{array}{ccc} F & F & FF \\ \diagup & \diagup & \diagup\diagup \end{array} \quad \begin{array}{ccc} F & T & TF \\ \diagup & \diagup & \diagup\diagup \end{array}$$

EXERCISES 3.4

Find the truth value of the following formulae given the possible situation:

Universe of Discourse: $\{0, 1\}$; p: $0, 1$; q: 1; r: 0; s: 1; t: $0, 1$

1. $\exists (p \supset q) \equiv \forall (s \cdot t)$
2. $\forall ((p \lor r) \cdot -q) \supset \exists (s \lor \exists r)$
3. $\exists s \equiv \forall ((p \cdot -t) \lor r)$
4. $(\exists s \cdot \exists t) \lor (\forall p \cdot \forall q)$
5. $\forall s \supset \exists (r \equiv t) \cdot \forall p$

VALIDITY

FINDING COUNTEREXAMPLES

We can now consider counterexamples for monadic arguments because we are able to find the truth values of formulae having one indefinite pronoun (that is, monadic formulae).

To review, recall what we must show to give a counterexample. We must specify some situation (called a possible situation) in which the assumptions are true and the conclusion is false. So in monadic logic our counterexample will be a possible situation. Remember that a possible situation consists of a universe of discourse and a subset of things on which each atomic formula in the formula is true. Let us look at a simple example: $\exists p$, so $\underline{p}$. First, we expand any formulae in the argument that have quantifiers. Are there any? Yes. We have just one assumption and it is a quantified formula. So we expand $\underline{\exists p}$. We do not have a possible situation yet. That is what we are going to construct. So, let us just assume we will have two objects in our universe of discourse. Then, $\underline{\exists p}$ expands like this:

$$p_0 \lor p_1$$

We have a conclusion which is not quantified and so it can be given a 0 or a 1—whatever will work. Let us try 0. Now we have:

$$\underline{p_0 \lor p_1}$$

So, p_0

Can we make the assumption true and the conclusion false? Yes. Begin by making the conclusion false. To do this we must not make $\underline{p}$ true for 0. So let us make $\underline{p}$ true for 1. Thus, if our possible situation has a universe of discourse of 0 and 1, and $\underline{p}$ is true of 1, then this possible situation should work. Let us try it:

$$p_0 \vee p_1$$
$$\overset{F}{\underset{\sqrt{}}{}} \overset{\textcircled{T}}{} \overset{T}{\underset{\sqrt{}}{}}$$
So, p_0
$$\textcircled{F}$$

$p_0 \vee p_1$ is true by S Rule 3. It does work. The assumption is true and the conclusion is false. So $\exists p$ is true by S Rule 7. Now, how do we state our counterexample? We simply give the possible situation that will make the assumptions true and the conclusion false. For our example, it is the following:

Universe of Discourse: $\{0, 1\}$; p: 1

This is a counterexample for the argument $\exists p$, so, p. This is what a counterexample in monadic logic would look like. It is all that is necessary. Until you become proficient at giving counterexamples, however, you should show your expanded formula as well as the assignment of truth values to the atomic formulae as shown above. Shall we try another, more difficult, example?

$$\exists p$$
$$\exists ((q \supset r) \vee -p)$$
_____
So, $\forall (q \supset r)$

How do we start? First assume that we will use a universe of discourse with two objects and then expand all the formulae that are quantified. First $\exists p$. This one is easy:

$(p_0 \vee p_1)$

Next we expand $\exists ((q \supset r) \vee - p)$:

$(((q_0 \supset r_0) \vee -p_0) \vee ((q_1 \supset r_1) \vee - p_1))$

Finally, we expand $\forall (q \supset r)$:

$(q_0 \supset r_0) \cdot (q_1 \supset r_1)$

Next we have to assign truth values to the atomic formulae so that the conclusion is false and the assumptions are true. First let us try to make the conclusion false. If we make q true for 0 and r false for 0 but true for 1, then the conclusion will be false by S Rules 1 and 4.

q: 0
r: 1
$$(q_0 \supset r_0) \cdot (q_1 \supset r_1)$$
$$\overset{T}{\underset{\sqrt{}}{}} \overset{F}{\underset{\sqrt{}}{}} \overset{F}{} \textcircled{F} \overset{F}{\underset{\sqrt{}}{}} \overset{T}{} \overset{T}{\underset{\sqrt{}}{}}$$

Now let us try to make the assumptions true. First consider $(p_0 \vee p_1)$. If we make p true for 0 and false for 1, then $p_0 \vee p_1$ will still be true by S Rule 3.

p: 1

$p_0 \lor p_1$
F ⓣ F
√   √

We have just one assumption left to worry about. We have already given a denotation to all the atomic formula that appear in that assumption.

q: 0
r: 1
p: 1

So, we only need to determine the truth value of the whole formula by using the appropriate S rules.

$(((q_0 \supset r_0) \lor - p_0) \lor ((q_1 \supset r_1) \lor \sim p_1))$
T F T   TT F   ⓣ   F TT   TF T
√   √√   √√√   √   √√   √√√

Now the whole solution looks like this:

Assumption 1. $p_0 \lor p_1$
                 F ⓣ T

Assumption 2. $(((q_0 \supset r_0) \lor - p_0) \lor ((q_1 \supset r_1) \lor \sim p_1))$
                 T F F   TT F   ⓣ   F TT   TF T
                 √   √√   √√√   √   √√   √√√
                 _____

So, $((q_0 \supset r_0) \cdot (q_1 \supset r_1))$
                 T F F   ⓕ   F TT
                 √   √√   √   √√

The assumptions are true and the conclusion is false so the following argument is invalid:

    $\exists p$
    $\exists ((q \supset r) \lor -p)$

So, $\forall (q \supset r)$

The counterexample is this possible situation:

Universe of Discourse: {0, 1}; q: 0; r: 1; p: 1

The important thing to remember when doing counterexamples in monadic logic is that you make up the possible situation. You pick a universe of discourse that you think will work and you decide what the denotation of each atomic formula will be. Some students think they need to be given a possible situation before they can try to develop a counterexample. This is not so. It is up to you to create a possible situation which will give you what you want. To do counterexamples in monadic logic you must be able to do expansion on quantified formulae and you must know the S rules. If you do not know these two things go back and learn how to do expansions and review the S rules.

Give counterexamples for the following arguments:

1. $\exists(q \cdot r)$; so, $(q \cdot r)$
2. $(q \vee s)$; so, $\forall(q \vee s)$
3. $\forall(s \supset t)$, $\forall t$; so, $\forall s$
4. $\forall(q \supset p)$, $\exists p$; so, $\forall q$
5. $\forall(r \supset s)$, $\exists -r$; so, $\exists -s$
6. $\forall(t \vee q)$, $\forall -t$; so, $\exists -q$
7. $\exists r$, $\exists t$; so $\exists(r \cdot t)$
8. $\forall s$, $\forall p$; so, $\forall -(s \cdot q)$
9. $\forall(t \supset p)$, $\forall q$; so, $\forall((p \supset t) \cdot q)$
10. $\forall(r \equiv (p \cdot s))$, $\forall p$; so, $\forall r$

PROOFS

VALID ARGUMENTS USED FOR PROOFS

Before discussing proofs, we should first review the new valid arguments given to you in the text.

For Some Introduction ($\exists$I)

$\dot{s}$; so, $\exists s$

Suppose $\underline{p}$ occurs on the line somewhere in a proof. If $\underline{p}$ is assumed to be true (which it must be or it would not appear on a line in a proof), then it must be true of at least one of the objects in the universe of discourse. If this is so, then it is also true that for some object(s) $\underline{p}$ is true. If $\underline{p}$ is true for one object then it is true for some object. Thus $\exists p$ is true. We have added or introduced a <u>for some</u> quantifier to the $\underline{p}$ that we had initially. Thus, we refer to this as an instance of For Some Introduction ($\exists$I).

For Some Elimination ($\exists$E)

$\exists s$, $\forall(S \supset U)$; so, U

Remember that in this argument the atomic formulae in $\underline{U}$ must be bound. If they are not bound, then the argument is invalid.

Although this argument poses some difficulty in explaining how and why it works, we will try to make our explanation as clear as possible. Suppose we have the following argument:

$\exists(q \cdot r)$
$\forall((q \cdot r) \supset \exists t)$
_____

So, $\exists t$

This argument has the form of the For Some Elimination argument. If $(q \cdot r)$ is substituted for $\underline{S}$ and $\exists t$ is substituted for $\underline{U}$, then we have the For Some Elimination argument. Because $\underline{t}$ is bound by the <u>for some</u> quantifier, it satisfies the criterion that $\underline{U}$ must be bound. Let us consider why the argument is valid.

Suppose we have a universe of discourse with two objects, 0 and 1. If we expand the formulae, they will look like this:

$$(q_0 \cdot r_0) \lor (q_1 \cdot r_1)$$
$$((q_0 \cdot r_0) \supset (t_0 \lor t_1)) \cdot ((q_1 \cdot r_1) \supset (t_0 \lor t_1))$$

So, $t_0 \lor t_1$

We know that either $(q_0 \cdot r_0)$ is true or $(q_1 \cdot r_1)$ is true or both are true. If neither of them were true, then $\exists(q \cdot r)$ would not be true. This much we know by S Rule 3.

$$(q_0 \cdot r_0) \lor (q_1 \cdot r_1)$$
$$\text{F} \quad \textcircled{F} \quad \text{F}$$

One or the other of these formulae must be true because we are given that $\exists(q \cdot r)$ is true. Now suppose for the time being that $(q_0 \cdot r_0)$ is true. If so, then $(t_0 \lor t_1)$ must be true also, since if it were false, then $(q_1 \cdot r_1) \supset (t_0 \lor t_1)$ would be false by S Rule 4:

$$(q_0 \cdot r_0) \supset (t_0 \lor t_1)$$
$$\underset{7}{\text{T}} \quad \textcircled{F} \quad \underset{7}{\text{F}}$$

And if $(q_0 \cdot r_0) \supset (t_0 \lor t_1)$ is false, then $((q_0 \cdot r_0) \supset (t_0 \lor t_1))$ $\cdot ((q_1 \cdot r_1) \supset (t_0 \lor t_1))$ would also be false by S Rule 1:

$$((q_0 \cdot r_0) \supset ((t_0 \lor t_1)) \cdot ((q_1 \cdot r_1) \supset (t_0 \lor t_1))$$
$$\text{F} \quad \textcircled{F} \quad \text{T or F}$$

Notice that it does not matter whether $(q_1 \cdot r_1) \supset (t_0 \lor t_1)$ is true or false. If one side of a conjunction (an <u>and</u> formula) is false, then the whole conjunction is false regardless of the truth value of the other side of the conjunction. But $((q_0 \cdot r_0) \supset (t_0 \lor t_1))$ $\cdot ((q_1 \cdot r_1) \supset (t_0 \lor t_1))$ cannot be false because $\forall((q \cdot r) \supset \exists t)$ is true and $((q_0 \cdot r_0) \supset (t_0 \lor t_1)) \cdot ((q_1 \cdot r_1) \supset (t_0 \lor t_1))$ is simply $\forall((q \cdot r) \supset \exists t)$ expanded. And we know $\forall((q \cdot r) \supset \exists t$ is true because it is one of our given assumptions.

What this all means is that $(t_0 \lor t_1)$ is true if $(q_0 \cdot r_0)$ is true. Now, let us suppose that $(q_0 \cdot r_0)$ is false and $(q_1 \cdot r_1)$ is true. If so, then $(q_0 \cdot r_0) \lor (q_1 \cdot r_1)$ is still true by S Rule 3:

$$(q_0 \cdot r_0) \lor (q_1 \cdot r_1)$$
$$\underset{7}{\text{F}} \quad \textcircled{T} \quad \underset{7}{\text{T}}$$

So, if $(q_1 \cdot r_1)$ is true, then we know again that $(t_0 \lor t_1)$ is true. We know this since, if $(t_0 \lor t_1)$ were false, then $(q_1 \cdot r_1) \supset (t_0 \lor t_1)$ would be false by S Rule 4:

$$(q_1 \cdot r_1) \supset (t_0 \lor t_1)$$
$$\underset{7}{\text{T}} \quad \textcircled{F} \quad \underset{7}{\text{F}}$$

And if $(q_1 \cdot r_1) \supset (t_0 \lor t_1)$ is false, then $((q_0 \cdot r_0) \supset (t_0 \lor t_1))$ $\cdot ((q_1 \cdot r_1) \supset (t_0 \lor t_1))$ would also be false by S Rule 1. But we know that $((q_0 \cdot r_0) \supset (t_0 \vee t_1)) \cdot ((q_1 \cdot r_1) \supset (t_0 \vee t_1))$ is true by assumption. So, no matter which formula $(q_0 \cdot r_0)$ or $(q_1 \cdot q_1)$ is true, the conclusion of the argument $(t_0 \vee t_1)$ is true. What it all boils down to is that $(t_0 \vee t_1)$ is true by Or Elimination:

$(q_0 \cdot r_0) \vee (q_1 \cdot r_1)$
$(q_0 \cdot r_0) \supset (t_0 \vee t_1)$
$(q_1 \cdot r_1) \supset (t_0 \vee t_1)$
_____

So, $(t_0 \vee t_1)$

Thus, if $(t_0 \vee t_1)$ is true then $\exists t$ is true and the argument is complete.
We could also look at For Some Elimination in the following way. Suppose we now have a different argument: $\exists p$, $\forall (p \supset \exists q)$; so, $\exists q$. This argument has the form of a For Some Elimination argument. Suppose we have a whole set of p's—one for each object in the Universe of Discourse: $\{0, 1, 2, 3, 4\}$.

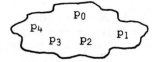

Again, let us suppose we have another set. This set contains all the $(p \supset \exists q)$'s—one for each object in the universe of discourse:

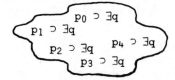

If $\forall (p \supset \exists q)$ is true, then each one (that is, all) in the set are true. And if $\exists p$ is true, then at least one of the p's in the set is true. Suppose we eliminate p_0 from the set. p_0 may or may not be true. But if p_0 is true, we can eliminate $p_0 \supset \exists q$ from the other set to obtain $\exists q$. This follows because we know that $p_0 \supset \exists q$ is true and that by using If-then Elimination we can obtain $\exists q$:

$p_0 \supset \exists q$
p_0
_____

So, $\exists q$

Someone may object, however, that we do not know whether p_0 is true and so we cannot conclude $\exists q$. In fact, we do not know and so let us try p_1. If p_1 is true, then we can eliminate $p_1 \supset \exists q$ and obtain $\exists q$ again by If-then Elimination. Once again, however, we do not know whether p_1 is true. p_1 could be false. So, we will eliminate p_2 and repeat the same process. This process can be repeated for p_3 and if we still do not know whether p_3 is true, then we proceed to consider p_4. But should p_4 be any different from the others? If we try p_0, p_1, p_2, and p_3 and they all turn out to be false, then p_4 must be true. p_4 must be true because we were given that $\exists p$ is true and if p_4 is not true, then no p is true and $\exists p$ would be false. So, p_4 is true and we eliminate $p_4 \supset \exists q$ from its set. By If-then Elimination $\exists q$ is true. It does not matter that we do not know which of the five $\underline{p}$'s is true. We only need to know that one is true. If $\exists \underline{p}$ is true, then we can be certain that $\underline{p}$ is true for at least one object in the universe of discourse. And since $\underline{\forall (p \supset \exists q)}$ is true, then we know that $p \supset \exists q$ is true of every object in the universe of discourse. From these considerations we derive $\exists q$ by If-then Elimination. In a sense we eliminate the for some assumption in the argument and thus we refer to this as For Some Elimination.

BOUNDNESS

In monadic logic our notion of boundness changes slightly. The text says the following about boundness in monadic logic: A formula is bound if and only if every occurrence of an atomic formula in it is bound. This concept is extremely important in regard to the For Some Elimination argument.

Notice that although the $\underline{q}$ in the previous argument was bound with a for some quantifier, this is not necessary. $\underline{q}$ could be bound by a for every quantifier as well. For this reason we say that the argument:

$\exists p, \forall (p \supset \forall q)$; so $\forall q$

is an instance of the For Some Elimination argument.

It is very important for you to understand that the $\underline{U}$ in the following argument:

$\exists S, \forall (S \supset U)$; so, U

be a bound formula. Suppose our last example was changed slightly as follows:

$\exists p, \forall (p \supset q)$; so, q

In this case, if $\underline{p}$ is substituted for $\underline{S}$ and $\underline{q}$ is substituted for $\underline{U}$, then we would seem to have an instance of For Some Elimination. But there is something missing. The $\underline{q}$ is not bound. Remember that for the For Some Elimination argument, the $\underline{U}$ must be bound. Someone may point out that the $\underline{q}$ is bound, since the formula $p \supset q$ is preceded by a for every quantifier. This is true, but the atomic formula $\underline{q}$ must be bound before the argument is valid. Another way to state the For Some Elimination argument might be like this:

$\exists S, \forall (S \supset U)$; so, U where the formula $\underline{U}$ can be either atomic or not and $\underline{U}$ has each atomic formula preceded by either a for some or a for every quantifier.

Let us examine this argument more carefully to determine whether we can find a counterexample. First we expand all the quantified formulae for a universe of discourse containing 0 and 1:

$p_0 \vee p_1$
$(p_0 \supset q_0) \cdot (p_1 \supset q_1)$

So, q

64

Now we assign p and q to be true of some object in the universe of discourse. So, our possible situation will look like this:

Universe of Discourse: $\{0, 1\}$; p: 0; q: 0

Since the conclusion q is not quantified, we can make it either q_0 or q_1. If we make the conclusion q_1, then it will be false, which is what we want. So, given the possible situation above, we have the following:

$$p_0 \lor p_1$$
$$\text{T} \quad \underline{\text{T}} \; \text{F}$$
$$(p_0 \supset q_0) \; \lor \; (p_1 \supset q_1)$$
$$\underset{\checkmark}{\text{T}} \; \underset{\checkmark}{\text{T}} \; \underset{\checkmark}{\text{T}} \quad \text{(T)} \quad \underset{\checkmark}{\text{F}} \; \underset{\checkmark}{\text{T}} \; \underset{\checkmark}{\text{F}}$$

So, q_1
(F)

Thus, the assumptions are true and the conclusion is false. So, the argument is invalid. You must remember that U must be a bound formula; otherwise the argument is invalid.

If you understand the reasoning behind the For Some Elimination argument, you should appreciate its usefulness. Other examples of this argument are given in the text as well as in this Study Guide. You will use this argument in the chapters to follow, so learn it well. Also, the For Some Elimination argument will be discussed when we come to Proof Strategy 12 later in this chapter.

EXERCISES 3.6

Determine which of the following are valid arguments (that is, instances of the For Some Elimination argument). For those which are not valid, give a counterexample.

1. $\forall((p \supset q) \lor r) \supset \exists(s \supset t)$, $\exists((p \supset q) \lor r)$; so, $\exists(s \supset t)$
2. $\exists((q \equiv t) \cdot w)$, $\forall((q \equiv t) \cdot w) \supset (p \supset \exists s))$; so, $p \supset \exists s$
3. $\exists(s \lor -t)$, $\forall((s \lor -t) \supset (\exists p \lor q))$; so, $\exists p \lor q$
4. $\forall((s \lor (t \equiv p)) \supset (p \cdot \exists(r \supset w))$, $\exists(s \lor (t \equiv p))$; so, $(p \cdot \exists(r \supset w))$
5. $\exists p$, $\forall(p \supset \exists(s \equiv ((t \supset p) \lor q))$; so, $\exists(s \equiv ((t \supset p) \lor q))$

For Every Elimination (∀E)

$\forall S$; so, S

If $\forall q$ is true and the universe of discourse is: $\{1, 0\}$, then $(q_0 \cdot q_1)$ is also true. You will remember from S Rule 1 that in order for $(q_0 \cdot q_1)$ to be true both q_0 must be true and q_1 must be true. If a formula is true for every object in the universe of discourse, then no matter which object we choose, the formula must be true. So if $\forall q$ is true, then q is true also. Thus, we have in a sense eliminated the for every quantifier and so we call this argument For Every Elimination (∀E). Whenever you see a formula that is preceded by a for every quantifier (∀), you are allowed to rewrite the

formula on a new line without the quantifier. For example, if we had
$\forall((s \lor t) \equiv (q \cdot r))$ on some line of proof, then we could write
$(s \lor t) \equiv (q \cdot r)$ on another line. This argument is very useful.

For Every Introduction ($\forall$I)

If $\underline{S}$ follows from a set of bound formulae, then $\forall\underline{S}$ also follows from
that set of formulae.

Rules of Proof

In conjunction with this argument (For Every Introduction ($\forall$I)) is
a new rule of proof. This rule is added to the previous rules of proof
you received in the chapter on truth-functional logic. Previously, we
stated three rules so this new rule of proof is Rule 4.

P Rule 4. A line, $\forall$S, is justified (by $\forall$I) if it is directly below
its predecessor, and up to an earlier line S still in
force, all assumptions of the argument and all temporary
assumptions in force are bound formulae.

This rule basically means this: If you arrive at a conclusion in
a proof and all the assumptions, including the temporary assumptions,
are bound formulae, then we can bind the conclusion also. Consider this
example: $\forall(q \supset r)$, $\forall(r \supset s)$; so, $\forall(q \supset s)$.

1. $\forall(q \supset r)$	As
2. $\forall(r \supset s)$	As
Show $\forall(q \supset s)$	
3. $(q \supset r)$	($\forall$E, 1)
4. $(r \supset s)$	($\forall$E, 2)
5. $(q \supset s)$	(H, 3, 4)

Line 5 has been arrived at by the proper P rules and all the assumptions
(that is, $\forall(q \supset r)$ and $\forall(r \supset s)$) are bound formulae. So, by P Rule 4
we can conclude: $\forall(q \supset s)$; this is what we are asked to show in our
conclusion. So, line 6 in our proof would be:

6. $\forall(q \supset s)$ ($\forall$I, 5)

Quantifier Exchange (Q)

These rules simply allow you to change from one quantifier to
another. For example, if you had $-\exists-(q \cdot p)$ on one line, then you
could write $\forall(q \cdot p)$ on the next line by Quantifier Exchange (Q).

PROOF STRATEGIES

STRATEGIES

There are four new proof strategies to add to the eight we were
given for truth-functional logic. If you examine these strategies
closely, you will discover that they correspond to the new valid arguments we have just discussed: For Some Elimination; For Some Introduction; For Every Elimination; and For Every Introduction.

Strategy 9. To show $\forall$S when all the assumptions in force are bound, show S and use $\forall$I.
Strategy 10. To show S from $\forall$S, use $\forall$E.
Strategy 11. To show $\exists$S, show S and use $\exists$I.
Strategy 12. To show a bound formula U when you still have $\exists$S in force, show $\forall$(S $\supset$ U) and use $\exists$E. In other words, if all assumptions still in force are bound, assume S and show U and use IfI, then $\forall$I, and finally $\exists$E.

Strategy 9

Whenever the conclusion of any argument is of the form $\forall$S, you need to use Strategy 9. Suppose we have the following argument: $\forall$(q · s), $\forall$(r · p); so, $\forall$(r · s). Here our conclusion is of the form $\forall$s where (r · s) is substituted for S. So Strategy 9 tells us that we need to show (r · s) with all the assumptions in force being bound. We set up the proof in the following way:

```
1. ∀(q · s)          As
2. ∀(r · p)          As
Show ∀(r · s)
[Show (r · s)]
```

By stating that we need to show (r · s), we are adopting Strategy 9 for this proof. We can proceed no further for the moment, however, until we can show (r · s). To do so, we need to apply Strategy 1. Recall that Strategy 1 advises us to eliminate wherever possible. The only elimination argument that we can possibly use at this point is For Every Elimination, one of our new arguments. So, let us do just that wherever we can:

```
1. ∀(q · s)          As
2. ∀(r · p)          As
Show ∀(r · s)
[Show (r · s)]
3. (q · s)           (∀E, 1)
4. (r · p)           (∀E, 2)
5. q                 (&E, 3)
6. s                 (&E, 3)
7. r                 (&E, 4)
8. p                 (&E, 4)
```

Because For Every Elimination is an elimination argument, Strategy 1 applies to it. And since For Every Elimination is the argument discussed by Strategy 10, we find that Strategy 10 is an instance of Strategy 1.

Recall that we are trying to show (r · s). Can we obtain this formula? Yes, from lines 6 and 7 as follows:

```
1. ∀(q · s)              As
2. ∀(r · p)              As
Show ∀(r · s)
[Show (r · s)]
3. (q · s)               (∀E, 1)
4. (r · p)               (∀E, 2)
5. q                     (&E, 3)
6. s                     (&E, 3)
7. r                     (&E, 4)
8. p                     (&E, 4)
9. (r · s)               (&I, 6, 7)
```

We have arrived at our show statement (r · s) and we are now ready to complete Strategy 9. Are all the assumptions that are in force bound? There are only two of them, lines 1 and 2. They are both bound, so we can apply For Every Introduction (∀I) in line 10:

```
10. ∀(r · s)             (∀I, 9)
```

Actually, this proof uses another strategy which we did not mention. Whenever we need to show (r · s), Strategy 2 applies. Let us look at the proof done in this way:

```
1. ∀(q · s)              As
2. ∀(r · p)              As
Show ∀(r · s)
[Show (r · s)]           (Strategy 9)
[Show r]                 (Strategy 2)
3. (r · p)               (∀E, 2)
4. r                     (&E, 3)
[Show s]                 (Strategy 2)
5. q · s                 (∀E, 1)
6. s                     (&E, 5)
7. r · s                 (&I, 4, 6)
8. ∀(r · s)              (∀I, 7)
```

Strategy 10

Strategy 10 simply tells us that if you want to show an unbound formula S and you are given, or you can derive, ∀S, then use the For Every Elimination argument. Here is an example of Strategy 10 used in a proof:

```
1. ∃p ⊃ ∀q
2. ∀(s ⊃ r) · ∃p
Show q
```

Simply work through the proof until you obtain ∀q, then use For Every Elimination as in the following:

```
1. ∃p ⊃ ∀q              As
2. ∀(s ⊃ q) · ∃p         As
Show q
[Show ∀q]                (Strategy 10)
3. ∃p                    (&E, 2)
4. ∀q                    (IfE, 1, 3)
5. q                     (∀E, 4)
```

Strategy 11

If we want to show a formula is true for something in the universe of discourse (that is, ∃S) then just show it is true for S and use For Some Introduction (∃I) as in the following example:

1. q ⊃ (r ≡ t)   As
2. ∀r · q   As

Show ∃t

Strategy 11 is used to show t. Then, use For Some Introduction:

```
1. q ⊃ (r ≡ t)          As
2. ∀r · q                As

Show ∃t
[Show t]                 (Strategy 11)
3. q                     (&E, 2)
4. r ≡ t                 (IfE, 1, 3)
5. r ⊃ t                 (IffE, 4)
6. ∀r                    (&E, 2)
7. r                     (∀E, 6)
8. t                     (IfE, 5, 7)
9. ∃t                    (∀I, 8)
```

In line 8 we showed t, so we just had to use For Some Introduction in line 9 and we were done.

Strategy 12

Suppose we have the following argument:

1. ∀(p ⊃ t)
2. ∃(p · r)

Show ∃(t · r)

Because this argument has a formula that is quantified with a for some quantifier, we will use Strategy 12 in our proof. Almost every argument that has one of its assumptions quantified with a for some quantifier, use Strategy 12. In other words, if you see an argument that has a for some formula as one of its assumptions, then you should consider using Strategy 12 in your proof.

The first step of this strategy is easy. You temporarily assume the quantified portion of the for some assumption. In this example the assumption that has a for some quantifier is ∃(p · r). So, assume (p · r) to begin Strategy 12.

Be careful not to derive (p · r) from ∃(p · r). This is not correct and usually happens because the erring student notices the ∃S and thinks of it as ∀S. Thus, he derives S and believes he is using For Some Elimination. But ∃E does not work that way. So, be careful not to make this common error.

We begin by assuming (p · r), then we work toward showing U. U in this example is (t · r). After we derive (t · r), we use For Some Introduction, then If-then Introduction, then For Every Introduction, and, finally, For Some Elimination, as follows:

69

```
1. ∀(p ⊃ t)                    As
2. ∃(p · r)                    As
Show ∃(t · r)
[Show ∀(p · r) ⊃ ∃(t · r)]]   (Strategy 12)
[Show (p · r) ⊃ ∃(t · r)]]    (Strategy 9)
   3. (p · r)                  Tas
```

Our first show statement, ∃(t · r), is the desired conclusion. The
second show statement, ∀((p · r ⊃ ∃(t · r), is the formula we need in
order to use For Some Elimination. If we substitute (p · r) for S
and ∃(t · r) for U, then we will have an instance of the argument
∀(S ⊃ U), ∃S; so, U, which is an instance of For Some Elimination. So,
we need to show ∀((p · r) ⊃ ∃(t · r). But since ∀((p · r) ⊃ ∃(t · r)
is a formula that begins with a for every quantifier, Strategy 9 is
appropriate. Strategy 9 tells us that if we want to show a for every
formula, then we must first show the formula with all the assumptions
in force bound and then use For Every Introduction. So, we need to
show (p · r) ⊃ ∃(t · r) with all the assumptions in force being bound.
This accounts for our third show statement. Now, since our third show
statement is a conditional (that is, an If-then formula), Strategy 9
is appropriate. Thus, we first assume the antecedent and then show the
consequent. Line 3, (p · r), is a temporary assumption.

   Next, we need to show the consequent, ∃(t · r). Since ∃(t · r) is
a for some formula, Strategy 11 applies. This means that to show
∃(t · r), we must first show (t · r) and then use For Some Introduction. To show (t · r) we use Strategy 11.

   Our proof should now look like this:

```
1. ∀(p ⊃ t)                      As
2. ∃(p · r)                      As
Show ∃(t · r)
[Show ∀((p · r) ⊃ ∃(t · r))]     (Strategy 12)
[Show (p · r) ⊃ ∃(t · r)]        (Strategy 9)
   3. (p · r)                    Tas
   [Show ∃(t · r)]
   [Show (t · r)]                (Strategy 11)
   [Show r]
   4. r                          (&E, 3)
   [Show t]
   5. p                          (&E, 3)
   6. p ⊃ t                      (∀E, 1)
   7. t                          (IfE, 5, 6)
   8. (t · r)                    (&I, 4, 7)
```

So now we have arrived at our show statement (t · r). Strategy 11 tells
us to use For Some Introduction, which gives us ∃(t · r). Next, use
If-then Introduction to obtain (p · r) ⊃ ∃(t · r) followed by the For
Every Introduction. Remember to check whether all the previous assumptions are bound. There are only two assumptions still in force, lines
1 and 2, and both are bound. So, we conclude with ∀((p · r) ⊃ ∃(t · r)),
which finally gives us what we need to finish the proof by using For
Some Elimination. The For Some Elimination argument can now be used
because we have obtained in line 11 or been given in line 2, the two
necessary formulae which has the form ∃S, ∀(S ⊃ U). So we can conclude
U.

70

```
 1. ∀(p ⊃ t)                          As
 2. ∃(p · r)                          As
 Show ∃(t · r)
 [Show ∀((p · r) ⊃ ∃(t · r))]        (Strategy 12)
 [Show (p · r) ⊃ ∃(t · r)]           (Strategy 9)
 3. (p · r)                           Tas
 [Show ∃(t · r)]
 [Show (t · r)]                       (Strategy 11)
 [Show r]
 4. r                                 (&E, 3)
 [Show t]
 5. p                                 (&E, 3)
 6. p ⊃ t                             (∀E, 1)
 7. t                                 (IfE, 5, 6)
 8. (t · r)                           (&I, 4, 7)
 9. ∃(t · r)                          (∃I, 8)
10. (p · r) ⊃ ∃(t · r)               (IfI, 3, 9)
11. ∀((p · r) ⊃ ∃(t · r))            (∀I, 10)
12. ∃(t · r)                          (∃E, 2, 11)
```

You should recognize that this proof required the use of several other proof strategies. This will almost always be the case. Usually, when a proof requires Strategy 12, it will also use Strategies 9, 11, and often others as well.

EXERCISES 3.7

Determine the major proof strategy needed for the following arguments. The conclusion of the argument will in most cases determine the major proof strategy.

Example: p, q; so, ∃((p · q) v s)

Since the conclusion of this argument is a <u>for some</u> formula, we use Strategy 11.

Example: ∃(p ≡ s); so, ∃(s ⊃ p)

The conclusion of this argument is also a <u>for some</u> formula, but the assumption is also a for some formula. In this case the assumption determines the proof strategy. The correct strategy is number 12.

```
 1. ∀p; so, ∃p
 2. ∃p, ∀q; so, ∃(p · q)
 3. ∀(p ≡ t), ∀(t ≡ s); so, ∀(s ⊃ p)
 4. ∃s · ∀q; so, q
 5. ∀(p ⊃ s), ∃(q ≡ -r); so, ∃(-r ⊃ q)
 6. ∀((q · r) · w); so, ∃(r · w)
 7. r ⊃ ∀((s ⊃ t) · q), ∀(r · w); so, q
 8. ∀(p ⊃ q), ∃-q, ∀(q ≡ r); so, ∀(p ⊃ r)
 9. ∃(s · t), ∀(w · q); so, ∃(w · t)
10. ∀((p v q) · t), ∀(s ⊃ w); so, ∃((w · t) v r)
```

You now have all the tools you need to examine arguments for validity. At this point all you will need is practice.

For each of the following arguments evaluate for validity. For those that are valid give a proof. For those that are invalid give a counter-example.

1. $\forall((s \lor w) \cdot p$, $\forall(q \supset r)$; so, $\exists((r \cdot p) \lor t)$
2. $\forall s$, $\forall t$; so, $\forall(s \cdot t)$
3. $(\forall q \supset r)$, $\exists q$; so, $r \lor s$
4. $\forall(s \equiv t)$, $\exists t$; so, $s \lor w$
5. $\exists(q \supset r)$, $\forall((q \supset r) \supset p \cdot \exists t)$; so, $\exists t$
6. $\exists(r \cdot w)$, $\forall(q \cdot p)$; so, $\exists(q \cdot w)$
7. $\exists(q \cdot s)$, $\exists(t \cdot w)$; so, $\exists(s \cdot w)$
8. $\exists q$, $\exists t$, $\exists s$; so, $\exists((s \cdot t) \cdot q)$
9. $\forall((p \cdot q) \cdot r)$, $\exists(s \equiv -w)$, $\forall(w \cdot t)$; so $\exists(q \cdot -s)$
10. $\exists((s \equiv t) \lor r)$, $\forall(-r \cdot t)$, $\forall(s \supset (p \cdot q))$; so, $\exists(q \lor (p \equiv w))$

TRANSLATION

Rules of Translation

The key to translating from English into symbols is simply prac-tice. The more you practice the better you become. We will first state the new rules of translation which will allow us to translate monadic formulae. The first seven rules from truth-functional logic still ap-ply, so we begin this new set at T Rule 8.

T Rule 8. <u>All S are U</u>, <u>U are S</u>, <u>only U are S</u>, <u>none but U are S</u> translate as $\forall(S \supset U)$.

T Rule 9. <u>No S are U</u>, <u>none of the S are U</u> translate as $\forall(S \supset -U)$.

T Rule 10. <u>Some S are U</u> translates as $\exists(S \cdot U)$.

T Rule 11. <u>S exist</u>, <u>there are S</u> translate as $\exists S$.

T Rule 12. <u>There are no S</u>, <u>S do not exist</u> translate as $\forall -S$.

T Rule 13. <u>W is one of the U</u> translates as $\exists w \cdot \forall(w \supset U)$.

T Rule 14. <u>W is not one of the U</u> translates as $\exists w \cdot \forall(w \supset -U)$.

T Rule 15. <u>S that are U</u> translates as $(S \cdot U)$.

T Rule 16. <u>Not S</u> translates as $-S$.

T Rule 17. A word or phrase <u>W</u> with an underlined letter translates as that letter. Written in English, the letter would be translated as <u>it is one of the W</u>. For example: <u>fast horses</u> translates as <u>h</u>, which into English would trans-late into <u>it is one of the fast horses</u>.

You will notice that these rules are the same as appear in the text except for two minor changes. First, these are called T rules to sig-nify that they are rules of translation as distinguished from the F rules, S rules, and P rules. Second, in T Rule 17 we changed the example from <u>old men</u> to <u>fast horses</u>. T Rule 17 usually can be shortened to: A word or phrase <u>W</u> with an underlined letter translates as that letter. For example, <u>fast horses</u> translates as <u>h</u>. The part of T Rule 17 that was omitted reads as follows: and written in English would be translated as <u>it is one of the W</u>. For example <u>fast horses</u> translates into English as <u>it is one of the fast horses</u>. Translating this way may seem strange to you, but there is a good reason for it. An example from the text will help to explain why: <u>All dogs are mammals</u>. According to T Rule 8 this is translated as $\forall(d \supset m)$. We can rewrite the sentence using T Rule 17 to obtain <u>for everything, if it is one of the dogs, then it is one of the mammals</u>. This English translation would produce the symbolic formula $\forall(d \supset m)$. In other words, translating <u>dogs</u> by <u>it is one of the dogs</u> enables us to give a correct translation in symbolic notation. This is all necessary because of the nature of monadic sentences. Without this rule, we would have no reason to translate <u>all dogs are mammals</u> as $\forall(d \supset m)$. With this rule, it makes sense to provide this symbolic translation for the English phrase.

EXERCISES 3.9

Translate the following formulae into symbolic notation using T Rules 1 through 17.

Example: There are Marxists if and only if all Communists are Socialists.

Solution: 1. There are <u>M</u>arxists if and only if all <u>C</u>ommunists are <u>S</u>ocialists.
2. There are M if and only if all C are S by line 1 and T Rule 17.
3. ∃M if and only if all C are S by line 2 and T Rule 11.
4. ∃M ≡ all C are S by line 3 and T Rule 5.
5. ∃M ≡ $\forall(C \supset S)$ by line 4 and T Rule 8.

1. There are no <u>U</u>nicorns, but there are <u>H</u>obbits if you have read the <u>R</u>ing trilogy.
2. If all <u>b</u>achelors are <u>u</u>nmarried then none but <u>m</u>arried are not bachelors.
3. Either <u>J</u>esse James is one of the <u>g</u>uilty or he is not.

Quantificational Logic

KEY TERMS

Variable Indefinite pronouns such as that individual.

Terms Expressions that have a reference to something. Terms can be either variables or constants.

Constants Names or phrases that apply to just one thing.

Relations Predicates. Words that describe a property of something.

Sets A group of objects. Generally, the members of sets are enumerated within a pair of parentheses.

Ordered Pairs Two objects in a specific order.

Denotation That to which terms refer.

We have now arrived at the point where a system of greater complexity is necessary to handle certain, more difficult arguments. As was pointed out in the text, truth-functional logic analyzed arguments that were not exclusively dependent on truth-functional connectors. We were not concerned about the content of the sentences in the argument; that is, we did not ask if the sentences were true of specific objects from a chosen universe of discourse.

In monadic logic we expanded on truth-functional logic to consider arguments with formulae that contained one indefinite pronoun. By using the pronoun it, we were able to consider the content of atomic formulae. This one indefinite pronoun can be called a variable. In quantificational logic we will consider formulae that have two variables or more. Thus, quantificational logic will require more symbols, F rules, S rules, P rules, and T rules.

Just as monadic logic extended the principles first stated in truth-functional logic, so too quantificational logic extends the principles of monadic logic. Monadic logic was slightly more complex than truth-functional logic. Similarly, quantificational logic is slightly more complex than monadic logic. We are simply taking another step upward in complexity, giving us the necessary tools to analyze arguments that monadic logic cannot handle. Whereas monadic logic had formulae with one indefinite pronoun, quantificational logic will have formulae with two or more.

In Chapter 2 we used the atomic sentences Cows moo, Dogs bark, and so on rather than the sentences Evil exists, Good is pleasant, and so forth, which were used in the text. Similarly, in Chapter 3 we used the atomic sentences It is blue, It is red, and so on instead of the sentences used in the text. This was meant to show you that it does not matter what the atomic formulae are. What matters is how they are put together. In this chapter we will also use a different set of sentences. Again, this serves only to emphasize that the words and phrases which make up the sentences are not important. What is important is how the words are connected according to the rules.

SYNTAX

ENGLISH SYNTAX

Consider the following sentences: That city is large, That first city is near Washington, and That city is near New York. Just as before, we can use these atomic formulae and the connectors to construct formulae. For example, That city is near New York or that city is large; If that first city is near Washington, then that city is near New York; and That city is large if and only if that city is near New York, and so on. We can also use quantifiers like those introduced in Chapter 3. The quantifiers in this chapter will quantify the variables in the sentences. The text uses the quantifier for some individual. The universe of discourse is the set of individuals. In the set of sentences listed above, the universe of discourse is cities. So, what will the quantifiers in this chapter be like? We will use for some city and for every city, as well as for some first city or for some second city. The quantifiers can also be read in a different way, which is useful in analyzing certain sentences. For example, for some second city can be read as some second city is such that. For every first city can be read as every first city is such that, and so on. In quantificational logic how the quantifier is stated will depend on the content of the sentence. Now that we have quantifiers to work with let us look at some examples of quantified sentences. For example:

For every city if that city is large then that city is near Washington.

This sentence could also be written:

Every city is such that if that city is large, then that city is near Washington.

Another example is as follows:

Every first city is such that for every second city if that first city is near that second city, then that second city is near that first city.

We now need to state the rules of syntax.

Rules of Syntax

An expression is a variable, constant, term, one-place or two-place relation, or formula if and only if it is so according to the following rules:

F Rule 1. The following are variables and also terms: that city; that first city; that second city.

F Rule 2. The following are constants and also terms: New York, Washington.

F Rule 3. The following are, respectively, a one-place and a two-place relation symbol: is large; is near.

F Rule 4. If u and w are terms and H and I are, respectively, a one-place and a two-place relation symbol, then the following are formulae: uH; uHw.

F Rule 5. If U and W are formulae, then so are the following: U and W; it is not the case that U; U or W; if U then W; U if and only if W.

F Rule 6. If that u is a variable and W is a formula, then the following are formulae: for every u, W (or, every u is such that W); for some u, W (or, some u is such that W).

Let us consider what these new rules of syntax tell us.

A. There are two kinds of terms:
   1. Constants.
   2. Variables.
B. There are two kinds of relation symbols:
   1. One-place relation symbols.
   2. Two-place relation symbols.
C. Formulae can be made by connecting terms to relation symbols. Since there are two kinds of terms and two kinds of relation symbols, there must be several ways to make formulae:
   1. One constant together with one one-place relation symbol.
   2. One variable together with one one-place relation symbol.
   3. Two constants together with one two-place relation symbol.
   4. Two variables together with one two-place relation symbol.
   5. One constant and one variable together with one two-place relation symbol.
D. Formulae can be made in the normal way, that is, by using truth-functional connectors.
E. A formula connected correctly to a variable is also a formula.

Paragraphs C, D, and E give us a lot more ways to construct formulae than before. Let us consider some examples:

C1. One constant together with one one-place relation symbol. By F Rule 2 we have two constants: New York and Washington. By F Rule 3 we have only one one-place relation symbol. So by F Rule 4 we can construct two formulae:
   1. New York is large.
   2. Washington is large.
   Obviously, if we were given more constants and more one-place relation symbols we could make more formulae.
C2. One variable together with one one-place relation symbol. By F Rule 1 we have three different variables: That city; that first city; and that second city. Again, by F Rule 3, we have

76

only one one-place relation symbol. So, by F Rule 4, we can construct three formulae:
1. That city is large
2. That first city is large.
3. That second city is large.

C3. Two constants together with one two-place relation symbol. Our two-place relation symbol is <u>is near</u>. Since we only have one two-place relation symbol, we can only construct the following formulae using our two constants:
1. New York is near Washington.
2. Washington is near New York.

C4. Two variables together with one two-place relation symbol. Since we have three variables, we could construct many different formulae. Here is one example:
1. That first city is near that second city.

C5. One variable and one constant together with one two-place relation symbol. There are many combinations of variables and constants, so we will give you only a few:
1. That city is near Washington
2. New York is that second city.
3. That second city is near New York.

D. We already know how to make formulae by using the truth-functional connectors. Consider one example:
1. If New York is near Washington, then Washington is near New York.
This is a formula by F Rule 5.

E. Our variables are: that city; that first city; and that second city. We have many formulae which we can connect to the quantifiers to make other formulae from C2:
1. For every city that city is large.
2. For some city that city is large.
Also, here is an example from C4:
1. For every first city that first city is near that second city.
These formulae can also be written using the other reading given in F Rule 6. For example:
1. For every first city that first city is near that second city.
This can be restated as:
1. Every first city is such that that first city is near that second city.
Many times it will be much easier to state a formula this way.

EXERCISES 4.1

Give a formal construction of the following formulae.

Example: New York is near Washington.
  1. <u>New York</u> is a term by F Rule 2.
  2. <u>Washington</u> is a term by F Rule 2.
  3. <u>Is near</u> is a two-place relation symbol by F Rule 3.
  4. <u>New York is near Washington</u> is a formula by lines 1, 2, and 3 and F Rule 4.

1. Washington is near that city.
2. That first city is near that second city.

3. That second city is large.
4. For every first city that first city is near Washington.
5. If for every first city that first city is near that second city, then Washington is near New York.
6. New York is near Washington if and only if Washington is near that first city or New York is near that second city.
7. It is not the case that if New York is near that first city, then for some second city that second city is near that first city.

SYMBOLIC NOTATION

As was done in both the text and in previous chapters of this Study Guide, we will express the F rules (rules of syntax) in symbolic notation.

Rules of Syntax

An expression is a variable, constant, term, one-place or two-place relation symbol, or formula if and only if it is so according to the following rules:

F Rule 1. The following are variables and also terms: x, y, z, ...
F Rule 2. The following are constants and also terms: c, d.
F Rule 3. The following are, respectively, a one-place and a two-place relation symbol: R, P.
F Rule 4. If u and w are terms and H and I are, respectively, a one-place and a two-place relation symbol, then the following are formulae: Hu, Iuw.
F Rule 5. If W and U are formulae, then so are the following: (w · U), -W, (W v U), (W ⊃ U), (W ≡ U).
F Rule 6. If u is a variable and W is a formula, then the following are formulae: (u)W, ∃uW.

EXERCISES 4.2

Give a formal construction for the following formulae:

Example: ∃xRx ⊃ (x)(Rx ≡ Pxd)

1. x is a variable and a term by F Rule 1.
2. R is a one-place relation symbol by F Rule 3.
3. Rx is a formula by lines 1 and 2 and F Rule 4.
4. ∃xRx is a formula by line 3 and F Rule 6.
5. d is a constant by F Rule 2.
6. P is a two-place relation symbol by F Rule 3.
7. Pxd is a formula by lines 1, 5, and 6 and F Rule 4.
8. Rx ≡ Pxd is a formula by lines 3 and 7 and F Rule 5.
9. (x)(Rx ≡ Pxd) is a formula by line 8 and F Rule 6.
10. ∃xRx ⊃ (x)(Rx ≡ Pxd) is a formula by lines 4 and 9 and F Rule 5.

1. Rd ⊃ -Pcd
2. -(Pdc ≡ (x)(Rx ⊃ Pxd))
3. ∃xPdx ⊃ (-Rd v Rc)

4. (x)(y)(Pxy ⊃ (Pdc · Pcd))
5. (∃x)(∃y)((Rx · -Ry) ≡ -Pxy))

BOUNDNESS

In monadic logic you learned about the concept of boundness. When an atomic formula is bound, that atomic formula is preceded by a quantifier. For example: ∃p, or ∀q. When a formula was bound, the whole formula was preceded by a quantifier. For instance, ∀(p ⊃ q) or ∃(q ∨ s). In quantificational logic we bind the variables that occur in the formula. Boundness in quantificational logic is defined as follows: An occurrence of a variable u is bound in a formula if and only if it occurs in a part of the formula that begins with a quantifier using u in other words, either (u) or ∃u ; otherwise it is free.

Consider the formula:

(x)(Pxd ≡ Rc) ⊃ ∃xRx ∨ Rd

Are the variables bound or free? Which occurrences are bound or free? The only variable we have is x. It occurs four times in the formula. Twice x occurs as a quantifier and the other two times x is bound, although both occurrences are not bound by the same quantifier.

Consider another formula:

(x)(z)Pzx ≡ -Pzx.

In this formula we have two variables x and z. Except for those in the quantifiers, there are two occurrences of x and two occurrences of z. Which are bound and which are free? The first occurrence of x is bound but the second is not. The first occurrence of z is bound but the second is not. How could we change the formula to make both occurrences of x and z bound? All we would have to do is add a single set of parentheses and both occurrences of x and z would be bound as shown in the following:

(x)(z)(Pzx ≡ Pzx)

EXERCISES 4.3

In the following formulae, each variable occurs at least twice. Determine which occurrences, if any, are bound.

Example: (x)Pxd ⊃ -Rx ∨ ∃xPdx

The first and third occurrences of x are bound. The second occurrence is not.

1. (x)∃yPxy ⊃ ((Rx ∨ Ry) · (Rc · Rd))
2. ∃xPxy ⊃ (x)Ry · Pcd
3. Rx · Ry ≡ Pxy · -Pyx
4. Pxy ⊃ (x)(Rx ∨ ∃yRy) · -(x)Pxy
5. (x)(Pdx ⊃ Ry) ≡ ∃x∃y(Pxy ∨ Pyx)

79

SEMANTICS

Because quantificational logic treats formulae that have two-place relation symbols and terms, it is necessary to consider whether these formulae are true or false not of just one object but of a pair of objects. Suppose our relation symbol is P and it stands for is near. Suppose our universe of discourse contains the following: New York, San Francisco, and Washington. Suppose also we are given the following formula Pcd, in which c is New York and d is Washington. Now, if we say that P is true of New York, then our possible situation looks like this:

Universe of Discourse: {New York, San Francisco, Washington};
c: New York; d: Washington; P: New York

Is Pcd true? Let us check. Pcd stands for New York is near Washington. Is that a true statement? It may be, but remember that our possible situation determines what is true or not. Then, is Pcd true according to our possible situation? According to the possible situation, Pcd is true only of the following statement: New York is near. But something is obviously wrong. New York is near is not even a formula. It does not conform to the rules of syntax. So what is wrong? P is only assigned one object. P must be assigned to two objects to represent a formula properly. Suppose we change our possible situation so that P contains a pair of objects instead of just New York. Suppose our possible situation looks like this:

Universe of Discourse: {New York, San Francisco, Washington};
c: New York; d: Washington; P: (New York,
San Francisco)

Now is Pcd true or false? Remember, Pcd stands for New York is near Washington. According to the assignment of objects given to P, P is true of New York and San Francisco. In other words, according to the assignment of objects given to P, the formula New York is near San Francisco is true. It does not matter that New York and San Francisco are three thousand miles apart. It only matters that the denotation of P says that P is true of the pair (New York, San Francisco). So if our formula is Pcd, then according to the above possible situation, Pcd is false. If P were denoted as follows:

P: (New York, Washington)

then Pcd would be true. The important thing to keep in mind is that since P is a two-place relation symbol, P must be assigned a pair of objects rather than just one.

The order in which the objects are stated is also important. Suppose we have the formula Pdc. Is Pdc true or false given the previously stated possible situation, that is, P: New York, Washington ? Pdc stands for Washington is near New York. Is P true of the pair of objects (Washington, New York)? You may want to say yes, but the answer is no. P is true of (New York, Washington) but not (Washington, New York). The order makes a difference.

ORDERED PAIRS AND SETS

As pointed out in the text, sets are enclosed in braces and ordered pairs are enclosed by parentheses. For example, {New York, Washington} is the set that contains New York and Washington, and (New York, Washington) is the ordered pair that contains New York and Washington in that order.

The set {Washington, New York} is equivalent to the set {New York, Washington}, but (Washington, New York) is not the same ordered pair as (New York, Washington).

Universes of discourse are always stated as sets. These sets can contain one, two, three, or any number of objects. But two-place relations will always be true of a pair of objects—an ordered pair. We can, however, allow two-place relations to be true of many different ordered pairs. In other words, it is perfectly correct to assign the following ordered pairs to P:

P: (New York, Washington)
   (Washington, New York)
   (San Francisco, Washington)

A two-place relation need not be true of only one ordered pair.

With these concepts in mind, let us now state the rules of semantics.

Rules of Semantics

According to any possible situation, if u and w each denote one thing in the universe of discourse and R and P are a one-place and a two-place relation symbol, respectively, then:

S Rule 1, S Rule 2, S Rule 3, S Rule 4, and S Rule 5 are the same as the corresponding rules for the connectives of truth-functional logic.

S Rule 6. Ru is true if R is true of what u denotes but false otherwise.

S Rule 7. Puw is true if P is true of the ordered pair consisting of what u denotes and what w denotes but false otherwise.

Consider S Rule 6. If we have a formula, say Rc ⊃ Rd, and we are given the following situation:

Universe of Discourse: {0, 1}; c: 1, d: 0; R: 1

then Rc is true, but Rd is false, because c denotes 1 and R is true of 1 and d denotes 0 and R is not true of 0. We would write this out in the following way:

$$R\ c \supset R\ d$$
$$\underline{T}\ \underline{1} - \underline{F}\ \underline{0}$$

By S Rule 6 and by S Rule 4 Rc ⊃ Rd is false.

$$R\ c \supset R\ d$$
$$\underline{T}\ \underline{1}\ \textcircled{F}\ \underline{F}\ \underline{0}$$

81

Now let us consider S Rule 7. S Rule 7 allows us to find the truth value of formulae that are made up of two-place relation symbols and terms. S Rule 6 is only for one-place relations. Suppose we have the formula Rc ⊃ Pcd and the same possible situation as before. We need only provide an assignment of objects for P. Because P is a two-place relation symbol, we must assign ordered pairs. So let us have P be true of the ordered pair (0, 1). Now, given the following possible situation:

Universe of Discourse: {0, 1}; R: 1; P: (0, 1); d: 0; c: 1

What is the truth value of Rc ⊃ Pcd. Since c is denoted 1, we put 1's under each c, and since d is denoted 0, we put a 0 under the d as follows:

```
R c ⊃ P c d
  1     1 0
```

Now is R true of 1? Look at our possible situation. It is true of 1, so Rc is true by S Rule 6. Is P true of (1, 0)? Again, look at our possible situation. P is true of (0, 1) but not (1, 0), so Pcd is false by S Rule 7.

```
R c ⊃ P c d
T 1   F 0 1
  √     √ √
```

Now by S Rule 4 we find that Rc ⊃ Pcd is false:

```
R c ⊃ P c d
T 1 (F) F 0 1
√ √    √ √ √
```

EXERCISES 4.4

Determine the truth value of the following formulae. Possible situation: Universe of Discourse: {0, 1}; c: 1; d: 0, x: 0; y: 0; R: 1; P: (0, 0), (0, 1).

Example: Pxd ⊃ (Ry · Pxc)

Since x denotes 0, then 0 is placed below every occurrence of x as follows:

```
P x d ⊃ (R y · P x c)
  0          0
```

Both y and d denote 0, so every occurrence of them in the formula is marked by a 0 beneath the letter:

```
P x d ⊃ (R y · P x c)
  0 0      0     0
```

Lastly, c denotes 1, so it is marked by a 1:

```
P x d ⊃ (R y · P x c)
  0 0      0     0 1
```

Now, P is true of (0, 0) and (0, 1), so both Pxd and Pxc are true by S Rule 7.

```
P x d ⊃ (R y · P x c)
T 0 0      0    T 0 1
̲ ̲̌ ̌            ̲   ̌ ̌
```

But R is not true of 1, so Ry is false by S Rule 6.

```
P x d ⊃ (R y · P x c)
T 0 0      F 0    T 0 1
̲ ̌ ̌      ̲ ̌    ̌ ̌
```

Ry · Pxc is false by S Rule 1.

```
R y · P x c
F 0 F T 0 1
̌ ̌ = ̌ ̌ ̌
```

So, by S Rule 4, the whole formula is false.

```
P x d ⊃ (R y · P x c)
T 0 0 (F) F 0 F T 0 1
̌ ̌ ̌ (=) ̌ ̌ ̌ ̌ ̌
```

1. Pxy ≡ -(Rd ∨ Rc)
2. -Pxy · (Pcd · Pdc)
3. Ry ⊃ (Rc ≡ (-Pxy ∨ Pyd)
4. (Rd · Pdc) ⊃ (Pxy ∨ Rc)
5. Pdx ⊃ (-Rx · (Pxd ≡ Rc))
6. --Pxx ⊃ (Pxx ∨ (Rd · Ry))
7. ((Pcd · Pdc) ∨ (Pxy · Pyx)) ≡ (Ry · Rx)

Now, let us change the possible situation and work through a few more exercises. Possible situation: Universe of Discourse: {0, 1}; c: 0; d: 1; x: 0; y: 1; R: 0, 1; P: (1, 1), (1, 0).

8. (Ry · Rx) ⊃ -(Rd ∨ Rc)
9. (-Pxx ∨ Rd) ⊃ (-Pxy · Pdc)
10. (Pxd ⊃ Rc) ≡ -(Rd · Rx) ∨ (Ry · Rc)
11. (Rc ⊃ -Rx) ≡ -(Pyx ∨ Pyy)
12. -Pcc · Pdd ⊃ -(-Pxy ∨ Pyx)

Rules of Semantics for the Quantifiers

The rules of semantics for formulae that contain quantifiers are much like the rules that were given in Chapter 3.

S Rule 8. (r)W is true if every denotation for r makes W true but false if some denotation for r makes W false.

S Rule 9. ∃rW is true if some denotation for r makes W true but false if every denotation for r makes W false.

If we can find one case in which the formula W is true for some object in the universe of discourse, then ∃rW is true by S Rule 9. And if W is true for every object in the universe of discourse, then (r)W is false.

The method of expansion that we used in Chapter 3 will be quite handy here as well. Let us look at some examples:

$(x)(R x \supset P x d)$

This formula can be expanded by rewriting it twice without the quantifier and connecting the two resultant formulae with an *and* as follows:

$(x)(R x \supset P x d) \cdot (R x \supset P x d)$

Now, suppose we have the following possible situation:

Universe of Discourse: $\{0, 1\}$; d: 1, P: (0, 0), R: 0, 1

Since our universe of discourse is 0 and 1, we subscript each occurrence of x first with 0 and then with 1:

$(R x_0 \supset P x_0 d) \cdot (R x_1 \cdot P x_1 d)$

We know from our reading of the text that if a variable is subscripted with a 0, then that occurrence of the variable denotes 0. If the variable is subscripted with a 1, then that occurrence of the variable denotes 1. If a variable is not subscripted, then that variable was not bound by a quantifier in the original quantified formula. The formula now looks like this:

$(R \underline{x_0} \supset P \underline{x_0}d) \cdot (R \underline{x_1} \supset P \underline{x_1}d)$
$\quad\ \underline{0} \qquad\ \underline{0} \qquad\quad \underline{1} \qquad\ \underline{1}$

Since $\underline{d}$ denotes 1 in our possible situation we have:

$(R x_0 \supset P x_0\underline{d}) \cdot (R x_1 \supset P x_1\underline{d})$
$\quad\ \underline{0} \qquad\ \underline{0}\,\underline{1} \qquad\quad \underline{1} \qquad\ \underline{1}\,\underline{1}$

By S Rule 6, $\underline{Rx_0}$ is true and $\underline{Rx_0}$ is true:

$(R x_0 \supset P x_0 d) \cdot (R x_1 \supset P x_1 d)$
$\ \underline{\text{T}}\,\underline{0} \qquad\ \underline{0}\,\underline{1} \qquad\quad \underline{\text{T}}\,\underline{1} \qquad\ \underline{1}\,\underline{1}$

And by S Rule 7, $\underline{Px_0 d}$ is false and $\underline{Px_1 d}$ is false:

$(R x_0 \supset P x_0 d) \cdot (R x_1 \supset P x_1 d)$
$\ \underline{\text{T}}\,\underline{0} \qquad \underline{\text{F}}\,\underline{0}\,\underline{1} \qquad\quad \underline{\text{T}}\,\underline{1} \qquad \underline{\text{F}}\,\underline{1}\,\underline{1}$

So, by S Rule 4 $\underline{(Rx_0 \supset Px_0 d)}$ is false and $\underline{(Rx_1 \supset Px_1 d)}$ is also false:

$(R x_0 \supset P x_0 d) \cdot (R x_1 \supset P x_1 d)$
$\ \underline{\text{T}}\,\underline{0} \qquad \underline{\text{F}}\,\underline{0}\,\underline{1} \qquad\quad \underline{\text{T}}\,\underline{1}\,\underline{\text{F}} \quad \underline{\text{F}}\,\underline{1}\,\underline{1}$

And, finally, by S Rule 1 we arrive at the following:

$(R \ x_0 \supset P \ x_0 d) \cdot (R \ x_1 \supset P \ x_1 d)$

$\underset{\displaystyle\sqrt{}}{T} \ \underset{\displaystyle\sqrt{}}{0} \quad \underset{\displaystyle\sqrt{}}{F} \ \underset{\displaystyle\sqrt{}}{F} \ \underset{\displaystyle\sqrt{}}{0} \ \underset{\displaystyle\sqrt{}}{1} \ \textcircled{\underset{\displaystyle\sqrt{}}{F}} \ \underset{\displaystyle\sqrt{}}{T} \ \underset{\displaystyle\sqrt{}}{1} \quad \underset{\displaystyle\sqrt{}}{F} \ \underset{\displaystyle\sqrt{}}{F} \ \underset{\displaystyle\sqrt{}}{1} \ \underset{\displaystyle\sqrt{}}{1}$

Since $(Rx_0 \supset Px_0 d) \cdot (Rx_1 \supset Px_1 d)$ is false, the formula <u>$(x)(Rx \supset Pxd)$</u> is also false. Thus, we have found the truth value of a quantified formula by using our method of expansion, the S rules, and the given possible situation.

EXERCISES 4.5

Expand the following formulae. Assume a universe of discourse with two elements, 0 and 1.

Example: $\exists x Pxy \supset (x)Rx$

$(Px_0 y \lor Px_1 y) \supset (x)Rx$

$(Px_0 y \lor Px_1 y) \supset Rx \cdot Rx$

$(Px_0 y \lor Px_1 y) \supset (Rx_0 \cdot Rx_1)$

<u>Part A</u>

1. $(x)(y)Pxy$
2. $\exists x Rx \supset (y)Pxy$
3. $Pxy \supset ((x)Rx \lor \exists x(y)Pxy)$
4. $(y)\exists x Pyx \equiv (Rx \cdot \exists y Ry)$
5. $(x)(y)Pxy \supset -Pcd$
6. $\exists x \exists y Pxy \supset -\exists z Rz \lor Pdc$
7. $\exists z(y)(Pzy \equiv (Ry \supset Pzy))$

<u>Part B</u>

Now that you have mastered the art of expansion, try to find the truth values of the formulae in Exercise 4.5 according to the rules of semantics. Assume the following possible situation:

Universe of Discourse: $\{0, 1\}$; x: 1; y: 0; z: 0; c: 0; d: 0; R: 0, 1; P: (0, 1), (1, 1), (1, 0)

Example: $P \ x_0 y \lor P \ x_1 y \supset R \ x_0 \cdot R \ x_1$

$\quad\quad\quad \underline{0} \ \underline{0} \quad\quad \underline{1} \ \underline{0} \quad\quad \underline{0} \quad\quad \underline{1}$

$(P \ x_0 y \lor P \ x_1 y) \supset (R \ x_0 \cdot R \ x_1)$

$\underset{\displaystyle\sqrt{}}{F} \ \underset{\displaystyle\sqrt{}}{0} \ \underset{\displaystyle\sqrt{}}{0} \ \underset{\displaystyle\sqrt{}}{T} \ \underset{\displaystyle\sqrt{}}{T} \ \underset{\displaystyle\sqrt{}}{1} \ \underset{\displaystyle\sqrt{}}{0} \ = \ \underset{\displaystyle\sqrt{}}{F} \quad \underset{\displaystyle\sqrt{}}{T} \ \underset{\displaystyle\sqrt{}}{0} \quad \underset{\displaystyle\sqrt{}}{T} \ \underset{\displaystyle\sqrt{}}{T} \ \underset{\displaystyle\sqrt{}}{1}$

VALIDITY

As in Chapters 2 and 3, our first check for validity is to find counterexamples. Remember that to show a counterexample for an argument, we must give a possible situation in which the assumptions are true and the conclusion is false. There is no sure procedure for doing this. But if you follow some basic guidelines, you should gain skill in this area.

Remember, you decide what the possible situation is. So start by making your universe of discourse 0 and 1. As was pointed out in the text, most invalid arguments do not require counterexamples that have more than two objects in the universe of discourse. Thus, you should begin most of your counterexamples by stating your universe of discourse to be {0, 1}. Next, if there are formulae in the argument that contain quantifiers, then expand the formulae by restating them twice without the quantifier and then connecting the resultant formulae with the appropriate and or or connectors. Subscript each occurrence of the free variables with 0's and 1's. Then, decide what denotation of each variable, constant, and relation symbol will make the conclusion false. Once you have done this, determine whether the possible situation will make the assumptions true. If not, then you must try again. For some arguments, it is best first to make the conclusion false and then determine whether the assumptions will be true. For others, it is best first to made the assumptions true and then determine whether the conclusion will be false. There is no established method that always works. Until you gain experience at doing counterexamples, any method will involve some trial and error. So be patient and practice.

EXERCISES 4.6

The following arguments are invalid. Give a counterexample for each.

Example: $\exists x R\ x$, $\exists y R\ y$, so $(x)(y)(R\ x \supset R\ y)$

Since all of the formulae in this argument are quantified formulae, the first step is to expand each of them. So, we assume a universe of discourse of {0, 1} and start the expansions. First, the first assumption:

$R\ x_0 \lor R\ x_1$

Next, the second assumption:

$R\ y_0 \lor R\ y_1$

And, finally, the conclusion:

$(x)(y)(R\ x \supset R\ y)$
$(y)(R\ x_0 \supset R\ y) \cdot (y)(R\ x_1 \supset R\ y)$
$((R\ x_0 \supset R\ y_0) \cdot (R\ x_0 \supset R\ y_1)) \cdot ((R\ x_1 \supset R\ y_0) \cdot (R\ x_1 \supset R\ y_1))$

Next, we decide what assignment of objects for the variables and the relation symbols will make the conclusion false. Since all of our variables are subscripted, we do not need to denote them. But we do need to assign objects to the one-place relation symbol, R. If we make R true of 0, then what truth value will our expanded formula have?

$$((R\ x_0 \supset R\ y_0) \cdot (R\ x_0 \supset R\ y_1)) \cdot ((R\ x_1 \supset R\ y_0) \cdot (R\ x_1 \supset R\ y_1))$$
$$\underset{\underline{T}\ \underline{0}}{} \quad \underset{\underline{T}\ \underline{0}}{} \quad \underset{\underline{T}\ \underline{0}}{} \quad \underset{\underline{F}\ \underline{1}}{} \quad \underset{\underline{F}\ \underline{1}}{} \quad \underset{\underline{T}\ \underline{0}}{} \quad \underset{\underline{F}\ \underline{1}}{} \quad \underset{\underline{F}\ \underline{1}}{}$$

According to S Rule 4, $R\ x_0 \supset R\ y_0$ is true, $(R\ x_0 \supset R\ y_1)$ is false, $(R\ x_1 \supset R\ y_0)$ is true, and $(R\ x_1 \supset R\ y_1)$ is true:

$$((R\ x_0 \supset R\ y_0) \cdot (R\ x_0 \supset R\ y_1)) \cdot ((R\ x_1 \supset R\ y_0) \cdot (R\ x_1 \supset R\ y_1))$$

$$\underset{\checkmark\ \checkmark}{T\ 0}\ \underset{\checkmark\ \checkmark}{T\ T\ 0}\ \underset{\checkmark\ \checkmark}{T\ 0}\ \underset{\checkmark\ \checkmark}{F\ F\ 1}\qquad \underset{\checkmark\ \checkmark}{F\ 1}\ \underset{\checkmark\ \checkmark}{T\ T\ 0}\ \underset{\checkmark\ \checkmark}{F\ 1}\ \underset{\checkmark\ \checkmark}{T\ F\ 1}$$

And by S Rule 1, $\underline{(R\ x_0 \supset R\ y_0) \cdot (R\ x_0 \supset R\ y_1)}$ is false and $\underline{(R\ x_1 \supset R\ y_1)}$ $\underline{\cdot\ (R\ x_1 \supset R\ y_1)}$ is true. So we add the $\underline{T}$ and $\underline{F}$ where appropriate to obtain:

$$((R\ x_0 \supset R\ y_0) \cdot (R\ x_0 \supset R\ y_1)) \cdot ((R\ x_1 \supset R\ y_0) \cdot (R\ x_1 \supset R\ y_1))$$

$$\underset{\checkmark\ \checkmark}{T\ 0}\ \underset{\checkmark\ \checkmark}{T\ T\ 0}\ \underset{\checkmark}{F}\ \underset{\checkmark\ \checkmark}{T\ 0}\ \underset{\checkmark\ \checkmark}{F\ F\ 1}\quad -\quad \underset{\checkmark\ \checkmark}{F\ 1}\ \underset{\checkmark\ \checkmark}{T\ T\ 0}\ \underset{\checkmark}{T}\ \underset{\checkmark\ \checkmark}{F\ 1}\ \underset{\checkmark\ \checkmark}{T\ F\ 1}$$

Finally, by S Rule 1 again, the following formula is false:

$$((R\ x_0 \supset R\ y_0) \cdot (R\ x_0 \supset R\ y_1)) \cdot ((R\ x_1 \supset R\ y_0) \cdot (R\ x_1 \supset R\ y_1))$$

So, our possible situation at this point is:

Universe of Discourse: $\{0, 1\}$; R: 0

We have made the conclusion false. So, now we need to determine whether the assumptions are true. First we will consider $\underline{Rx_0 \lor Rx_1}$. The subscription on the variables tells us this much:

$$R\ x_0 \lor R\ x_1$$
$$\underline{0}\qquad \underline{1}$$

The possible situation tells us that $\underline{R}$ is true of 0 as follows:

$$R\ x_0 \lor R\ x_1$$
$$\underline{T\ 0}\ \underset{\checkmark}{}\qquad \underline{F\ 1}\ \underset{\checkmark}{}$$

By S Rule 3 we have:

$$R\ x_0 \lor R\ x_1$$
$$\underset{\checkmark\ \checkmark}{T\ 0}\ \bigoplus\underset{\checkmark\ \checkmark}{F\ 1}$$

So, the first assumption is true. Next, we check the second assumption:

$$R\ y_0 \lor R\ y_1$$

Again the subscription on the variables tells us:

$$R\ y_0 \lor R\ y_1$$
$$\underline{0}\qquad \underline{1}$$

And, since $\underline{R}$ is true of 0:

$$R\ y_0 \lor R\ y_1$$
$$\underline{T\ 0}\ \underset{\checkmark}{}\qquad \underline{F\ 1}\ \underset{\checkmark}{}$$

Again, by S Rule 3:

$$R \ y_0 \ v \ R \ y_1$$

$$\frac{T}{\checkmark} \ \frac{0}{\checkmark} \ \textcircled{T} \frac{F}{\checkmark} \ \frac{1}{\checkmark}$$

Thus, both assumptions are true and the conclusion is false. Therefore, the argument is invalid and the counterexample is simply:

Universe of Discourse: {0, 1}; R: 0

Now, try the following exercises:

1. (x)(Rx ⊃ Pxx), ∃x(Pxx · Bx) so, ∃x(Rx · Bx)
2. (x)(y)(Cx ⊃ Dy), (y)(Dy ⊃ Ey) so, (y)(x)(Ey ⊃ Cx)
3. ∃x∃y∃z((Rx · Dy) ⊃ Ez) so, (x)(y)(z)-Ez ⊃ (Rx · Dy)
4. Pcd ⊃ (x)(Rx ⊃ Dx), (x)(Rx · Pxd) so, -Dc
5. (x)(y)(Rxy ≡ Sxy), (x)(y-Sxy so, (y)(x)Rxy

PROOFS

Now that we are able to show invalidity by constructing counter-examples, our next step is to construct proofs to show validity. Before doing so, we must first understand completely how to use replacement notation. Replacement notation is used in two of the new valid arguments that will be discussed later. These new valid arguments are essential in doing proofs and replacement notation is likewise essential in using the new valid arguments. So, in order to do proofs you must understand replacement notation. As stated in the text S w/t should be read as: The formula S, with the variable w replaced by the term t. S w/t results from replacing every free occurrence of the variable w in S with the term t, provided that every substituted occurrence of t in the result is free. Remember that S is any formula, w is any variable, and t is any term. What does all this mean? Let us look at some examples. Suppose S is (x)(y)(Pyx ⊃ Dxy). Then, S x/d is (x)(y)(Pyx ⊃ Dxy). Notice that nothing is changed, because x does not occur free in any part of the formula. The x in Pyx is bound and the x in Dxy is also bound. Remember, S w/t is the result of replacing every free occurrence of the variable w in S with the term t. Let us try another example. Suppose S is (x)Pxy ⊃ (y)Dxy. Then, what is S x/y? Again, nothing changes. The formula becomes (x)Pxy ⊃ (y)Dxy. But why? In the antecedent, (x)Pxy, the x is bound. But what about the consequent? Why is it not (y)Dyy? The x is not bound in Dxy so why not change the x to a y? You must remember how the entire restriction was worded: The formula S, with the variable w replaced by the term t. S w/t is the result of replacing every free occurrence of the variable w in S with the term t, provided that every substituted occurrence of t in the result is free. If, in our example, (x)Pxy ⊃ (y)Dxy, if we replaced the free x in (y)Dxy with a y we would obtain (y)Dyy. But then the substituted occurrence of y would be bound. So, the substitution cannot be made.

Let us keep the same formula but change the notation from S x/y to S y/x. Now, what is substituted? In the antecedent, (x)Pxy, the y is free. Can we change the y to x? If we make the change, we will obtain (x)Pxx. But then the substituted x will be bound. So, we cannot do anything to the antecedent. How about the consequent, (y)Dxy? Here there are no free occurrences of y, so we can again make no replacements.

Try another example: If S is Pxd ⊃ ∃xDxd, then what is S x/d? Since the antecedent Pxd has a free x, we can replace it with a d to obtain Pdd. The x in the consequent, ∃xDxd, is bound, so we cannot replace the x. Thus, we obtain Pdd ⊃ ∃xDxd.

EXERCISES 4.7

1. If S is ∃xPyx, what is S y/d?
2. If S is (x)Hxx ⊃ Pyx, what is S x/y?
3. If S is (x)(y)(Pxy ≡ -Hyx), what is S x/y?
4. If S is (∃xHxx ∨ (x)Pxy), what is S y/c?
5. If S is (Pxx ∨ -Hyy), what is S x/y?
6. If S is (x)(y)(Pxy ⊃ Hxz), what is S x/z?
7. If S is (x)(y)(∃z)(Hxz ∨ Pxx) ⊃ Tzy, what is S y/z?

VALID ARGUMENTS USED FOR PROOFS

Now that we understand replacement notation, we can discuss the valid arguments that we will need to use in doing proofs in quantificational logic. First, we will state these arguments. They are very similar to the ones introduced in the chapter on monadic logic.

For Some Introduction (∃I)

S w/t; so, ∃wS

For Some Elimination (∃E)

∃wS, (w)(S ⊃ U); so, U

For Every Introduction (∀I)

If S follows from a set of formulae in which the variable w occurs only bound, then (w)S follows from this set of formulae.

For Every Elimination (∀E)

(w)S; so, S w/t

Quantifier Exchange (Q)

∃wS; so, -(w)-S, and -(w)-S; so, ∃wS
(w)S; so, -∃w-S, and -∃w-S; so, (w)S
∃w-S; so, -(w)S, and -(w)S; so, ∃w-S
(w)-S; so, -∃wS, and -∃wS; so, (w)-S

As in monadic logic, these new valid arguments have been stated exactly as they appear in the text with the exception of the Quantifier Exchange (Q) arguments. In the text, the set of Q arguments is first stated and then followed by the words "and conversely." Here we actually state the converse arguments. For instance, the text says: ∃wS; so, -(w)-s, and conversely. We would state the arguments in this way: ∃wS; so, -(w)-S, and -(w)-S; so, ∃wS.

These arguments are valid for every formula S, every variable w, every term $\underline{t}$, and every formula $\underline{U}$ in which $\underline{w}$ occurs only bound. Many times this last phrase, "and every formula $\underline{U}$ in which $\underline{w}$ occurs only bound," is confusing. This phrase, however, only applies to the For Some Elimination argument, since among these new arguments, For Some Elimination is the only one that contains a $\underline{U}$. This means that if in the formula $\underline{U}$ there occurs the variable $\underline{w}$, then that occurrence of $\underline{w}$ must be bound. Note that the variable $\underline{w}$ is found in both the assumptions of the For Some Elimination argument. If $\underline{w}$ occurs in $\underline{U}$ and is not bound, then the argument is not valid. For example: (x)(Tx ⊃ Rxx); ∃xTx; so, Rxx. In this case $\underline{w}$ is $\underline{x}$, $\underline{S}$ is $\underline{Tx}$, and $\underline{U}$ is $\underline{Rxx}$. So we have ∃xTx substituted for ∃wS, (x)(Tx ⊃ Rxx) substituted for (w)(S ⊃ U) and Rxx substituted for $\underline{U}$. You should see that the variable $\underline{x}$ occurs in $\underline{U}$ (it occurs twice, in fact) but that these occurrences of $\underline{x}$ are not bound. The formula $\underline{Rxx}$ has the variable $\underline{x}$, but it is no preceded by a quantifier. So, the occurrences of $\underline{x}$ in $\underline{Rxx}$ are free occurrences. Since $\underline{x}$ is the same variable that occurs in both the assumptions, ∃xTx and (x)(Tx ⊃ Pxx), this argument does not satisfy the criteria for the valid For Some Elimination argument. If we change the argument and bind the occurrence of $\underline{x}$ in $\underline{U}$, then the argument is valid. For instance: ∃xTx, (x)(Tx ⊃ ∃xRxx); so, ∃xRxx. Now, the variable $\underline{x}$ in the formula $\underline{U}$ is bound.

The only difference between these new valid arguments and those introduced in monadic logic is the use of replacement notation and the use of different quantifier symbols. But the concepts are exactly the same as those discussed in the chapter on monadic logic.

In the next section we will discuss each of these new arguments briefly.

THE FOR SOME ARGUMENTS

For Some Introduction (∃I)

$\underline{S}$ w/t; so, ∃wS

If we have a formula, say $\underline{Pdd}$, then we can conclude ∃xPxx by For Some Introduction. Remember that $\underline{S}$ w/t is read as: The formula $\underline{S}$, with the variable $\underline{w}$ replaced by the term $\underline{t}$. So if our assumption is $\underline{S}$ /d, then all that we have left to do is choose a variable. We could choose $\underline{y}$, so that our assumption would be $\underline{S}$ y/d. But let us choose $\underline{x}$, so that we have $\underline{S}$ x/d. According to the argument, if we have $\underline{S}$ x/d, then we can conclude ∃xS. And since $\underline{S}$ is $\underline{Pdd}$, the $\underline{x}$ replaces the occurrences of $\underline{d}$, so that we have ∃xPxx. Thus, we substituted a nonquantified formula, $\underline{Pdd}$, with a formula quantified by a for some quantifier, ∃xPxx. So, in a sense, we have "introduced" a for some quantifier, which is the reason we call this For Some Introduction.

If $\underline{R}$ is true of $\underline{c}$ (that is, if we know that $\underline{Rc}$ is true), then $\underline{R}$ is true of something, namely $\underline{c}$. So, if $\underline{R}$ is true of something, then ∃xRx is true.

For Some Elimination (∃E)

∃wS; (w)(S ⊃ U); so, U

We have already discussed this argument to some extent when we explained the meaning of the phrase "and every formula $\underline{U}$ in which $\underline{w}$

occurs only bound." Also, this argument was discussed at length in the chapter on monadic logic. In quantificational logic, the symbolic notation is different but the concept is the same. To use this argument we must have two formulae—a formula that is quantified by a <u>for some</u> quantifier and an if-then formula that is quantified by a <u>for every</u> quantifier.

For example, suppose <u>S</u> is Rx. Then, to have a formula of the form ∃wS, Rx must be quantified by a <u>for some</u> quantifier or, in symbols of symbolic notation, ∃xRx. Also, we must have a formula of the form (w)(S ⊃ U) in which <u>w</u> occurs only bound in <u>U</u>. Since <u>S</u> is Rx in this case and <u>w</u> is the variable <u>x</u>, then our other formula will look like this: (x)(Rx ⊃ U), in which <u>U</u> is some formula and if the variable <u>x</u> occurs in <u>U</u>, then it must be a bound occurrence. So, if we choose <u>U</u> to be Tzx, our formula will be (x)(Rx ⊃ ∃Tzx). But now we have a problem. The formula Tzx (our <u>U</u> in this case) has an occurrence of <u>x</u> that is not bound. So, we have not yet satisfied all the criteria for the valid argument. We must first make the occurrence of <u>x</u> in Tzx a bound occurrence. To do so, we will simply change <u>U</u> to be ∃xTzx rather than Tzx. Now, the occurrence of <u>x</u> is bound and we have an instance of the valid For Some Elimination argument:

∃xRx, (x)(Rx ⊃ ∃xTzx); so, ∃xTzx

Let us try another example:

∃xRy, (x)(Rx ⊃ Tzy; so, Tzy

In this argument <u>U</u> is the formula Tzy. Notice that Tzy is not a bound formula. But there are no occurrences of the variable <u>x</u> in Tzy, so Tzy need not have quantifiers. In the For Some Elimination argument the formula <u>U</u> has to be a quantified formula only when there is an occurrence of the bound variable in the two assumptions. So, if the two assumptions have quantified z's (that is, ∃zRz, (z)(Rz ⊃ U)), then, if <u>U</u> contains an occurrence of <u>z</u>, then that occurrence of <u>z</u> must be bound by quantifiers. If <u>U</u> is, say, Pxy, then there is no occurrence of <u>z</u> and, thus, Pxy, (U) need not be a quantified formula. We will discuss this argument further when we come to the proof strategies.

THE FOR EVERY ARGUMENTS

For Every Introduction (∀I)

If <u>S</u> follows from a set of formulae in which the variable <u>w</u> occurs only bound, then (w)S follows also from this set of fomrulae.

If we arrive at a formula <u>S</u>, say Tx, somewhere in a proof and the variable <u>x</u> occurs only bound in assumptions that are in force (that is, the assumptions in which every <u>x</u> occurs bound), then we can conclude that (x)Tx is true. This argument is used in conjunction with P Rule 4 (Rule of Proof 4).

Rules of Proof

As pointed out in the text, the rules of proof in truth-functional logic are used in quantificational logic as well. But in quantificational logic we need one more rule of proof. Although P Rule 4 was

used in monadic logic, it must be stated now in a way that conforms
to the different notation used in quantificational logic.

P Rule 4. A line, (w)S, is justified by ∀I if, up to an earlier
line S still in force, all assumptions of the argument
and all temporary assumptions in force have the variable
w not occurring free.

To return to our example, if we arrive at a formula, say Tx, then
if all the assumptions in force (both temporary assumptions and given
assumptions) that contain an occurrence of x that is bound, then we
can bind the formula that was derived from these bound assumptions.
Suppose we are given the argument:

(x)(Bx ⊃ Rx), (x)(Rx ⊃ Tx), (x)Bx; so, (x)Tx

We can show the proof as follows:

1. (x)(Bx ⊃ Rx)   As
2. (x)(Rx ⊃ Tx)   As
3. (x)Bx   As
Show (x)Tx

Using the For Every Elimination argument that we will discuss shortly,
we obtain the following:

1. (x)(Bx ⊃ Rx)   As
2. (x)(Rx ⊃ Tx)   As
3. (x)Bx   As
Show (x)Tx
4. Bx ⊃ Rx   (∀E, 1, x/x)
5. Rx ⊃ Tx   (∀E, 2, x/x)
6. Bx   (∀E, 3, x/x

By If then Elimination we can obtain Rx and by If-then Elimination
again we can obtain Tx:

1. (x)(Bx ⊃ Rx)   As
2. (x)(Rx ⊃ Tx)   As
3. (x)Bx   As
Show (x)Tx
4. Bx ⊃ Rx   (∀E, 1, x/x)
5. Rx ⊃ Tx   (∀E, 2, x/x)
6. Bx   (∀E, 3, x/x)
7. Rx   (IfE, 4, 6)
8. Tx   (IfE, 5, 7)

We have arrived at Tx and all the previous assumptions still in force
(that is, lines 1, 2, and 3) having the variable x, have the x bound. In
other words x occurs in all three assumptions, but nowhere does it occur free. So, by the For Every Introduction argument and P Rule 4, we
conclude that (x)Tx is true from line 8 and ∀I. If, say line 3 (assumption 3), were simply Bx rather than (x)Bx, then the criteria for the
argument would not be totally satisfied. Thus, we could not conlcude
(x)Tx in line 8. In a sense, we have introduced a for every quantifier
into the formula Tx; thus the argument is called For Every Introduction.

For Every Elimination (∀E)

   (w)S; so, S w/t

   In this argument, if we know that S is true of every variable w, then it is true of any term we choose. If (x)Rxd is true, then Rxd is true of any x we wish to choose. It is true of d, cE, e, or f or any other term. So, if (x)Rxd is true, then we can conclude that Rdd is true also—or, if you like, Rcd, Red, Rfd. We simply replace the variable w (in this case x) in S w/t, with the term t (in this case c, d, e, or f).

   Suppose we had the following argument: (x)Pdx; so, Pdf. Since the variable x is quantified for every x, then we can choose whatever term we need to do our proof. So we chose f.

   1. (x)Pdx   As
   Show Pdf
   2. Pdf   (∀E, 1, x/f)

Notice that we used For Every Elimination (∀E) and replaced the variable x with the term f. We state this by writing: ∀E, 1, x/f. This reads: For Every Elimination, line 1, where the variable x is replaced by the term f. It is sometimes helpful, though not necessary, to write it that way. Before we finish our discussion of For Every Elimination, there is one other point that deserves attention. Suppose we have the formula (x)(y)Pyx. Can we use For Every Elimination to obtain the formula (y)Pyy in which we replace the variable x with the term y (x/y)? No! Someone may reason that if it is true of every x, then it should be true of y or for that matter c, d, e, and so on. This kind of reasoning makes sense except that it disregards the restriction mentioned earlier: . . . provided that *every* substituted occurrence of t in the result is free. Recall the discussion in both the text and the Study Guide on replacement notation. When a variable is replaced by a term, the term must be free in the resulting formula. In our example, if we replace the variable x with the term y; then our result will be (y)Pyy. But, as you can see, the y is bound. So, we cannot replace the variable x with the term y.

   Beginning with a formula that contains a *for every* quantifier, the For Every Elimination argument derives a formula that does not have a quantifier. Thus, in a sense, we eliminate the *for every* quantifier and so we call this argument For Every Elimination.

Quantifier Exchange (Q)

   These arguments simply allow us to change a formula that is quantified by a *for some* quantifier to a formula that is quantified by a *for every* quantifier and vice versa. Suppose we have ∃yPyy; by Quantifier Exchange we can conclude -(y)-Pyy.

   Lastly, before we begin doing proofs, it will help to know and understand the proof strategies. Strategies 1 through 8 are the same as the corresponding strategies of truth-functional logic. Strategies 9 through 12 are similar to the corresponding strategies in monadic logic. The only major difference is in the symbolic notation of quantificational logic.

PROOF STRATEGIES

STRATEGIES

Strategy 9. To show (w)S, show S in which w occurs bound in any assumption still in force, and use ∀I.

Almost every time you need to show a for every formula (that is, a formula which is quantified with a for every quantifier), you will use Strategy 9. You simply work toward showing S with the variable w bound in all the previous assumptions in force. This means that, whenever you intend to use this argument, you should check all the assumptions still in force, including temporary assumptions, to determine whether the variable that you intend to bind is also bound in all the previous assumptions in force. Consider this argument, for example:

(x)Tx, Px; so, (x)(Tx · Px)

The proof would proceed as follows:

1. (x)Tx   As
2. Px   As
Show (x)(Tx · Px)

Since our statement, (x)(Tx · Px), is a formula bound with a for every quantifier, then Strategy 9 is appropriate. So, we adopt Strategy 9 and work to show S (in this case (Tx · Px)).

1. (x)Tx   As
2. Px   As
Show (x)(Tx · Px)
[Show Tx · Px
3. Tx   (∀E, 1)
4. Tx · Px   (&I, 2, 3)

We are now ready to complete the proof. But before we use For Every Introduction (as Strategy 9 suggests), we must check if w (in this case x) occurs bound in any assumption still in force. Both lines 1 and 2 are assumptions in force, so we need to determine whether x is bound in both. Assumption 1 has an occurrence of x that is bound. But assumption 2 has an occurrence of x that is not bound. So, since every assumption that contains the variable x is not bound, we cannot use the For Every Introduction argument. In fact, the argument is invalid. Let us change the argument slightly and see if it works:

(x)Tx, (x)Px; so, (x)(Tx · Px)

Here is the proof:

1. (x)Tx   As
2. (x)Px   As
Show (x)(Tx · Px)
[Show Tx · Px]
3. Tx   (∀E, 1)
4. Px   (∀E, 2)
5. Tx · Px   (&I, 3, 4)

94

Now, we check our assumptions. Are the occurrences of x bound? Yes! In both cases x is bound, so we can conclude as follows in line 6:

6. (x)(Tx · Px)   (∀I, 5)

It is a good idea to get into the habit of checking your assumptions before you use the For Every Introduction argument.

Strategy 10. From (w)S, conclude S w/t, and use ∀E.

If we want to show a formula S w/t, just show (w)S and use ∀E. Remember, S w/t is read as: The formula S with the variable w replaced by the term t. Suppose we have the following argument:

Bx ⊃ (y)Ty, Bx · Ry; so, Td

The conclusion of this argument has the form S w/d in which T is S, w is a variable, and d is the term that replaced the variable. So, we only need to find a case of (w)S (in our case (y)Ty):

1. Bx ⊃ (y)Ty   As
2. Bx · Ry   As
Show Td
[Show (w)Tw (in which w is any variable)
3. Bx   (&E, 2)
4. (y)Ty   (IfE, 1, 3)
5. Td   (∀E, 4, y/d)

Strategy 11. To show ∃wS, show S w/t, and use ∃I.

If we need to show a for some formula (that is, a formula that is quantified by a for some quantifier), simply show the formula with the variable replaced by a term (that is, S w/t) and use ∃I. For example, if you need to show ∃xPxx, just show Pdd and use ∃I. Suppose we have the argument:

(x)(Rx · Tx); so ∃yTy

Since the conclusion of this argument is of the form ∃wS (in our case ∃yTy), Strategy 11 is appropriate. So, we try to show S w/t (in our case, Td, Tc, Te or any other term) and then use ∃I. Let us try this proof:

1. (x)(Rx · Tx)   As
Show ∃yTy
2. Rd · Td   (∀E, 1)
3. Td   (&E, 2)
4. ∃yTy   (∃I, 3, d/y)

Strategy 12. To show U when ∃wS is still in force and w only occurs bound in U, show (w)(S ⊃ U), and use ∃E. In other words, if all assumptions in force only have w occurring bound, assume S and show U. Then use IfI, followed by ∀I, followed by ∃E.

This strategy is the most difficult to understand of all; yet is is

really very straightforward if only we follow the steps of the strategy
very carefully. Suppose we have an argument:

$\exists y Ry$, $(y)(Ry \supset (Bx \cdot Tx))$; so $\exists y Ty$

This argument will use Strategy 12. If we proceed slowly, we can follow
the steps of the strategy without any problems. First, we determine
which formula is U and which is S. Our conclusion is $\exists x Tx$, so that is
U. We have a $\exists w S$ still in force, namely $\exists y Ry$. So, S is Ry. Following
the strategy, we assume S. This will be a temporary assumption:

```
1. ∃yRy                     As
2. (y)(Ry ⊃ (Bx · Tx))      As
Show ∃xTx
┌─7 3. Ry                    Tas
```

Now we work to show $\exists x Tx$ (U):

```
1. ∃yRy                     As
2. (y)(Ry ⊃ (Bx · Tx))      As
Show ∃yTy
┌─7 3. Ry                    Tas
│   4. Ry ⊃ (Bx · Tx)        (∀E, 2)
│   5. Bx · Tx               (IfE, 3, 4)
│   6. Tx                    (&E, 5)
│   7. ∃yTy                  (∃I, 6, x/y)
```

Next, we use If-then Introduction:

```
1. ∃yRy                     As
2. (y)(Ry ⊃ (Bx · Tx))      As
Show ∃yTy
┌─7 3. Ry                    Tas
│   4. Ry ⊃ (Bx · Tx)        (∀E, 2)
│   5. Bx · Tx               (IfE, 3, 4)
│   6. Tx                    (&E, 5)
├─ 7. ∃yTy                   (∃I, 6, x/y)
8. Ry ⊃ ∃yTy                 (IfI, 3, 7)
```

Now, Strategy 12 advises us to use ∀I. Remember, before we can use ∀I,
we first need to check whether all of the assumptions still in force
have y bound. This proof has three assumptions. The first two (lines 1
and 2) are given assumptions. The third assumption is a temporary assumption. So, which assumptions are still in force? Our temporary assumption in line 3 is not in force, but our given assumptions are. Now,
check whether y is bound in both assumptions. It is bound in both assumptions so it is alright to use For Every Introduction in line 9:

```
1. ∃yRy                     As
2. (y)(Ry ⊃ (Bx · Tx))      As
Show ∃yTy
┌─7 3. Ry                    Tas
│   4. Ry ⊃ (Bx · Tx)        (∀E, 2, y/y)
│   5. Bx · Tx               (IfE, 3, 4)
│   6. Tx                    (&E, 5)
│   7. ∃yTy                  (∃I, 6)
```

```
8. Ry ⊃ ∃yTy                  (IfI, 3, 7)
9. (y)(Ry ⊃ ∃yTy)             (∀I, 8)
```

Now we are ready to do the final step of the strategy, namely, use ∃E
Looking at the proof you should note that in line 1 we have ∃yRy which
has the form ∃wS in which Ry is S and y is w.

In line 9 we have (y)(Ry ⊃ ∃yTy) which has the form (w)(S ⊃ U) in
which Ry is again S, U is ∃yTy and y is again w. Also, notice that y is
bound in U. So, we have everything we need in order to conclude U by
For Some Elimination:

```
 1. ∃yRy                       As
 2. (y)(Ry ⊃ (Bx · Tx))        As
Show ∃yTy
      ┌─ 3. Ry                 Tas
         4. Ry ⊃ (Bx · Tx)     (∀E, 2, y/y)
         5. Bx · Tx            (IfE, 3, 4)
         6. Tx                 (&E, 5)
      └─ 7. ∃yTy               (∃I, 6, x/y)
 8. Ry ⊃ ∃yTy                  (IfI, 3, 7)
 9. (y)(Ry ⊃ ∃yTy)             (∀I, 8)
10. ∃yTy                       (∃E, 1, 9)
```

You now have at your disposal several Basic Valid Arguments, P Rule
4, and Proof Strategies 9 through 12 for use in quantificational logic.
So, you have all you need to do the following proofs.

EXERCISES 4.8

Give proofs for the following arguments:

1. (x)(Bx ⊃ Qx), (x)(Qx ⊃ Rx); so, (x)(Bx ⊃ Rx)
2. (y)(x)Hxy; so, (x)(y)Hxy
3. (x)(y)Tyx; so, (y)(x)Tyx
4. ∃x(y)Qxy; so, (y)∃xQxy
5. (x)(Bx · Rx); so, (x)Bx · (x)Rx
6. (x)Bx · (x)Rx; so, (x)(Bx · Rx)
7. (z)(Tz ⊃ Rz); so, (z)Tz ⊃ (z)Rz
8. ∃z(Bz · Tz); so, ∃zBz · ∃zTz
9. ∃x∃y∃zKxyz; so, ∃z∃y∃xKxyz (in which K is a three-place relation)
10. (z)Bz v ∃yRy; so, (z)∃y(Bz v Ry)

AXIOMATIZATION

In the text you are asked to axiomatize a set of formulae. Most of
you will probably scratch your heads not knowing what to do or how to
start. The idea behind axiomatizing a set is to eliminate the formulae
that are not needed. In other words, if we have a set of formulae and
two of the formulae in the set can be derived from the other formulae
in the set, then we do not need those two. They are redundant. Axiomatizing is showing (proving) that this is the case.

Suppose we have five formulae: A, B, C, D, and E. Suppose we are
asked to axiomatize this set of formulae. What do we do? First you
might look to see if one or more of the formulae might be obviously

```
```

derivable from the others. Suppose you guess that both B and E are derivable from the other formulae. Next, you try to construct a proof to show that from A, C, and D, you can derive B. Then, you construct a proof to show that from A, C, and D, you can derive E. Now, our set of formulae is reduced to the minimum number that cannot be derived. To prove that the formulae that are left cannot be derived, show counterexamples. A, C, and D are left, so first let us show that D does not follow from A and C. This requires that we show a counterexample with A and C as assumptions and D as the conclusion. Next, show that from A and D, we cannot derive C. So, we will need to provide another counterexample with A and D as assumptions and C as the conclusion. Lastly, we must show that from C and D, A does not follow. Now, one last counterexample is necessary, in which C and D are the assumptions and A is the conclusion.

Every axiomatization will require at least one proof and one counterexample and, frequently, will require many more. How many will be determined by the number of formulae in the original set. In our example, two proofs and three counterexamples were necessary. The proofs were as follows:

1. A, C, D; so, E
2. A, C, D; so, B

The counterexamples were:

1. A, C; so, D
2. A, D; so, C
3. D, C; so, A

TRANSLATION

Quantificational logic enables us to translate sentences that are more complex than we encountered before. But this means that the rules for translating are correspondingly more complex. They are much like those from the previous chapters, however, and with practice you should not have too much trouble doing translations in quantificational logic.

Why sentences are translated a certain way is another question altogether. In the text, there is some discussion as to why, for example, all S are U is translated (x)(Sx ⊃ Ux). For the most part, you should accept these rules and use them. Why a formula translates a certain way is the subject of a different course. We will first state the rules of translation and then do some exercises.

Rules of Translation

T Rule 1. All S are U and All S U translate as (x)(Sx ⊃ Ux).
T Rule 2. No S are U and No S U translate as (x)(Sx ⊃ -Ux).
T Rule 2. Some S are U and Some S U translate as ∃x(Sx · Ux).
T Rule 4. [S that U]x translates as (Sx · Ux).
        [S that U]y translates as (Sy · Uy).
T Rule 5. [W all U]x translates as (y)(Uy ⊃ Wxy).
        [W all U]y translates as (x)(Ux ⊃ Wyx).
T Rule 6. [W no U]x translates as (y)(Uy ⊃ -Wxy).
        [W no U]y translates as (x)(Ux ⊃ -Wyx).
T Rule 7. [W some U]x translates as ∃y(Uy · Wxy).

98

[W some J]y translates as ∃x(Ux · Wyx).

T Rule 8. A word or phrase with an underlined letter translates as that letter capitalized.

EXERCISES 4.9

Translate the following sentences using the above rules.

Example: All criminals rob some citizens that gamble.
1. All criminals rob some citizens that gamble.
2. All C R some I that G by T Rule 8.
3. (x)(Cx ⊃ ∃[R some I that G]x by T Rule 1.
4. (x)(Cx ⊃ ∃y[I that G]y · Rxy)) by T Rule 7.
5. (x)(Cx ⊃ ∃y(Iy · Gy) · Rxy) by T Rule 4.

1. Some pilots fly some airplanes that glide.
2. All dog catchers catch all dogs that smell.

For the following use also T rules from previous chapters.

3. Some welders work all jobs if and only if all foremen pay some wages.
4. It is not the case that if some bankers save all pennies that shine then no citizens spend all nickels.
5. If William mows all lawns that need no care, then some neighbors yell.

Quantificational Logic with Identity and Operations

KEY TERMS

<u>Function</u> Names for constructing more complex denoting expressions. Functional symbols, together with terms, make complex terms.

<u>Tuple</u> A number of ordered objects. An ordered pair is a two-tuple, an ordered triple is a three-tuple, and so on.

<u>Identity</u> The relation between two objects that are equal.

<u>Iota Operator</u> The iota operator uses a formula that refers to a set with only one object in it, together with a variable, to form a term.

<u>Set Abstraction Operator</u> The set abstraction operator uses a formula that refers to a set containing more than one object, together with a variable, to form a term.

As in previous chapters, in this section we will learn to evaluate even more complex arguments, giving counterexamples for the invalid arguments and proofs for the valid ones. To do this, we will add another method for constructing formulae to those methods we already know. Also, we will consider what are called function symbols, which are used to construct complex terms.

SYNTAX

Rules of Syntax

An expression is a variable, constant, term, one-place or two-place relation symbol or function symbol, or formula if and only if it is so according to the following rules:

F Rule 1 through F Rule 6 are the same as in quantificational logic.

F Rule 7. If <u>u</u> and <u>w</u> are terms, then the following is a formula: U is w.

F Rule 8. The following are, respectively, a one-place and a two-place function symbol: the father of, the nearest common ancestor of.

F Rule 9. If <u>u</u> and <u>w</u> are terms and <u>k</u> and <u>l</u> are, respectively, a one-place and a two-place function symbol, then the following are terms: <u>ku</u>, <u>lu and w</u>.

You will notice that these rules are exactly the same as those given in the text except that here they are called F rules, the F standing for <u>formula</u>. In this chapter we will also use the same terms and one- and two-place function symbols as given in the text.

What can we do with these new F rules? In the chapter on quantificational logic, we constructed formulae by connecting terms with relation symbols. But here, we can construct formulae by using two terms, together with the word <u>is</u>. <u>Hume is Kant</u> is a formula by F Rule 7 because <u>Hume</u> is a term and <u>Kant</u> is a term and these two terms are connected by an <u>is</u>. The formula happens to be false, but that does not matter. We are concerned presently with syntax, not semantics. If <u>New York</u> is a term and <u>Washington</u> is also a term, then <u>New York is Washington</u> is another false formula.

F Rule 8 explains how to use function symbols. Function symbols are similar to relation symbols. There are two kinds of function symbols just as there are two kinds of relation symbols. The one-place function symbol we are given in the text is <u>the father of</u>. How do we use it? First, we add a term to the right side of the symbol. For example, if <u>Socrates</u> is a term, then we can add <u>Socrates</u> to the right side of the one-place function symbol, <u>the father of</u>, to obtain <u>the father of Socrates</u>. So, is <u>the father of Socrates</u> a formula? No! When we connected terms to relation symbols, we obtained formulae. But when we connect terms to functions, we obtain terms (complex terms). Since complex terms are still terms, they can be used as such. So, we can add our new term, <u>the father of Socrates</u>, to a function symbol to obtain another new term. For instance, the function <u>the father of</u> can be added to the new term, <u>the father of Socrates</u>, to obtain the term, <u>the father of the father of Socrates</u>. Constructed formally, the process would look like this:

1. <u>Socrates</u> is a term by F Rule 1.
2. <u>The father of</u> is a function by F Rule 8.
3. <u>The father of Socrates</u> is a term by lines 1 and 2 and F Rule 9.
4. <u>The father of the father of Socrates</u> is a term by lines 2 and 3 and F Rule 9.

This brings us to F Rule 9, for we used it in lines 3 and 4 of this construction. F Rule 9 tells us how we can put function symbols together with terms to obtain other terms. Suppose we have the terms <u>Henry James, Sr.</u>, <u>Henry James, Jr.</u>, and <u>William James</u>. F Rule 9 allows us to construct a term using the two-place function symbol <u>the nearest common ancestor of</u> as follows: <u>The nearest common ancestor of Henry James, Jr., and William James</u>. Now, by F Rule 7, we can construct a formula by connecting our new term with one of our given terms: <u>Henry James, Sr., is the nearest common ancestor of Henry James, Jr., and William James</u>. This formula happens to be true, but we could construct many other formulae that would be false as, for example, <u>Henry James, Jr., is the father of William James</u>. This is false.

EXERCISES 5.1

If <u>Great Britain</u>, <u>France</u>, <u>Germany</u>, <u>Hitler</u>, <u>Churchill</u>, and <u>DeGaulle</u> are all terms and <u>the father of</u> and <u>the ally of</u> are one-place function symbols and <u>the nearest common ancestor of</u> is a two-place function symbol, then which of the following are formulae? Give a formal construction for those that are formulae. For those that are not formulae, explain why they are not and how they could be changed to be made formulae.

1. Great Britain is the ally of the ally of France.
2. If France is the ally of Germany and Great Britain, then Hitler is the nearest common ancestor of Churchill and De Gaulle.
3. France and Great Britain are the nearest common ancestor of Germany if and only Churchill is the ally of DeGaulle.
4. Churchill is the ally of the nearest common ancestor of the ally of France.
5. Hitler is the ally of Germany or it is not the case that Churchill is the nearest common ancestor of DeGaulle and Roosevelt.

SYMBOLIC NOTATION

As before we will shorten these formulae by using symbolic notation.

Rules of Syntax

An expression is a variable, constant, term, one-place or two-place relation symbol or function symbol, or formula, if and only if it is so according to the following rules:

F Rule 1 through F Rule 6 are the same as those used in quantificational logic.

F Rule 7. If u and w are terms, then the following is a formula: $(u = w)$.

F Rule 8. The following are, respectively, a one-place and a two-place function symbol: f, g.

F Rule 9. If u and w are terms and k and l are, respectively, a one-place and a two-place function symbol, then the following are terms: ku, luw (read as the k of u and the l of u and w.

EXERCISES 5.2

If a, b, c, d, e, are terms, f is a one-place function symbol and g is a two-place function symbol, then which of the following are formulae? Give a formal construction for those that are formulae. For those that are not formulae, explain why not and how they could be changed to be made formulae. Remember that F Rules 1 through 6 still hold.

1. $(x)((fx = gcc) \equiv (\exists y lyx))$
2. $lab \equiv (x)(fx = gxx)$
3. $(x)(fx = gxx) = lab$
4. $ffgce$
5. $(fffd = e) \equiv (x)(\exists y)(Pxy \supset Rc)$

SEMANTICS

TRUTH

When we formulated our three new F rules, we increased our capability for constructing formulae and we also learned another way to construct new terms from both function symbols and terms. Now, we will also need a method for determining the truth values of these new formulae, as well as the denotations of the new terms. Do the nine rules of semantics as we have already stated them enable us to find the truth value of, for example, (fd = gea)? They do not. So, we will need some new rules that will instruct us in how to handle these new formulae.

Rules of Semantics

S Rule 1 through S Rule 9 are the same as those used in quantificational logic.

S Rule 10. (u = w) is true if what u denotes equals (or is the same as) what w denotes but false otherwise.

S Rule 11. If k is a one-place function symbol true of an ordered pair whose first component is what u denotes, then ku denotes the second component of the pair.

S Rule 12. If l is a two-place function symbol true of an ordered triple whose first two components are what u denotes and what w denotes, then luw denotes the third component of the triple.

These new rules of semantics need to be explained in more detail. S Rule 10 says that if u is denoted to be 0, then w must also be denoted to be 0. If both u and w are 0, then (u = w) is true. If u and w are denoted to be different things, then (u = w) is false. For example, determine whether (c = e) is true, given the following possible situation:

Universe of Discourse: {0, 1}; c: 0; e: 1.

According to this possible situation, (c = e) is false:

c = e
0   1

The formula is false, because, according to S Rule 9, the two terms must denote the same thing. In this case c denotes 0 and e denotes 1. So, by S Rule 9 (c = e) is false:

(c = e)
0 Ⓕ 1

It may help to remind you that terms are not true or false; they denote objects in the universe of discourse. Usually, terms denote 0 or 1. Formulae are, however, true or false. Before, the truth or falsity of formulae was simply determined by the truth or falsity of their constituent formulae or atomic formulae. Now, we have to consider the formulae that are constructed by connecting two terms with an equals sign (=). S Rule 10 tells us how to do this.

103

S Rules 11 and 12 use a slightly different method for determining truth values than the method we have used before. The text makes the following comment: We now say that a function symbol is true of the tuples assigned to it. Tuples are any ordered number of objects. For instance, an ordered pair is a tuple, that is, a 2-tuple. An ordered triple is a 3-tuple. We could also have 4-tuples, 5-tuples, and so on. S Rule 11 does not tell us how to determine the truth value of a term because terms are not true or false; terms denote objects in the universe of discourse. You must not confuse functions and relations. From our F rules we know that $\underline{R}$ is a one-place relation and $\underline{f}$ is a one-place function. It will help you to see the difference between them by considering the following example. Suppose we have the formula $\underline{Rc \supset Pdfc}$ with the possible situation: R: 1; P: (0, 0); f: (0, 1); c: 0; d: 0. What is the truth value of the formula? First, you should notice that $\underline{R}$, the one-place relation, is true of a single object. (We might call it a one-tuple.) $\underline{P}$, however, a two-place relation, is true of ordered pairs (two-tuples). But the function $\underline{f}$, a one-place function symbol, is assigned an ordered pair. S Rule 11 explains why we have this difference. Since part of the consequent $(\underline{fc})$ of our formula, $(\underline{Pdfc})$, is a term constructed from the one-place function symbol $\underline{f}$ and the term $\underline{c}$, then we need to consider the meaning of $\underline{f}$ being assigned (0, 1). $\underline{fc}$ must denote 0 or 1 because it is a term. The formula $\underline{Pdfc}$ is composed of a two-place relation symbol $\underline{P}$ and two terms $\underline{d}$ and $\underline{fc}$. In the last chapter, we determined the truth value of $\underline{P}$ by showing that $\underline{P}$ was true of an ordered pair. The first object in the ordered pair corresponded to the first term that followed the relation symbol and the second object in the ordered pair corresponded to the second term following the first term. For example, the formula $\underline{Pcd}$ is true when $\underline{c}$ denotes 0, $\underline{d}$ denotes 1, and $\underline{P}$ is assigned the ordered pair (0, 1) as follows:

```
P c d
T 0 1
  √ √
```

In a similar way, the formula $\underline{Pdfc}$ can be analyzed to determine its truth value. But in this formula the second term is $\underline{fc}$. So, $\underline{fc}$ must denote 0 or 1. Our possible situation assigns (0, 1) to $\underline{f}$, so when $\underline{f}$ is followed by a term that denotes 0, the $\underline{f}$ denotes 1. In this case, $\underline{c}$ denotes 0, so $\underline{fc}$ denotes 1 by S Rule 11:

```
f c
1 0
  √
```

Now, let us proceed to consider $\underline{Pdfc}$. $\underline{d}$ denotes 0 and $\underline{fc}$ denotes 1. So, $\underline{Pdfc}$ is false because $\underline{P}$ is true of only the ordered pair (0, 0). $\underline{P}$ is not true of the ordered pair (0, 1), which is what $\underline{Pdfc}$ would require to make the formula true:

```
P d f c
  0 1 0
      √
```

```
P d f c
F 0 1 0
  √ √ √
```

104

Continuing further, we show that R͟c is false by S Rule 6:

```
R c
F 0
≡ ‗
```

Next, we combine the two formulae to obtain a true formula by S Rule 4:

```
R c ⊃ P d f c
_ 0   _ 0 _ 0

R c ⊃ P d f c
F 0   _ 0 1 0
‗ 7   ‗ ‗ ‗ 7

R c ⊃ P d f c
F 0   F 0 1 0
‗ 7   ‗ 7 7 7

R c ⊃ P d f c
F O T F 0 1 0
7 7 ═ 7 7 7 7
```

Now, the question arises: What would happen if f͟ were assigned (1, 0) instead of (0, 1)? What would f͟c denote? Since c͟ denotes 0 and f͟ is as-signed (1, 0), then f͟c does not denote anything:

```
f c
  0
≡ ‗
```

The first component of the ordered pair (1, 0) is 1. And since the de-notation of the term c͟ plays a part in determining the denotation of f͟c, it must denote the first component of the ordered pair. If it does not, then there is no denotation for the complex term f͟c. Let us look at another example. Suppose we have the following possible situation:

Universe of Discourse: {0, 1}; R: 1; f: (0, 1), c: 0, d: 1

What is the truth value of the two formulae R͟f͟c and R͟f͟d? First, let us consider R͟f͟c. c͟ denotes 0 in our possible situation an͟d, since 0 is the first component of the ordered pair to which f͟ is assigned, then f͟c de-notes the second component of the ordered pair—namely, 1. So, f͟c de-notes 1.

```
R f c
  1 0
  ‗ 7
```

And, since R͟ is true of 1, then R͟f͟c is true.

```
R f c
T 1 0
‗ 7 7
```

Now, let us consider R͟f͟d. d͟ denotes 1 in our possible situation, but f͟ is assigned only (0, 1). The first component of the ordered pair is not the same as the denotation of d͟. When this happens, you cannot find a denotation for the complex term f͟c and thus, you also cannot find a truth value for the formula R͟f͟d. If f͟d does not denote anything, then we cannot find the truth value of R̲f̲c̲. Suppose this were the case and our possible situation were changed to:

Universe of Discourse: {0, 1}; R: 1, f: (0, 1), (1, 0); c: 0, d: 1

So now, R̲f̲c̲ is still true.

$$
\begin{array}{ccc}
\text{R} & \text{f} & \text{c} \\
\underline{\text{T}} & \underline{1} & \underline{0} \\
= & \diagup & \diagup
\end{array}
$$

And R̲f̲d̲ is determined to be false:

$$
\begin{array}{ccc}
\text{R} & \text{f} & \text{d} \\
\underline{\text{F}} & \underline{0} & \underline{1} \\
= & \diagup & \diagup
\end{array}
$$

S Rule 12 works the same way as S Rule 11 except that S Rule 12 involves two-place functions and ordered triples (3-tuples). A term constructed from a two-place function symbol denotes the last object in the ordered triple (that is, the third object in the 3-tuple). For example, the two-place function g̲ must be followed by two terms, for example, c̲ and d̲, to obtain g̲c̲d̲. To determine what g̲c̲d̲ denotes, first decide what c̲ denotes and then what d̲ denotes. Whatever follows this pair in the ordered triple, that is, whatever is assigned to g̲ in the possible situation, will be what g̲c̲d̲ denotes. Suppose we have the following possible situation:

Universe of Discourse: {0, 1}; g: (0, 1, 0); c: 1; d: 0; P: (0, 1)

What is the truth value of the formula P̲d̲g̲d̲c̲? First, we determine that d̲ denotes 0 and c̲ denotes 1:

$$
\begin{array}{ccccc}
\text{p} & \text{d} & \text{g} & \text{d} & \text{c} \\
\_ & \underline{0} & \_ & \underline{0} & \underline{1}
\end{array}
$$

Next, determine what g̲d̲c̲ denotes in our universe of discourse. The denotation of g̲d̲c̲ will be 0, because 0 is the last component of the ordered triple. Thus, since d̲ is 0 and c̲ is 1, then g̲d̲c̲ is 0 by S Rule 12:

$$
\begin{array}{ccc}
\text{g} & \text{d} & \text{c} \\
\underline{0} & \underline{0} & \underline{1} \\
& \diagup & \diagup
\end{array}
$$

Suppose for the moment that we wished to find the denotation of g̲c̲d̲. What would it be? Since c̲ denotes 1 and d̲ denotes 0, we form the ordering 1, 0. Now, we look to our possible situation and find that g̲ is assigned (0, 1, 0), which has the ordering 0, 1 for the first two components of the ordered triple. But 0, 1 is different from the ordering we obtain from g̲c̲d̲. g̲c̲d̲ gives us instead the ordering 1, 0 as the first two components of the ordered pair:

$$
\begin{array}{ccc}
\text{g} & \text{c} & \text{d} \\
& \underline{1} & \underline{0}
\end{array}
$$

Since g does not have an assignment in the possible situation, for an ordered triple that has 1, 0 as its first two components, then we conclude that gcd does not have a denotation under this possible situation. And a denotation cannot be found unless the possible situation is changed.

Now let us return to our original formula Pdgdc. gdc denotes 0 because 0 is the third component of the ordered triple that has 0, 1 as the first two components. So, now we have:

$$
\begin{array}{c}
\text{P d g d c} \\
\underline{0}\ \underline{0}\ \underline{0}\ \underline{1} \\
\checkmark\ \checkmark
\end{array}
$$

Since our possible situation says P is true of the ordered pair (0, 1), then Pdgdc is false by S Rule 7.

$$
\begin{array}{c}
\text{P d g d c} \\
\text{F }\underline{0}\ \underline{0}\ \underline{0}\ \underline{1} \\
=\ \checkmark\ \checkmark\ \checkmark\ \checkmark
\end{array}
$$

You should now understand that S Rule 10 tells us how to find the truth value of a formula (a formula constructed from two terms and an equals sign, and that S Rules 11 and 12 tell us how to find the denotation of complex terms.

EXERCISES 5.3

Determine the denotation of the following terms according to S Rule 11, S Rule 12, and the following possible situation:

Universe of Discourse: {0, 1}; P: (0, 1), (1, 1); R: 0; b: 1;
c: 1; d: 0; e: 1; f: (0, 1), (1, 1);
g: (0, 1, 0), (1, 1, 1), (1, 0, 1), (0, 0, 0)

Example:
$$
\begin{array}{c}
\text{g f e d} \\
\underline{1}\ \underline{1}\ \underline{1}\ \underline{0} \\
=\ \checkmark\ \checkmark\ \checkmark
\end{array}
$$

Part A

1. fe
2. ffe
3. gcfd
4. gfdgcd
5. fgeb
6. ffb
7. fgfdc
8. gfefd
9. fgfbgdc

Part B

Determine the truth value of the following formulae. Use the previously given possible situation.

107

1. Rfe ≡ Pfeffe
2. -Rgcfd ⊃ (Pgebd ∨ -Pffbc)
3. (Pgfefdc ≡ Rfgeb)
4. (fffgfcfe = gfefd)
5. (gfdgcd - fgfed) ∨ Rfgeb

Part C

Determine the truth value of the following formulae. Use the previously given possible situation. (Hint: Because these formulae contain
variables and quantifiers, you will need to expand them.)

Example: (x)(Rgdx ⊃ Pxfc)

$$(R\ g\ x_0 d \supset P\ x_0 f\ c) \cdot (R\ g\ x_1 d \supset P\ x_1 f\ c)$$
$$\underset{\overline{\sqrt{}}}{T}\ \underset{\overline{\sqrt{}}}{0}\ \underset{\overline{\sqrt{}}}{0}\ \underset{\overline{\sqrt{}}}{0}\ \underset{\overline{\sqrt{}}}{T}\ \underset{\overline{\sqrt{}}}{T}\ \underset{\overline{\sqrt{}}}{0}\ \underset{\overline{\sqrt{}}}{1}\ \underset{\overline{\sqrt{}}}{1}\ \textcircled{F}\ \underset{\overline{\sqrt{}}}{F}\ \underset{\overline{\sqrt{}}}{1}\ \underset{\overline{\sqrt{}}}{1}\ \underset{\overline{\sqrt{}}}{0}\ \underset{\overline{\sqrt{}}}{F}\ \underset{\overline{\sqrt{}}}{T}\ \underset{\overline{\sqrt{}}}{1}\ \underset{\overline{\sqrt{}}}{1}\ \underset{\overline{\sqrt{}}}{1}$$

1. ∃xRgxfc ≡ ∃y(Pgyd ⊃ Ry)
2. (x)(∃y)(Pgxy) · (∃y)(z)(Rgyz)
3. (x)(z)((Rz ∨ Pxd) ⊃ (Pzc ∨ Rfe))
4. ∃x∃y(Pfefd ⊃ (Ry · Pxfy))
5. (x)(∃y)(z)(Pfxgyz ⊃ --Rgxz)

VALIDITY

We will determine the validity of arguments in this chapter exactly
as we have done previously. First, the argument should be checked to
determine whether it is possible to give a counterexample. Counterexamples are done in the same way as in previous chapters.

EXERCISES 5.4

Give counterexamples for the following arguments:

1. (x)(Rx ⊃ Pffxd); ∃xRx; so, (x)(Pffxd)
2. Rfe · -Pfde; Pfde ⊃ ∃xRfgxd; so, -∃xRfgxd
3. (x)∃y(Pfye ⊃ Rfx), (x)-Rfx; so, (x)-Pfye

PROOFS

BOUNDNESS

If we find that an argument does not have a counterexample, then
our next step is to give a proof. Before we discuss proofs, however,
we need to define an occurrence of a bound term. The definition provided in the text reads as follows: An occurrence of a term is bound
in a formula just in case some occurrence of a variable in the term is
bound in the formula. This means that anytime a formula contains a complex term, and the complex term is made up of a function symbol and a
variable (which is also a term), then that occurrence of the term (that
is, the occurrence that contains the variable) is bound if the variable
is a bound term. What about the formula ∃y(x)(Pcgyx)? Is the term gyx
bound? Yes. Both the terms x and y that make up the complex term gyx

are bound, so the occurrence of the term gyx in the formula ∃y(x)Pcgyx
is bound. But the formula Rgxz has an occurrence of the term gxz in
which the x and z are variables that are not bound. So, the occurrence
of the term gxz in the formula Rgxz is not bound.

EXERCISES 5.5

Which of the following formulae have occurrences of terms that are
bound? For those that do not have occurrences of terms that are bound,
explain what changes would be necessary to make them bound.

1. ∃xRgxfa
2. Pgxdc · Rfgyc
3. Pfgdx ⊃ ∃yRfx
4. (x)(Rgyd) ≡ ∃y(Pyx ⊃ Pgxd)
5. (x)(y)(Pfz · Rfgcd)

VALID ARGUMENTS USED FOR PROOFS

Having been given the definition of an occurrence of a bound term,
we can now do proofs. Proofs will proceed just as they did before in
quantificational logic. Since we have been introduced to a new method
of constructing formulae (F Rule 7) and since all the ways of constructing formulae (by using the connectors and, not, or, If-then, If and only
if, for some, and for every) have introduction and elimination instances
of the Basic Valid Arguments, then it is not surprising that the new
connector, =, would also have Basic Valid Arguments of this type. These
new arguments are called Equality Introduction (=I) and Equality Elimination (=E). The following are valid arguments for every formula S
and all terms u and w.

Equality Introduction (=I)

So, (u = u)

This argument may seem trivial, but, nevertheless, it is a useful
argument and is necessary in order to complete the proofs of some arguments. Since u stands for any term, then all of the following are instances of Equality Introduction:

(fd = fd)
(gfdc = gfdc)
(fffgcfd = fffgcfd)

All of the above are formulae by F Rule 7.
Note that, at any time during a proof that it might be helpful, you
can enter an instance of this valid argument on a line and justify the
line by Equality Introduction (=I). No other lines of proof are necessary to use this argument.

Equality Elimination (=E)

S, (u = w); so, S' (where S' is the result of replacing any free occurrence of u or w in S with w or u, provided the substituted terms
remain free)

Suppose we have the following argument:

Rgfxd, (fx = c); so, Rgcd

By using Equality Elimination, the proof becomes simple. If (fx = c), then by Equality Elimination we simply substitute any or all free occurrences of fx with the c that we know fx is equal to. So, we obtain the following:

```
1. Rgfxd              As
2. (fx = c)           As
Show Rgcd
3. Rgcd               (=E, 1, 2)
```

Since fx in Rgfxd occurs freely, we are able to use this argument. Let us consider another argument:

Pfgfxc, (fx = c), Pfgcc ⊃ (x)Rgxfd, (x = d); so, Rgdfd

Here is the proof:

```
1. Pfgfxc             As
2. Pfgcc ⊃ Rgxfd      As
3. (fx = c)           As
4. (x = d)            As
Show Rgdfd
```

By Equality Elimination we can substitute c for fx in the formula Pfgfxc to obtain Pfgcc as follows:

```
1. Pfgxc              As
2. Pfgc ⊃ (x)Rgxfd    As
3. (fx = c)           As
4. (x = d)            As
Show Rgdfd
5. Pfgcc              (=E, 1, 3)
```

Now, in line 6 we can obtain (x)Rgxfd by If-then Elimination and lines 2 and 5. What next? Some may want to use assumption 4 (x = d) together with line 6 ((x)Rgxfd) and Equality Elimination to obtain the desired conclusion Rgdfd. But note that the occurrence of the term x in the formula (x)Rgxfd is bound. Since x is bound, then Equality Elimination cannot be used.

But this does not necessarily mean that the proof cannot be completed. In line 6 we have (x)Rgxfd. So, by For Every Elimination we can obtain Rgdfd by replacing x with d.

```
1. Pfgfxc             As
2. Pfgcc ⊃ (x)Rgxfd   As
3. (fx = c)           As
4. (x = d)            As
Show Rgdfd
5. Pfgcc              (=E, 1, 3)
6. (x)Rgxfd           (IfE, 2, 5)
7. Rgdfd              (∀E, 6, x/d)
```

Give proofs for the following arguments:

1. $(x)(fx = gxx)$, Pfc; so, Pgcc
2. $(x)(Bx \supset \exists yHyfx)$, $\exists xBx \cdot \exists yHy$, $fx = d$; so, $\exists yHyd$
3. $(x)(Rx \supset Pfxfy)$, Rc, $fc = x$; so, $(x)Pxfy$

TRANSLATION

Although this chapter does not require new proof strategies, we do need, however, more rules for translation. These rules are quite straightforward and are used just as the rules in the previous chapters. Their use should not require further explanation. What is needed at this point is practice.

Rules of Translation

T Rule 1. <u>w is r</u> translates as <u>w = r</u>.
T Rule 2. <u>w is a U</u> translates as <u>Uw</u>.
T Rule 3. <u>At most w is a U</u> translates $(x)(-(x = w) \supset -Ux)$.
T Rule 4. <u>w is the one and only U</u> translates as $(x)((x = w) \equiv Ux)$.
T Rule 5. <u>There is a U</u> translates as $\exists y(y \text{ is a U})$.
T Rule 6. <u>There is at most one U</u> translates as $\exists y$ (at most y is a U).
T Rule 7. <u>There is one and only one U</u> translates as
           $\exists y(y \text{ is the one and only U})$.
T Rule 8. <u>[S that is a U]x</u> translates as $Sx \cdot Ux$.
T Rule 9. A word with an underlined letter translates as that let-
           ter capitalized. Names, however, with an underlined let-
           ter translate as terms with small letters.

These rules will work for any formulae, <u>S</u>, <u>U</u>, and any terms <u>x</u>, <u>r</u>, and <u>w</u>. Notice that these new rules allow us to translate identity statements such as: <u>J</u>immy Carter is <u>A</u>merican. This translates as:

$(j = a)$

Translate the following sentences.

Example: Richard Nixon is the one and only president that resigned.
           1. <u>R</u>ichard Nixon is the one and only <u>p</u>resident that re-
              signed.
           2. r is the one and only P that D, by T Rule 9.
           3. $(x)((x = r) \equiv [P \text{ that } D]x$, by T Rule 4.
           4. $(x)((x = r) \equiv (Px \cdot Dx))$, by T Rule 4 from Chapter 4.

1. There is a <u>b</u>uilding that is a <u>f</u>iretrap.
2. At most the <u>s</u>on of <u>G</u>eneral George Patton is a <u>m</u>ajor. (Hint: Use a function symbol.)

For the following sentences, use the T rules from the previous chapters.

3. If Lewis Carroll is Charles Lutwidge Dodgson, then it is not the case that there is one and only one logician.
4. There is a vacuum if and only if there is at most one vacuum and space is the one and only vacuum.

OTHER OPERATIONS

THE IOTA OPERATOR AND SET ABSTRACTION

Before we move on to consider the topic of definitions in the next chapter, we should discuss briefly the iota and set abstraction operators. As usual, these new operators have a formal rule of syntax.

Rule of Syntax

If S is a formula and w is a variable, then the following are terms: (ιw)S, (read as the w such that S) and {w:s} (read as the set of all w such that S). The symbol ι is the iota (pronounced Ī-ō-tǎ) operator. With is we can partially translate a sentence such as: The elephant is grey.

1. The elephant is grey.
2. (ιx)(x is an elephant) is grey.

From this point, the translation becomes simple:

3. G(ιx)(x is an E), by T Rule 9.
4. G₍ιx₎Ex, by T Rule 2.

Note that the rule of syntax informs us that, given a formula and a variable, we can use the iota operator to construct a term.

You will recall from monadic logic that we used atomic formulae such as it is red, it is blue, and so on. Using these atomic formulae, together with the for some and for every quantifiers and the truth-functional connectors, we constructed more complex formulae such as: for everything it is red and it is blue. The iota operator works in a similar way. Take, for example, the sentence the elephant is grey. Is grey is translated simply as Gx in which is grey is a relation symbol. The elephant is somewhat more difficult to translate. We think of elephant as the atomic formula it is an elephant. When the word the precedes a phrase that describes a set with only one object in it (that is, one elephant), then we use the iota operator. Considering these things, then the translation (ιx) x is an elephant should make sense. The x is a variable that replaces the it in it is an elephant. The it is the indefinite pronoun we discussed in monadic logic. We use the iota operator because our sentence begins with the followed by a phrase that describes a singular object. So, according to the new rule of syntax, we have the necessary ingredients to construct a term (namely, a formula, a term, and the iota operator). So, (ιx)(x is an elephant) is a term by our new rule of syntax. If we add to it the rest of our sentence is grey, then we have a formula by F Rule 9. The relation symbol G together with a term will give us a formula. The term in this case is (ιx)Ex. So, G(ιx)Ex is a formula by F Rule 9.

The symbol {:} stands for the set abstraction operator. This operator, along with a formula and a term, will also produce a term. The set abstraction operator is used when a word or phrase describes a set that contains more than one object. This can be contrasted to the iota operator, which is used when the word is describing a set with only one object. For example:

The mouse would use the iota operator—(ιx)(x is a mouse).
The mice would use the set abstraction operator—{x:x is a mouse}

Suppose we have the phrase: The senators voted for Proposition 13. Because senators refers to a group or set that contains more than one object, the set abstraction operator is appropriate. Its translation should look like this:

{x:x is a senator} voted for Proposition 13

Again we have the variable x which stands for it in it is a senator. So, if we have an atomic formula it is a senator symbolized by the one-place relation symbol S, and a variable x that stands for it, then it is a senator is symbolized Sx. Using the set abstraction operator, we obtain the term {x:Sx}. Now, with V translated as voted for Proposition 13, which is a one-place relation symbol, together with our term {x:Sx}, we can construct the following formula:

V{x:Sx}

SEMANTICS

Because the iota and set abstraction operators give us terms, the rule of semantics for these operators will not enable us to determine truth or falsity. They will instead tell us how to determine what the terms denote.

Rules of Semantics

If ι or {:} is assigned an ordered pair whose first component is the set of all denotations for w that make S true, then $(\iota x)S$ or {w:S}, whichever is applicable, denotes the second component. In addition, if there is one and only one denotation for w that makes S true, then $(\iota w)S$ denotes that object. Suppose we have the following possible situation:

Universe of Discourse: {0, 1}; P: (0, 1), (1, 1); d: 1; c: 1; ι: ({1}, 1), {:}:({0, 1}, 0)

Given this possible situation, what does the term (ιx)(x = d) denote? According to the rule of semantics, the term $(\iota w)S$ denotes the second component of the ordered pair assigned to the ι symbol if the denotations of w that makes S true are the first component of the ordered pair. In our example, we have the variable x rather than w, and the formula (x = d) rather than S. So, the term (ιx)(x = d) has the form $(\iota w)S$. What denotations of w (in our case x) makes S (in our case x = d) true? Since d is assigned 1, then to make S (in our case x = d) true, x must also be 1:

$$(\imath x)(x = d)$$
$$\frac{1}{\checkmark} \ \underline{T} \ \frac{1}{\checkmark}$$

So, the set of all denotations of x that make $x = d$ true is the set containing 1; that is, {1}. Now, we look at our possible situation. What is the assignment for $\imath$? $\imath$ is assigned the ordered pair ({1}, 1). The first component of the ordered pair is the set containing 1. This is the same set as the set of all denotations of x that make $x = d$ true. So, since the set of all denotation of x that make $x = d$ true is the set that is the first component of the ordered pair ({1}, 1), then the denotation of the term $(\imath x)(x = d)$ denotes 1. But suppose for a moment that our possible situation was changed and d denoted 0 instead of 1. Then, assuming the rest of the possible situation stayed the same, what would $(\imath x)(x = d)$ denote? Since d now denotes 0, then the only denotation of x that would make $x = d$ true is 0. For $x = d$ to be true x must denote 0. So, in this case, the set of all denotations of x that make $x = d$ true is {0}. Now, what does $(\imath x)(x = d)$ denote? As usual, to find out we look at our possible situation. $\imath$ is assigned the ordered pair ({1}, 1). But we have {0} as the set of all denotations of x that make $x = d$ true. {0} is not the same as the first component of an ordered pair assigned to $\imath$. So, what do we do? What does $(\imath x)(x = d)$ denote?

To find out we must reall the rule of semantics. The last sentence says: In addition, if there is one and only one denotation for w that makes S true, then $(\imath w)S$ denotes that object. (This last requirement makes the iota rule, stated below, valid.) So, in our present example, we have only one denotation of x that makes $x = d$ true. This means that whatever that one denotation of x is, the denotation for $(\imath x)(x = d)$ is the same. Thus, since 0 is the only denotation that makes $x = d$ true when d denotes 0, then $(\imath x)(x = d)$ denotes 0. So, essentially, we need not state an assignment for $\imath$ in our possible situation, because there never should be more than one w that will make S and $(\imath w)S$ true.

This, however, is not the case when we consider the set abstraction operator. Although the iota operator concerns sets that have only one object, the set abstraction operator concerns sets that contain more than one object.

Consider the term {x:Pxc}. It is a term because it consists of a variable x, a formula Pxc, and the set abstraction operator. What does this term denote given our previous possible situation? We need to determine which x or x's will make Pxc true. Since c denotes 1 in our possible situation and P is true of the ordered pairs (0, 1) and (1, 1), then if x is 0, Pxc will be true and if x is 1, Pxc will still be true. So, there are two denotations of x that make Pxc true, namely 0 and 1. Therefore, the set of all denotations of x that make Pxc true is the set {0, 1}. So, what is the denotation of the term {x:Pxc}? To find out, we look at our possible situation. The {:} is assigned an ordered pair. The first component of the ordered pair is the set {0, 1}. The second component of the ordered pair is 0. So, since {0, 1} is the set of all denotations of x that make Pxc true and {0, 1} is also the first component of the ordered pair assigned to {:} in the possible situation, then the term {x:Pxc} denotes the second component of the ordered pair, namely 0. So, given our previously stated possible situation, the term {x:Pxc} denotes 0.

114

VALID ARGUMENTS

Using both of our new operators, we can construct valid arguments that will be quite useful in doing proofs. If S and U formulae and w, y, and z are variables and z does not occur free in S, then the following are valid arguments:

Extensionality (EX)

$(w)(S \equiv U)$; so, $\{w:s\} = \{w:U\}$
$(w)(S \equiv U)$; so, $(\imath x)S = (\imath x)U$
So, $\{w:S\} = \{z:S \ w/z\}$
So, $(\imath w)S = (\imath z)S \ w/z$

Iota Rule (IR)

So, $y = (\imath w)(w = y)$

We will not give explanations for these valid arguments, since the text provides a brief discussion of them. We will, however, give you two proofs that use three of these arguments. We will prove the following:

$(x)(Tx \supset Pxd)$; so, $\{x:Pxd \cdot Tx\} = \{X:Tx\}$

1. $(x)(Tx \supset Pxd)$
   Show $\{x:Pxd \cdot Tx\} = \{x:Tx\}$

To show our conclusion, we simply need to show $(x)(Pxd \cdot Tx \equiv Tx)$ and then use one of our four extensionality arguments:

1. $(x)(Tx \supset Pxd)$	As
Show $\{x:Pxd \cdot Tx\} = \{x:Tx\}$	
[Show $(x)(Pxd \cdot Tx \equiv Tx)$]	
[Show $Pxd \cdot Tx \equiv Tx$]	
[Show $Pxd \cdot Tx \supset Tx$]	
2. $Tx \supset Pxd$	$(\forall E, 1, x/x)$
3. $Pxd \cdot Tx$	Tas
4. Tx	$(\&E, 3)$
5. $Pxd \cdot Tx \supset Tx$	$(IfI, 3, 4)$
[Show $Tx \supset Pxd \cdot Tx$]	
6. Tx	Tas
7. Pxd	$(IfE, 2, 6)$
8. $Pxd \cdot Tx$	$(\&I, 6, 7)$
9. $Tx \supset Pxd \cdot Tx$	$(IfI, 6, 8)$
10. $Pxd \cdot Tx \equiv Tx$	$(IffI, 5, 9)$
11. $(x)(Pxd \cdot Tx \equiv Tx)$	$(\forall I, 10)$
12. $\{x:Pxd \cdot Tx\} = \{x:Tx\}$	$(EX, 11)$

Suppose now we have the argument: Everyone is such that he is a barber if and only if he is Jones. So, the barber is Jones. We first need to symbolize the argument as follows:

$(x)(Bx \equiv x = j)$; so, $(\imath x)Bx = j$

Now, we can do the proof:

1. (x)(Bx ≡ x = j)   As
Show (ɿx)Bx = j
2. (ɿx)Bx = (ɿx)x = j   (EX, 1)
3. j = (ɿx)(x = j)   (IR)
4. (ɿx)Bx = j   (=E, 2, 3)

Definitions

KEY TERMS

<u>Definition</u> An identity or an <u>if and only if</u> formula consisting of
(1) a left portion, called the <u>definiens</u>, that contains the symbol
being defined together with the appropriate number of variables
(all different); (2) a right portion, called the <u>definiendum</u>, that
does not contain the symbol being defined. The entire formula is
preceded by universal quantifiers (<u>for all</u> quantifiers for each
variable in the definiens).

<u>Definiens</u> The left part of a definition formula. The definiens is
that which is being defined.

<u>Definiendum</u> The right part of a definition formula. The definiendum
is that which defines the definiens.

<u>Eliminability</u> A property that every definition must possess. If in a
formula a symbol appears that is the definiens in a definition, the
symbol can be replaced by the definiendum of the definition or vice
versa.

<u>Noncreativity</u> A property that every definition must possess. A defi-
nition must not include information, other than the definiens, that
is not provable if the information was not provable before the definition was used.

TYPES OF DEFINITIONS

In this chapter we are mainly concerned with the method for defining one concept by using only other concepts. It would be of little
use to define a word or concept using the same word or concept. Imagine
trying to tell residents of the Sahara Desert what snow is.' You would
get nowhere if you defined snow in terms of snow. A definition is only
useful if you use terms that are known to define terms that are unknown.

As in the previous discussions on validity' in which the content of
the sentence was considered less important than the form of the sentences, so also in this chapter we will be more concerned with form
than with content. The form that definitions take are very important
and play a more significant role than the content. Indeed, we will

determine whether or not a formula is adequate as a definition by examining its form.

Consider Exercises 6.1 given in the text. The first exercise asks for a definition of female. Then, it states the definition in English, that is, a person who is not male. This definition assumes we know what it is to be male. But this is not the only way to define female, we could define a female as a person who can give birth to children. This definition is alright as long as we know what it means to give birth and what children are. It is probably acceptable, however, to define female as a person who is not male. First, how can we symbolize male? Mx is an adequate symbolization. How about not male? We simply add a not to obtain -Mx. So, we put this symbolization of not male in the blank to obtain the definition of female, namely, (x)(Ex ≡ -Mx). In English, this formula would read as follows: For every person x, x is a female if and only if x is not male. So, no matter which person we wish to consider (recall that the universe of discourse consists of all persons) that person is female if and only if that person is not male. Let us continue. The next exercise consists of defining what a mother of someone is. In English the definition is: A mother of someone is a female parent of that person. Notice that one of the terms used to define what a mother is is the word female. Luckily, we now know what a female is because we have just defined it. So, according to the English definition, in order to be a mother of someone you must be a female and you must be a parent of that person. We know how the word female is symbolized, so we need to choose a symbol for parent. P is given at the beginning of Exercises 6.1 as the symbol for parent. Remember that parent is a two-place relation. That is, someone is the parent of someone else. So, parent will be symbolized Pxy, which reads x is the parent of y. Now, we are ready to finish the definition. For anyone x and anyone y, x is the mother of y if any only if x is female and x is the parent of y. This can be symbolized as follows:

$$(x)(y)(Txy \equiv Ex \cdot Pxy)$$

Since x is the mother, then the same x must be female as well as the parent. Could the formula be symbolized $(x)(y)(Txy \equiv Ey \cdot Pyx)$? No! This is doubly incorrect. First, if x is the mother of y, then Ey would mean that the offspring is female rather than stating that the parent was female. Secondly, Pyx means that y is the parent of x. So, $(x)(y)(Txy \equiv Ey \cdot Pyx)$ obviously will not do. But does this mean that being a mother can only be defined one way? No. Remember that female was defined as anyone who is not male. So, instead of using female to define mother, we could also use not male as follows:

$$(x)(y)(Txy \equiv -Mx \cdot Pxy)$$

Substituting words in definitions like this makes use of the eliminability property, which will be discussed in greater detail below. The next exercise defines what a child is in terms of being a parent. You should already recognize that each successive definition uses words that were defined in previous definitions. For instance, in Exercise 2, we used female to define what a mother is. But we defined what a female was in Exercise 1. Similarly, in Exercise 3, we will use a term that was used in a definition in Exercise 2, namely the word parent, to define what a child is. You should recognize that most definitions given in terms of words that have already been defined. In other words, what was a definiens in, say Exercise 3, could very possibly appear as the definiendum or part of the definiendum in Exercise 4; or, what appears in the definiendum in, say Exercise 2, could also be used in the definiendum of Exercise 3. In Exercise 2 x was the parent of y:(Pxy). But in Exercise 3 y is the parent of x:(Pyx).

In Exercise 9 we are asked to define bachelor in terms of being both male and unmarried. We know what a male is, for we used it in previous definitions. But we have not used married before now. At the beginning of the exercises, married is given the symbol Axy: x is married to y. We now have a symbol for married and since we already had one for male, we can define a bachelor in terms of being unmarried and male.

Notice that in Exercises 12 through 17 we begin using terms and functions in our definitions. These are still treated as before and should give you no special problems. In Exercise 18, we begin using numbers and the function symbols + and X. These are two-place function symbols. Normally, a two-place function symbol is written with the two terms following the function symbol. For example +12 would be read as 1 + 2. But since everyone is in the habit of writing the + between two numbers, we will follow that convention.

In Exercise 25 we are asked to show that certain formulae are implied by the definitions stated above. Let us look at Problem 1, $s1 = 2$. This is read as: The successor of 1 is equal to 2. So, what do we do? We can use any of the definitions already given to show $s1 = 2$. Which one or ones do we use? What is a successor? Successor was defined in Exercise 21, so let us see if that will help us. If we use For Every Elimination and substitute a 1 for the x we obtain $s1 = 1 + 1$. This is just what we need:

1. $(x)(sx = 1 + x)$ Definition 21
   Show $s1 = 2$
2. $s1 = 1 + 1$ ($\forall$E, x/1)

Now, we have what we want or the left side of the formula, namely, $s1$. On the right side we have $1 + 1$, but we want 2. 2 is defined in Exercise 20. Can we use that definition to obtain what we want? Yes. $2 = 1 + 1$ is just what we need and, by using Equality Elimination, we can finish the proof:

1. $(x)(sx = 1 + x)$ Definition 21
   Show $s1 = 2$
2. $s1 = 1 + 1$ ($\forall$E, x/1)
3. $2 = 1 + 1$ Definition 20
4. $s1 = 2$ (=E, 2, 3)

So, we showed $s1 = 2$ using only the definitions and the valid arguments we had discussed previously. After you have done all the exercises given in the text (Exercises 6.1), you should be at least intuitively aware of just what a dfinition is.

CHARACTERIZING DEFINITIONS

Stated formally, a definition is an if and only if formula or an identity formula that must fulfill three criteria:

1. The left part of the definition is the symbol that is being defined. It includes as many variables as needed and these variables are all different. The left part of the definition is called the definiens.
2. The right part of the definition does not contain the symbol that is being defined, and it is called the definiendum.
3. The formula is preceded by universal quantifiers (for all quantifiers) for each variable in the definiens and only for those variables.

So, if you want to know if a formula is a definition, you must check whether it satisfies these three criteria. Consider the following:

1. $(y)(x)(Hxz \equiv Jx \cdot Ky)$
2. $(y)(Qyy \equiv Jy \cdot Ky)$
2. $(x)(y)(Qxy \equiv Jx \cdot Qyx)$
4. $j = gbj$
5. $(y)(Qxy \equiv Jx \cdot Ky)$
6. $(x)(y)(Qxyz \equiv (Jx \cdot Ky) \cdot Mz)$

Are these six formulae definitions? They are all formulae. They are all either if and only if formulae or identity formulae. They probably even look like definitions. But for one reason or another, none of these formulae are definitions. Let us determine why not. Example 1 is not a definition of the two-place relation symbol H because the variable z in Hxz is not quantified. Also, the variable y is quantified. But y only appears in the definiendum. This violates Criterion 3. Example 2 is not a definition of the two-place relation Q because the variable y occurs twice after Q (that is, Qyy). This violates Criterion 1. In Example 3, the left side of the formula (the definiens) is alright. Even both variables in Q are universally quantified. So, what is wrong? The problem in this example is in the definiendum. Q appears in the definiendum. This violates Criterion 2. Example 4 is an identity formula. The definiens (the left side) is the constant j. This formula is not a definition, because the constant j (the definiens) appears as part of the term gbj in the definiendum. So, this formula is not a definition because it violates Criterion 2. In Example 5 all the variables in the definiens are not quantified. So, Example 5 violates Criteria 3. Lastly, in Example 6 we have a three-place relation symbol. But only two of the variables (y and x) are quantified. So, Example 6 violates Criterion 3.

EXERCISES 6.1

We have just discussed six examples of formulae that at first glance looked like they were definitions, and we have shown why they were not. In Examples 2 through 6 make the necessary changes so that these formula do fulfill all the criteria for definitions. For example: $(y)(x)(Hxz \equiv Jx \cdot Ky)$ is not a definition because Criterion 3 is violated. If we changed all occurrences of the variable y to z, then Criterion 3 is fulfilled. So, $(z)(x)(Hxz \equiv Jx \cdot Kz)$ would be a correctly formed definition.

It should be emphasized that the content of a definition is not important as the form. Suppose that while on vacation in Africa we come across a very unusual plant. The natives call this plant a Bulbgrok. You ask the natives if the Bulbgrok plants grow wild, and they say no. They tell you that the Bulbgrok is a crossbreed from a Blub plant and a Krog plant. You find that these other plants are also unknown to the civilized world. We can easily define that a Bulbgrok is, namely, an offspring of a Blub plant and a Korg plant. So, B will stand for the Bulbgrok plant, L will stand for the Blub plant, and K will stand for the Korg plant. We have already assigned P for parent. Thus, we have:

Bz: z is a Bulbgrok
Ly: y is a Blub
Kx: y is a Korg
Pxz: x is the parent of z
Pyz: y is the parent of z

The definition will be as follows:

(z)(Bz ≡ ∃x∃y(Ly · Kx) · (Pxz · Pyz)

Even though we do not know what a Bulbgrok, a Blub, or a Korg plant is, we can still define these terms by giving them the form of a definition. This definition may not mean anything to most people, but it is, nevertheless, a correct definition.

PROPERTIES OF DEFINITIONS

ELIMINABILITY

Eliminability Property

A definition implies that any formula containing the defined symbol is equivalent to some other formula without the defined symbol.

This means that if we have a formula that contains the definiens of some definition, then we can replace the definiens with the definiendum. For example, if we had the formula (y)∃xSxy, then, because Sxy is the definiens of the definition (x)(y)(Sxy ≡ Mx · Cxy) we can replace the Sxy by Mx · Cxy. This gives us the new formula (y)(∃y)(Mx · Cxy). But we can go one step further. Since Cxy is defined as Pyx in another definition (that is, (x)(y)((Cxy ≡ Pyx)), then we can change this new formula (y)∃x(Mx · Cxy) to (y)∃x(Mx · Pyx).

If the eliminability property did not hold for definitions, then they would would not be very useful. Indeed, definitions are useful precisely because the definiendum can be used wherever the definiens appears in a formula. This concept is used a great deal in the proofs of the theorems done in Chater 6 of the text.

NONCREATIVITY

Noncreativity Property

A definition implies no formula that does not include the defined symbol, if that formula cannot be proven without using the defined sumbol.

This means that a definition should not give us the ability to prove new formulae, that is, formulae that contain symbols that are not being defined and that could not have been proved independently. In other words, if we have what we think is a definition, then we must not be able to use it to derive new information using old concepts. For example: $(x)(y)(Ex \equiv My)$ could not be a valid definition, because it is creative. That is, although the following argument is valid:

$(x)(y)(Ex \equiv My)$; so $-Mb \equiv -Mc$

the following is invalid: So, $\underline{-Mb \equiv -Mc}$. In this example, we have used the definition to prove something that does not include the new symbol and that could not be proved without the defined symbol.

Of course, we know that $\underline{(x)(y)(Ex \equiv -My)}$ is not a definition because it violates Criterion 3 stated above. Actually, it was because we wanted definitions to be noncreative that we had to include Criterion 3.

OTHER APPLICATIONS

ELEMENTARY SET THEORY

We now have the ability to give definitions that exhibit the properties of noncreativity and eliminability. We also have the ability to use the principles of quantificational logic with identities and operators. So, we are now prepared to study set theory. The text covers this material in eight sections, each one building upon the previous sections:

1. Set Abstraction and Extensionality
2. Boolean Operations
3. Subsets
4. Doubletons and Singletons
5. Relations
6. Orderings
7. Functions
8. Maxi-min Preference Relations

It is not within the scope of this Study Guide to explain these sections in any detail. It would take a great number of pages to provide even a brief discussion. Indeed, entire books have been written on just these topics alone. If you have been successful so far in doing proofs, you should have no trouble in proving many of the theorems that appear in these sections. Many theorems, however, are quite difficult. Continued review of previous materials should help, and we will attempt to give you some brief suggestions in the following pages.

There is one thing which you must remember in these sections. Each section begins with either assumptions or definitions and then proceeds to state theorems. These assumptions, definitions, and theorems will be listed without universal quantifiers in front binding the free variables, but they should be treated as if those quantifiers were present. You must keep this in mind. Many of the theorems cannot be proved if the variables in the definitions and theorems are not bound variables. So, you must treat them as if they had universal quantifiers on all the free variables. The quantifiers have been omitted simply to save time and space.

SET ABSTRACTION AND EXTENSIONALITY

Assumption 1, $A = \{x : x \in A\}$, allows us to prove Theorem 1, $(x)(x \in A \equiv x \in B) \supset A = B$ which says in effect that any two sets that have the same elements are equal. This is called set extensionality. To do this we have to use the previous extensionality property for set abstraction terms, (Ex), from Chapter 5.

It is interesting to note that although sets are extensional (that is, have the same elements and are equal), other collective entities that we might be inclined to call sets may not be extensional. For instance, two committees can have the same members, yet be different committees. So, committees are not extensional.

Assumption 1 also allows us to prove Theorem 2: $x \in \{x : x \in A\} \equiv x \in A$. From this it would seem natural to generalize and state for any formula S, $x \in \{x : S\} \equiv S$. For instance, $x \in \{x : x \text{ is red}\} \equiv x \text{ is red}$ or $x \in \{x : x \text{ is not a teapot}\} \equiv x \text{ is not a teapot}$. This is just what set theorists of the 19th century did. Unfortunately, as Bertrand Russell pointed out, this principle is not true in all cases. And this is exactly what Theorem 3 tells us. $\{x : x \notin x\}$ is called the Russell set. If we use this set in place of S in the generalized formula $x \in \{x : S\} \equiv S$, then we obtain $x \in \{x : x \notin x\} \equiv x \notin x$ which is false. The reason it is false is that the formula $\{x : x \notin x\}$ itself cannot be a member of itself if and only if it is not a member of itself. Thus, $x \in \{x : S\} \equiv S$ is not true in all cases and therefore $-(x)(x \in \{x : x \notin x\} \equiv x \notin x)$.

So, we cannot assume all instances on the set abstraction principle. The approach of the text is simply to assume the instances of the principle that are needed for the set abstraction terms used in subsequent definitions. A more advanced course in set theory would study this problem in greater detail.

BOOLEAN OPERATORS

Theorems 2.1 through 2.4 in this section are proved from Definitions 2.1 through 2.4. Theorems 2.5 through 2.11 are proved from Theorems 2.1 through 2.4. It is not necessary to use the definitions once Theorem 2.4 has been proved.

SUBSETS

The key to this set of theorems is Theorem 3.6. Once Theorem 3.6 has been proved, then you will need to use it often in proving those theorems that follow. For example, to prove Theorem 3.7, we begin by assuming $A \subseteq B \cdot B \subseteq C$. Then we use And Elimination:

```
1. A ⊆ B · B ⊆ C        As
2. A ⊆ B                (&E, 1)
```

Next, we temporarily assume $x \in A$ and use And Introduction. Then, we use Theorem 3.6 to obtain $x \in B$. Then, we use Theorem 3.6 again to obtain $x \in C$. Finally, we indent back using If-then Introduction and by Definition 3 we are done.

```
   ┌ 1. A ⊆ B · B ⊆ C              As
   │  2. A ⊆ B                     (&E, 1)
   └┌ 3. x ∈ A                     Tas
    │ 4. x ∈ A · A ⊆ B             (&I, 2, 3)
    │ 5. x ∈ A · A ⊆ B ⊃ x ∈ B     Theorem 3.6
    │ 6. x ∈ B                     (IfE, 4, 5)
    │ 7. B ⊆ C                     (&E, 1)
    │ 8. x ∈ B · B ⊆ C             (&I, 6, 7)
    │ 9. x ∈ B · B ⊆ C ⊃ x ∈ C     Theorem 3.6
    └ 10. x ∈ C                    (IfE, 8, 9)
   │ 11. x ∈ A ⊃ x ∈ C            (IfI, 3, 10)
   │ 12. (x)(x ∈ A ⊃ x ∈ C)       (∀I, 11)
   └ 13. A ⊆ C                     (Definition 3.1, x, 12)
    14. A ⊆ B · B ⊆ C ⊃ A ⊆ C     (IfI, 1, 13)
```

DOUBLETONS AND SINGLETONS

In this section you use the definitions to prove Theorems 4.1 and 4.2. After you have proved these two theorems, you will not need to return to the definitions. Theorems 4.1 and 4.2 are used in proving all the theorems that follow. For example, in proving Theorem 4.3 we first assume Theorem 4.2, substituting z's for x's. Then, we obtain $z = z$ by Equality Introduction and $z \in \{z\}$ by If-then Elimination:

```
1. z ∈ {z} ≡ z = z              Theorem 4.2, x/z
2. z = z                        (=I)
3. z = z ⊃ z ∈ {z}              (IffE, 1)
4. z ∈ {z}                      (IfE, 2, 3)
```

RELATIONS

In this section there are nine definitions that are used to prove the first 12 theorems. After Theorem 5.12, you will no longer need to use the definitions. Theorems 5.3 through 5.12 are used quite often to prove theorems 5.13 through 5.22.

The last three sections, orderings, functions, and maxi-min preference relations, have no patterns like those we have just discussed. You will find many of the theorems in these sections quite difficult though not impossible to prove. Remember that once a theorem has been proved, then that theorem can be used for later proofs.

ANSWERS TO EXERCISES

EXERCISES 2.1

The following exercises can be done in more than one way:

1. 1. <u>Dogs bark</u> is a formula by F Rule 1.
   2. <u>Fish breathe</u> is a formula by F Rule 1.
   3. <u>Birds sing</u> is a formula by F Rule 1.
   4. <u>Dogs bark and fish breathe</u> is a formula by lines 1 and 2 and F Rule 2.
   5. <u>Dogs bark and fish breathe if and only if birds sing</u> is a formula by lines 3 and 4 and F Rule 2.
2. This sentence is not a formula according to the F rules. To convert this sentence into a formula eliminate the initial <u>the</u>, leaving: <u>Lions meow or birds sing</u>.
3. This sentence is not a formula according to the F rules because <u>fish sing</u> is not a formula. To convert this sentence into a formula, change <u>fish</u> to <u>birds</u>, leaving: <u>Cows moo and birds sing</u>.
4. 1. <u>Fish breathe</u> is a formula by F Rule 1.
   2. <u>Dogs bark</u> is a formula by F Rule 1.
   3. <u>Lions meow</u> is a formula by F Rule 1.
   4. <u>Fish breathe or dogs bark</u> is a formula by lines 1 and 2 and F Rule 2.
   5. <u>It is not the case that lions meow</u> is a formula by line 3 and F Rule 2.
   6. <u>If fish breathe or dogs bark, then it is not the case that lions meow</u> is a formula by lines 4 and 5 and F Rule 2.
5. 1. <u>Cows moo</u> is a formula by F Rule 1.
   2. <u>It is not the case that cows moo</u> is a formula by line 1 and F Rule 2.
   3. <u>It is not the case that it is not the case that cows moo</u> is a formula by line 2 and F Rule 2.
6. This sentence is not a formula according to the F rules. To make this sentence into a formula, change <u>No</u> to <u>it is not the case that</u>, leaving: <u>It is not the case that fish breathe</u>.
7. This sentence is not a formula according to the F rules because <u>fish don't breathe</u> is not a formula. Change <u>fish don't breathe</u> to <u>it is not the case that fish breathe</u>, leaving: <u>Cows moo if and only if it is not the case that fish breathe</u>.
8. This sentence is not a formula according to the F rules because there is no formula preceding the <u>if and only if</u>. In order to make

125

this sentence into a formula, you need to place another formula in front of the sentence. For example: Dogs bark if and only if cows moo and lions meow.

9. This sentence is not a formula according to the F rules because only part of the if-then connector, namely, then, is present. To convert this sentence into a formula, place an If in front of the sentence, leaving: If fish breathe or it is not the case that dogs bark if and only if lions meow, then it is not the case that birds sing.

10. This sentence is not a formula according to the F rules because lions don't meow is not a formula. To make this sentence into a formula, change lions don't meow to it is not the case that lions meow, leaving: Birds sing or cows moo if and only if it is not the case that lions meow and dogs bark.

EXERCISES 2.2

The following exercises can be done in more than one way:

1. v q ≡ s is not a formula according to the F rules because the connecting symbol v appears next to only one formula, (q ≡ s). To make it a formula, add a formula in front of the v. Thus, if we add a p, we will have the formula p v (q ≡ s).

2. 1. p is a formula by F Rule 1
   2. q is a formula by F Rule 1.
   3. r is a formula by F Rule 1.
   4. p ⊃ q is a formula by lines 1 and 2 and F Rule 2.
   5. (p ⊃ q) · r is a formula by lines 3 and 4 and F Rule 2.

3. 1. s is a formula by F Rule 1.
   2. t is a formula by F Rule 1.
   3. p is a formula by F Rule 1.
   4. s ⊃ t is a formula by lines 1 and 2 and F Rule 2.
   5. -p is a formula by line 3 and F Rule 2.
   6. (s ⊃ t) ≡ -p is a formula by lines 4 and 5 and F Rule 2.

4. (q · r) ≡ v is not a formula according to the F rules because two connectors (- and v) have been placed next to one another. If we remove the connectors, we obtain q · r. If we add s and t, we obtain (q · r)· ≡ (s v t).

5. (p v q) ⊃ is not a formula according to the F rules because there is not a formula following the "hook" (⊃). To make this into a formula, either drop the "hook" symbol or add a formula after it. If we drop the "hook" symbol, we obtain p v q. If we add s we obtain (p v q) ⊃ s.

6. -(≡ t · r) is not a formula according to the F rules because there is not formula preceding the symbol ≡. To make this into a formula, drop the symbol or add a formula in front of it. If we drop the ≡ symbol, we obtain -(t · r). If we add p, we obtain -(p ≡ (t · r)).

7. -p((p ⊃ r)(s v t) is not a formula according to the F rules because there are two connectors missing. To make it a formula, we need to add connectors in the appropriate places. If we use a "hook" symbol first and an if and only if symbol second, we obtain the formula -p ⊃ ((p ⊃ r) ≡ (s v t).

8. 1. s is a formula by F Rule 1.
   2. t is a formula by F Rule 1.
   3. s v t is a formula by lines 1 and 2 and F Rule 2.

9. p ≡ (qr v t) is not a formula according to the F rules because **two** formulae (q and r) have been placed next to one another without a connector. To make this into a formula, either drop one of the formulae or add a connector between the q and the r. If we drop the q, we obtain p ≡ (r v t). If we add an <u>and</u> symbol, we obtain p ≡ ((q · r) v t).

10. 1. p is a formula by F Rule 1.
    2. r is a formula by F Rule 1.
    3. t is a formula by F Rule 1.
    4. q is a formula by F Rule 1.
    5. s is a formula by F Rule 1.
    6. p ⊃ r is a formula by lines 1 and 2 and F Rule 2.
    7. t v q is a formula by lines 3 and 4 and F Rule 2.
    8. -s is a formula by line 5 and F Rule 2.
    9. -p is a formula by line 1 and F Rule 2.
    10. (-s v -p) is a formula by lines 8 and 9 and F Rule 2.
    11. (p ⊃ q) · (t v q) is a formula by lines 6 and 7 and F Rule 2.
    12. ((p ⊃ q) · (t v q)) ≡ (-s v -p) is a formula by lines 10 and 11 and F Rule 2.
    13. -(((p ⊃ q) · (t v q)) ≡ (-s v -p)) is a formula by line 12 and F Rule 2.

EXERCISES 2.3

1. -p is true if p is false. -p is false if p is true.
2. p v q is false if p is false and q is false. In all other cases p v q is true.
3. p ⊃ q is false if p is true and q is false. In all other cases p ⊃ q is true.
4. If p and q have the same truth value, then p ≡ q is true. If p and q have different truth values, then p ≡ q is false.

EXERCISES 2.4

1. - - (p ⊃ s) ≡ (r · t)
   T̲ F̲ F̲ T̲ T̲ Ⓕ F̲ F̲ F̲

2. (((s ⊃ t) ⊃ r) ⊃ p) ⊃ q)
   T̲ F̲ F̲ T̲ F̲ F̲ F̲ Ⓣ T̲

3. (q ⊃ (r ⊃ (s ⊃ (t ⊃ r))))
   T̲ Ⓣ F̲ T̲ T̲ T̲ F̲ T̲ F̲

4. (p · r) v (s   t) ≡ (- q v - s)
   F̲ F̲ F̲ F̲ T̲ F̲ F̲ Ⓣ F̲ T̲ F̲ F̲ T̲

5. ((p ≡ q) v (s ≡ r)) ⊃ (t ≡ r)
   F̲ F̲ T̲ F̲ T̲ F̲ F̲   Ⓣ F̲ T̲ F̲

6. ((s ⊃ t) ⊃ (q ⊃ p)) ⊃ (- r ⊃ - t)
   T̲ F̲ F̲ T̲ T̲ F̲ F̲   Ⓣ T̲ F̲ T̲ T̲ F̲

7. ((t ≡ s) ⊃ (s ≡ r)) ⊃ (t ≡ r)
   F̲ F̲ T̲ T̲ T̲ F̲ F̲   Ⓣ F̲ T̲ F̲

8. (p ⊃ (q ⊃ (p ⊃ q))) ≡ (((s ⊃ t) ⊃ s) ⊃ t)
   F̲ T̲ T̲ T̲ F̲ T̲ T̲   Ⓕ   T̲ F̲ F̲ T̲ T̲ F̲ F̲

9. (r ≡ - s) ≡ ((- p ≡ - q) v - t
   F̲ T̲ F̲ T̲ Ⓣ   T̲ F̲ F̲ F̲ T̲ T̲ T̲ F̲

10. - - - (p v - - q) ≡ (- - s · - t)
    F̲ T̲ F̲ F̲ T̲ T̲ F̲ T̲ Ⓕ T̲ F̲ T̲ T̲ T̲ F̲

127

EXERCISES 2.5

1.
```
1. p ⊃ q                As
2. -r ⊃ p               As
Show -r ⊃ q
  3. -r                 Tas
  [Show q]
  4. p                 (IfE, 2, 3)
  5. q                 (IfE, 1, 4)
6. -r ⊃ q              (IfI, 3, 5)
```

2.
```
1. p · q                As
2. r · s                As
Show q · s
[Show q]
3. q                    (&E, 1)
[Show s]
4. s                    (&E, 2)
5. q · s                (&I, 3, 4)
```

3.
```
1. q · s                As
2. t · p                As
Show (t · q) v r
[Show t · q]
[Show t]
3. t                    (&E, 2)
[Show q]
4. q                    (&E, 1)
5. t · q                (&I, 3, 4)
6. (t · q) v r          (OrI, 5)
```

4.
```
1. r v s                As
2. -r · -t              As
Show s
3. -r                   (&E, 2)
4. s                    (DS, 1, 3)
```

5.
```
1. (s · t) · p          As
2. q ⊃ r                As
3. p ⊃ q                As
Show w v r
[Show r]
4. p                    (&E, 1)
5. q                    (IfE, 3, 4)
6. r                    (IfE, 2, 5)
7. w v r                (OrI, 6)
```

6.
```
1. p · s                As
2. q ≡ s                As
Show q
3. s ⊃ q                (IffE, 2)
4. s                    (&E, 1)
5. q                    (IfE, 3, 4)
```

7.
```
1. -(p v q)             As
2. -q ⊃ r               As
Show r v s
[Show r]
3. -p · -q              (De Morgans Law, 1)
```

128

```
     4. -q                    (&E, 3)
     5. r                     (IfE, 2, 4)
     6. r v s                 (OrI, 6)
8. 1. -r ⊃ (s ⊃ t)           As
   2. -(r v t)               As
   Show -s
   ‾‾‾‾‾‾
   3. -r · -t                (De Morgans Law, 2)
   4. -r                     (&E, 3)
   5. s ⊃ t                  (IfE, 1, 4)
   6. -t                     (&E, 3)
   7. -s                     (DC, 5, 6)
9. 1. p ⊃ q                  As
   2. p · (q ⊃ -p)           As
   Show s
   ‾‾‾‾‾‾
   [Show p · -p]
   3. p                      (&E, 2)
   4. q ⊃ -p                 (&E, 2)
   5. q                      (IfE, 1, 3)
   6. -p                     (IfE, 4, 5)
   7. p · -p                 (&I, 3, 6)
   8. s                      (A, 7)
10. 1. p ⊃ q                 As
    2. -s ⊃ -(q · r)         As
    Show r ⊃ (p ⊃ s)
    ‾‾‾‾‾‾‾‾‾‾‾‾‾‾‾‾
        3. r                 Tas
        [Show p ⊃ s]
        4. p                 Tas
        [Show s]
        5. q                 (IfE, 1, 4)
        6. q · r             (&I, 3, 5)
        7. s                 (DC, 2, 6)
        8. p ⊃ s             (IfI, 4, 7)
        9. r ⊃ (p ⊃ s)       (IfI, 3, 8)
```

EXERCISES 2.6

1. 1. L̲ions meow provided that f̲ish breathe or c̲ows moo.
   2. l̲ provided that f or c by T Rule 7.
   3. l̲ provided that (f v c) by T Rule 2.
   4. (f v c) ⊃ l by T Rule 6.
2. 1. T̲rees bloom if and only if s̲pring is here unless the t̲empera-
      tures rise.
   2. t̲ if and only if s̲ unless e̲ by T Rule 7.
   3. t̲ if and only if (s v e) by T Rule 2.
   4. t̲ ≡ (s v e) by T Rule 5.
3. 1. If a d̲og barks, then it makes a n̲oise unless M̲ary Jean is not
      there to hear it.
   2. If d̲, then n unless m by T Rule 7.
   3. If d̲, then (n v m) by T Rule 2.
   4. d̲ ⊃ (n v m) by T Rule 6.
4. 1. Either b̲irds sing or the M̲ormon Tabernacle Choir sings, but if
      birds sing, then L̲arry is happy.
   2. Either b̲ or m̲, but if b̲, then l̲ by T Rule 7.
   3. (b v m), but if b̲, then l̲ by T Rule 2.

4. (b ∨ m), but (b ⊃ l) by T Rule 6.
5. (b ∨ m) · (b ⊃ l) by T Rule 1.
5. 1. The sky is blue provided the sun is shining, but unless the sun is shining, the sky is black.
   2. b provided s, but unless s, k by T Rule 7.
   3. b provided s, but (s ∨ k) by T Rule 2.
   4. (b ⊃ s), but (s ∨ k) by T Rule 6.
   5. (b ⊃ s) · (s ∨ k) by T Rule 1.
6. 1. Picasso paints and Beethoven composes, but provided that Lyle has a bat and ball, baseball is in season.
   2. p and b, but provided that y, l by T Rule 7.
   3. p and b, but (y ⊃ l) by T Rule 6.
   4. (p · b), but (y ⊃ l) by T Rule 1.
   5. (p · b) · (y ⊃ l) by T Rule 1.
7. 1. Just in case the weather is nice, Aaron will plan a picnic unless Tom is in town but if Tom is in town, then they will go golfing.
   2. Just in case w, a unless t. If t, then g by T Rule 7.
   3. (w ≡ a), unless t. If t, then g by T Rule 5.
   4. (w ≡ a) ∨ t, but if t, then g by T Rule 2.
   5. (w ≡ a) ∨ t, but (t ⊃ g) by T Rule 6.
   6. ((w ≡ a) ∨ t) · (t ⊃ g) by T Rule 1.
8. 1. If Dean and Marva have the money, then they will buy a Mercedes only if a BMW is more expensive.
   2. If d then m, only if b by T Rule 7.
   3. d ⊃ m, only if b by T Rule 6.
   4. (d ⊃ m) ⊃ b by T Rule 6.
9. 1. Ellen will sew, if Jeff will mow provided that Simon does not cry or Jeremy does not sigh.
   2. e if j provided that s or r by T Rule 7.
   3. (j ⊃ e) provided that s or r by T Rule 6.
   4. (j ⊃ e) provided that (s ∨ r) by T Rule 2.
   5. (j ⊃ e) ⊃ (s ∨ r) by T Rule 6.
10. 1. David is an engineer just in case Julie is a teacher fair, but only if Trudy plants tomato vines will Eric have spaghetti come dinner time.
    2. d just in case j but only if t, e by T Rule 7.
    3. (d ≡ j) but only if t, e by T Rule 5.
    4. (d ≡ j) but (e ⊃ t) by T Rule 6.
    5. (d ≡ j) · (e ⊃ t) by T Rule 1.

EXERCISES 3.1

The following exercises can be done in more than one way:

1. 1. It is blue is a formula by F Rule 1.
   2. It has aesthetic beauty is a formula by F Rule 1.
   3. It is red is a formula by F Rule 1.
   4. It is red and it has aesthetic beauty is a formula by lines 2 and 3 and F Rule 2.
   5. It is blue, or it is red and it has aesthetic beauty is a formula by lines 1 and 4 and F Rule 2.
2. 1. It has aesthetic beauty is a formula by F Rule 1.
   2. It is not the case that it has aesthetic beauty is a formula by line 1 and F Rule 2.
   3. It is heavy is a formula by F Rule 1.

130

4. It is red is a formula by F Rule 1.
5. It is heavy or it is red is a formula by lines 3 and 4 and F Rule 2.
6. It is not the case that it has aesthetic beauty if and only if it is heavy or it is red is a formula by lines 2 and 5 and F Rule 2.

3. 1. It is red is a formula by F Rule 1.
   2. It has aesthetic beauty is a formula by F Rule 1.
   3. For something it has aesthetic beauty is a formula by line 2 and F Rule 3.
   4. It is not the case that for something it has aesthetic beauty is a formula by line 3 and F Rule 2.
   5. If it is red, then it is not the case that for something it has aesthetic beauty is a formula by lines 1 and 4 and F Rule 2.

4. This sentence is not a formula according to the F rules because the apple is red is not an atomic formula. To make it a formula, we remove the words the apple and replace them with the indefinite pronoun it.

5. This sentence is not a formula according to the F rules because neither it is aesthetically beautiful nor it isn't the case that it is blue is an atomic formula. To make these sentences into formulae we change it is aesthetically beautiful to it has aesthetic beauty and it isn't the case that it is blue to it is not the case that it is blue.

6. 1. It is blue is a formula by F Rule 1.
   2. It is not the case that it is blue is a formula by line 1 and F Rule 2.
   3. It is red is a formula by F Rule 1.
   4. For something it is red is a formula by line 3 and F Rule 3.
   5. It if is not the case that it is blue, then for something it is red is a formula by lines 2 and 4 and F Rule 2.
   6. For everything if it is not the case that it is blue, then for something it is red is a formula by line 5 and F Rule 3.

7. This sentence is not a formula according to the F rules because it's not red is not a formula nor is it's not beautiful. If we change it's not red to it is not the case that it is red and it's not beautiful to it is not the case that it is beautiful then we will have two formulae connected by a so. Therefore, the sentence is an argument made by connecting two formulae with the illative so.

8. This sentence is not a formula by the F rules because neither it is not red nor it is not blue is a formula. To make these into formulae, we change it is not red to it is not the case that it is red and it is not blue to it is not the case that it is blue.

9. 1. It is heavy is a formula by F Rule 1.
   2. It is not the case that it is heavy is a formula by line 1 and F Rule 2.
   3. For everything it is not the case that it is heavy is a formula by line 2 and F Rule 3.
   4. It is red is a formula by F Rule 1.
   5. It has aesthetic beauty is a formula by F Rule 1.
   6. It is red or it has aesthetic beauty is a formula by lines 4 and 5 and F Rule 2.
   7. If for everything it is not the case that it is heavy, then it is red or it has aesthetic beauty is a formula by lines 3 and 6 and F Rule 2.

10. 1. It is heavy is a formula by F Rule 1.
    2. It is red is a formula by F Rule 1.
    3. For something it is red is a formula by line 2 and F Rule 3.
    4. It is blue is a formula by F Rule 1.
    5. For everything it is blue is a formula by line 4 and F Rule 3.
    6. For something it is red or for everything it is blue is a formula by lines 3 and 5 and F Rule 2.
    7. It is heavy if and only if for something it is red or for everything it is blue is a formula by lines 1 and 6 and F Rule 2.
    8. It has aesthetic beauty is a formula by F Rule 1.
    9. It is not the case that it has aesthetic beauty is a formula by line 8 and F Rule 2.
    10. It is heavy if and only if for something it is red or for everything it is blue or it is not the case that it has aesthetic beauty is a formula by lines 7 and 9 and F Rule 2.

EXERCISES 3.2

The following exercises can be done in more than one way:

1. 1. p is a formula by F Rule 1.
   2. q is a formula by F Rule 1.
   3. p ⊃ q is a formula by lines 1 and 2 and F Rule 2.
   4. ∀(p ⊃ q) is a formula by line 3 and F Rule 3.
   5. r is a formula by F Rule 1.
   6. t is a formula by F Rule 1.
   7. ∃r is a formula by line 5 and F Rule 3.
   8. (∃r · t) is a formula by lines 6 and 7 and F Rule 2.
   9. ∀(p ⊃ q) ≡ (∃r · t) is a formula by lines 4 and 8 and F Rule 2.
2. ∃∀p ⊃ (q ∨ t) is not a formula according to the F rules because p is preceded by two quantifiers (∃ and ∀). To make this into a formula, simply drop one of the quantifiers.
3. ∃(p · q) ⊃ ∀(s ≡ (r · t) is not a formula according to the F Rules because a right parenthesis is missing. ∀(s ≡ (r · t) cannot be constructed using only the F rules. If we add a right parenthesis to ∀(s ≡ (r · t), we obtain ∀(s ≡ (r · t)). The entire formula can now be constructed from the F rules. Thus, it is a correct formula.
4. 1. p is a formula by F Rule 1.
   2. q is a formula by F Rule 1.
   3. s is a formula by F Rule 1.
   4. ∃p is a formula by line 1 and F Rule 3.
   5. ∃p ⊃ q is a formula by lines 2 and 4 and F Rule 2.
   6. ∀(∃p ⊃ q) is a formula by line 5 and F Rule 3.
   7. ∀(∃p ⊃ q) ∨ s is a formula by lines 3 and 6 and F Rule 2.
5. t ≡ ∃ ∨ (p · q) is not a formula according to the F rules because the quantifier (∃) does not precede a formula. To make this into a formula, we simply place a formula behind the ∃. If we add s, we obtain (t ≡ ∃s) ∨ (p · q).
6. ∀ ⊃ q is not a formula according to the F rules because the quantifier (∀) does not directly precede a formula. To make this a formula, we simply place another formula behind the ∀. If we add p, then we obtain ∀p ⊃ q.
7. 1. p is a formula by F Rule 1.
   2. q is a formula by F Rule 1.
   3. r is a formula by F Rule 1.

4. $(q \supset r)$ is a formula by lines 2 and 3 and F Rule 2.
5. $\exists p$ is a formula by line 1 and F Rule 3.
6. $\exists p \supset r$ is a formula by lines 3 and 5 and F Rule 2.
7. $\forall (\exists p \supset r)$ is a formula by line 6 and F Rule 3.
8. $(q \supset r) \supset \forall (\exists p \supset r)$ is a formula by lines 4 and 7 and F Rule 2.

8. $(r \equiv -s) \vee \exists$ is not a formula according to the F rules because the quantifier $(\exists)$ does not quantify any formula. To make this into a formula, we simply place another formula behind the $\exists$. If we add q, we obtain $(r \equiv -s) \vee \exists q$.

9. $\forall \vee \exists q$ is not a formula according to the F rules because the quantifier $(\forall)$ does not quantify any formula. To make this into a formula, we simply place another formula behind the $\forall$. If we add t, we obtain $\forall t \vee \exists q$.

10. 1. p is a formula by F Rule 1.
2. q is a formula by F Rule 1.
3. s is a formula by F Rule 1.
4. t is a formula by F Rule 1.
5. r is a formula by F Rule 1.
6. $p \supset q$ is a formula by lines 1 and 2 and F Rule 2.
7. $-(p \supset q)$ is a formula by line 6 and F Rule 2.
8. $q \supset r$ is a formula by lines 2 and 5 and F Rule 2.
9. $\forall (q \supset r)$ is a formula by line 8 and F Rule 3.
10. $\exists s$ is a formula by line 3 and F Rule 3.
11. $-t$ is a formula by line 4 and F Rule 2.
12. $\exists s \vee -t$ is a formula by lines 10 and 11 and F Rule 2.
13. $(\exists s \vee -t) \cdot \forall (q \supset r)$ is a formula by lines 9 and 12 and F Rule 2.
14. $-(p \supset q) \equiv ((\exists s \vee -t) \cdot \forall (q \supset r))$ is a formula by lines 7 and 13 and F Rule 2.

EXERCISES 3.3

There may be more than one correct answer to these exercises. Answers to the first part could be written as follows:

1. $s \equiv (p \vee \exists q) \cdot (q \supset p)$
2. $q \cdot (s \vee r) \equiv \exists -q$
3. $(p \supset -s) \vee (\forall -q \cdot q)$
4. $(t \cdot \forall -q) \equiv ((s \supset q) \vee p)$
5. $(r \supset s) \vee ((t \supset (p \cdot \exists q)) \vee (-q \cdot s)))$

The following are sample solutions to the second part of the exercise:

1. $s \equiv \exists ((p \vee q) \cdot (q \supset p))$
2. $\forall (q \cdot (s \vee r) \equiv -q)$
3. $(p \supset -s) \vee \exists (-q \cdot q)$
4. $\exists ((t \cdot -q) \equiv ((s \supset q) \vee p))$
5. $(r \supset s) \vee \forall ((t \supset (p \cdot q)) \vee (-q \cdot s))$

EXERCISES 3.4

1. $((p_0 \supset q_0) \vee (p_1 \supset q_1)) \equiv ((s_0 \cdot t_0) \supset (s_1 \cdot t_1))$
   $\underline{T}\ \underline{F}\underline{F}\ \ \underline{T}\ \underline{T}\ \underline{T}\underline{T}\ \ \textcircled{\underline{F}}\ \ \underline{F}\ \underline{F}\underline{F}\ \ \underline{F}\ \underline{T}\ \underline{T}\underline{T}$

2. $((p_0 \lor r_0) \cdot - q_0) \cdot ((p_1 \lor r_1) \cdot - q_1) \supset ((s_0 \lor s_1) \lor (r_0 \lor r_1))$
   T T TTF F T TF FFT (T) F TT T TTF

3. $(s_0 \lor s_1) \equiv ((p_0 \cdot - t_0) \lor r_0) \cdot ((p_1 \cdot - t_1) \lor r_1)$
   F TT (F) T FFT TT F T FTT FF

4. $((s_0 \lor s_1) \cdot (t_0 \lor t_1) \lor ((p_0 \cdot p_1) \cdot (q_0 \cdot q_1)$
   F TT T TTT (T) T TT F FFT

5. $(s_0 \cdot s_1) \supset (((r_0 \equiv t_0) \lor (r_1 \equiv t_1)) \cdot (p_0 \cdot p_1)$
   F FT (T) T TT T FFT T TTT

EXERCISE 3.5

There may be more than one correct answer for the following:

1. Universe of Discourse: $\{0, 1\}$; q: 0; r 0, 1
   $(q_0 \cdot r_0) \lor (q_1 \cdot r_1)$
   T TT (T) F FT
   So, $(q_1 \cdot r_1)$
   F (F)T

2. Universe of Discourse: $\{0, 1\}$; q: 0; s: 0
   $(q_0 \lor s_0)$
   T (T)T
   So, $(q_0 \lor s_0) \cdot (q_1 \lor s_1)$
   T TT (F) F FF

3. Universe of Discourse: $\{0, 1\}$; s: 1; t: 0, 1
   $(s_0 \supset t_0) \cdot (s_1 \supset t_1)$
   F TT (T) T TT
   $t_0 \cdot t_1$
   T (F)T
   So, $s_0 \cdot s_1$
   F (F)T

4. Universe of Discourse: $\{0, 1\}$; q: 0, 1; p: 0
   $(q_0 \supset p_0) \cdot (q_1 \supset p_1)$
   F TT (T) F TF
   $p_0 \lor p_1$
   T (T)F
   So, $q_0 \lor q_1$
   F (F)F

5. Universe of Discourse: $\{0, 1\}$; r: 1; s: 0, 1
   $(r_0 \supset s_0) \cdot (r_1 \supset s_1)$
   F TT (T) T TT
   $- r_0 \lor - r_1$
   T F (T)F T

6. Universe of Discourse: $\{0, 1\}$; t: ; q: 0, 1
   $(t_0 \lor q_0) \cdot (t_1 \lor q_1)$
   F TT (T) F TT
   $- t_0 \cdot - t_1$
   T F (T)T F
   So, $- q_0 \lor - q_1$
   F T (F)F T

134

7. Universe of Discourse: {0, 1}; r: 0; t: 1
$r_0 \lor r_1$
T (T) F
$t_0 \lor t_1$
F (T) T
So, $(r_0 \cdot t_0) \lor (r_1 \cdot t_1)$
T F F (F) F F T

8. Universe of Discourse: {0, 1}; s: 0, 1; p: 0; q: 0
$s_0 \cdot s_1$
T (T) T
$p_0 \cdot p_1$
T (F) T
So, $-(s_0 \cdot q_0) \cdot -(s_1 \cdot q_1)$
F T T T (F) T T F F

9. Universe of Discourse: {0, 1}; t: 1; p: 0, 1; q: 0, 1
$(t_0 \supset p_0) \cdot (t_1 \supset p_1)$
F T T (F) T T T
$q_0 \cdot q_1$
T (T) T
So, $((p_0 \supset t_0) \cdot q_0) \cdot ((p_1 \supset t_1) \cdot q_1)$
T F F F T (F) T T T T T

10. Universe of Discourse: {0, 1}; r: ; p: 0, 1; s:
$(r_0 \equiv (p_0 \cdot s_0)) \cdot (r_1 \equiv (p_1 \cdot s_1))$
F T T F F (T) F T T T F F
$p_0 \cdot p_1$
T (T) T
So, $r_0 \cdot r_1$
F (F) F

EXERCISES 3.6

The following exercises may have more than one solution.

1. Valid.

2. Universe of Discourse: {0, 1}; p: 1; q: 1; t: ; w: 1, 0; s:
$((q_0 \equiv t_0) \cdot w_0) \lor ((q_1 \equiv t_1) \cdot w_1)$
F TF TT (T) T FF TF
$(((q_0 \equiv t_0) \cdot w_0) \supset (p_0 \supset (s_0 \lor s_1))) \cdot (((q_1 \equiv t_1) \cdot w_1) \supset (p_1 \supset (s_0 \lor s_1)))$
F TF TT T FTF FF (F) T FF FT T T F F FF
So, $p_1 \supset (s_0 \lor s_1)$
T (F) F FF

3. Universe of Discourse: {0, 1}; s: 0; t: 0, 1; p: ; q: 0
$(s_0 \lor -t_0) \lor (s_1 \lor -t_1)$
T TFT (T) F FFT
$((s_0 \lor -t_0) \supset ((p_0 \lor p_1) \lor q_0)) \cdot ((s_1 \lor -t_1) \supset ((p_0 \lor p_1) \lor q_1))$
F FFT T F FF TT (T) F FFT T F FF FF
So, $(p_0 \lor p_1) \lor q_1$
F FF (F) F

135

4. Universe of Discourse: $\{0, 1\}$; s: 1; t: 0, 1; p: 1; r: 0, 1; w: 0, 1

$(s_0 \lor (t_0 \equiv p_0)) \supset (p_0 \cdot ((r_0 \supset w_0) \lor (r_1 \supset w_1)) \cdot (s_1 \lor (t_1 \equiv p_1))$

$\underline{F}$ $\underline{F}$ $\underline{T}$ $\underline{F}$ $\underline{F}$ $\underline{T}$ $\underline{F}$ $\underline{F}$ $\underline{T}$ $\underline{T}$ $\underline{T}$ $\underline{T}$ $\underline{T}$ $\underline{T}$ $\underline{T}$ $Ⓣ$ $\underline{F}$ $\underline{F}$ $\underline{T}$ $\underline{F}$ $\underline{F}$

$\supset (p_1 \cdot ((r_0 \supset w_0) \lor (r_1 \supset w_1)) (s_0 \lor (t_0 \equiv p_0)) \lor (s_1 \lor (t_1 \equiv p_1))$

$\underline{T}$ $\underline{T}$ $\underline{T}$ $\underline{T}$ $\underline{T}$ $\underline{T}$ $\underline{T}$ $\underline{T}$ $\underline{T}$ $\underline{T}$ $\underline{F}$ $\underline{F}$ $\underline{T}$ $\underline{F}$ $\underline{F}$ $Ⓣ$ $\underline{T}$ $\underline{T}$ $\underline{T}$ $\underline{T}$ $\underline{T}$

So, $p_0 \cdot ((r_0 \supset w_0) \lor (r_1 \supset w_1))$

$\underline{F}$ $Ⓕ$ $\underline{T}$ $\underline{T}$ $\underline{T}$ $\underline{T}$ $\underline{T}$ $\underline{T}$ $\underline{T}$

5. Valid.

EXERCISES 3.7

1. Strategy 11.	6. Strategy 11.
2. Strategy 12.	7. Strategy 10.
3. Strategy 9.	8. Strategy 9.
4. Strategy 10.	9. Strategy 12.
5. Strategy 12.	10. Strategy 11.

EXERCISES 3.8

1. Universe of Discourse: $\{0, 1\}$; s: 0; w: 1; p: 0, 1; r: ; q:

$((s_0 \lor w_0) \cdot p_0) \cdot ((s_1 \lor w_1) \cdot p_1)$

$\underline{T}$ $\underline{T}$ $\underline{F}$ $\underline{T}$ $\underline{T}$ $Ⓣ$ $\underline{F}$ $\underline{T}$ $\underline{T}$ $\underline{T}$ $\underline{T}$

$(q_0 \supset r_0) \cdot (q_1 \supset r_1)$

$\underline{F}$ $\underline{T}$ $\underline{F}$ $\underline{T}$ $\underline{F}$ $\underline{T}$ $\underline{F}$

So, $((r_0 \cdot p_0) \lor t_0) \lor ((r_1 \cdot p_1) \lor t_1)$

$\underline{F}$ $\underline{F}$ $\underline{T}$ $\underline{F}$ $\underline{F}$ $Ⓕ$ $\underline{F}$ $\underline{F}$ $\underline{T}$ $\underline{F}$ $\underline{F}$

2.
```
   1. ∀s                    As
   2. ∀t                    As
   Show ∀(s · t)
   [Show s · t]
   [Show s]
   3. s                     (∀∃, 1)
   [Show t]
   4. t                     (∀∃, 2)
   5. s · t                 (&I, 3, 4)
   6. ∀(s · t)              (∀I, 5)
```

3. Universe of Discourse: $\{0, 1\}$; q: 0; r: 0; s:

$(q_0 \supset r_0) \cdot (r_1 \supset r_1)$

$\underline{T}$ $\underline{T}$ $\underline{T}$ $Ⓣ$ $\underline{F}$ $\underline{T}$ $\underline{F}$

$q_0 \lor q_1$

$\underline{T}$ $Ⓣ$ $\underline{F}$

So, $r_1 \lor s$

$\underline{F}$ $Ⓕ$ $\underline{F}$

4. Universe of Discourse: $\{0, 1\}$; s: 1; t: 1; w:

$(s_0 \equiv t_0) \cdot (s_1 \equiv t_1)$

$\underline{F}$ $\underline{T}$ $\underline{F}$ $Ⓣ$ $\underline{T}$ $\underline{T}$ $\underline{T}$

$t_0 \lor t_1$

$\underline{F}$ $Ⓣ$ $\underline{T}$

136

So, $s_0 \vee w$
   F Ⓕ F

5. 1. $\exists(q \supset r)$ As
   2. $\forall((q \supset r) \supset p \cdot \exists t)$ As
   Show $\exists t$
   [Show $\forall((q \supset r) \supset \exists t)$]
   [Show $((q \supset r) \supset \exists t)$]
       3. $q \supset r$ Tas
       [Show $\exists t$]
       4. $(q \supset r) \supset p \cdot \exists t$ ($\forall$E, 2)
       5. $p \cdot \exists t$ (IfE, 3, 4)
       6. $\exists t$ (&E, 5)
   7. $(q \supset r) \supset \exists t$ (IfI, 3, 6)
   8. $\forall((q \supset r) \supset \exists t)$ ($\forall$I, 7)
   9. $\exists t$ ($\exists$E, 1, 8)

6. 1. $\exists(r \cdot w)$ As
   2. $\forall(q \cdot p)$ As
   Show $\exists(q \cdot w)$
   [Show $\forall((r \cdot w) \supset \exists(q \cdot w))$]
   [Show $(r \cdot w) \supset \exists(q \cdot w)$]
       3. $r \cdot w$ Tas
       [Show $\exists(q \cdot w)$]
       [Show $(q \cdot w)$]
       [Show q]
       4. $q \cdot p$ ($\forall$E, 2)
       5. q (&E, 4)
       [Show w]
       6. w (&E, 3)
       7. $q \cdot w$ (&I, 5, 6)
       8. $\exists(q \cdot w)$ ($\exists$I, 7)
   9. $(r \cdot w) \supset \exists(q \cdot w)$ (IfI, 3, 8)
   10. $\forall((r \cdot w) \supset \exists(q \cdot w))$ ($\forall$I, 9)
   11. $\exists(q \cdot w)$ ($\exists$E, 1, 10)

7. Universe of Discourse: $\{0, 1\}$; q: 0; s: 0; t: 1; w: 1
   $(q_0 \cdot s_0) \vee (q_1 \cdot s_1)$
   T T T Ⓣ F F F

   $(t_0 \cdot w_0) \vee (t_1 \cdot w_1)$
   F F F Ⓣ T T T

   So, $(s_0 \cdot w_0) \vee (s_1 \cdot w_1)$
        T F F Ⓕ F F T

8. Universe of Discourse: $\{0, 1\}$; q: 1; t: 0; s: 1
   $q_0 \vee q_1$
   F Ⓣ T

   $t_0 \vee t_1$
   T Ⓣ F

   $s_0 \vee s_1$
   F Ⓣ T

   So, $((s_0 \cdot t_0) \cdot q_0) \vee (s_1 \cdot t_1) \cdot q_1)$
        F F T F F Ⓕ T F F F T

137

9. | 1. ∀((p · q) · r))   As
   | 2. ∃(s ≡ -w)   As
   | 3. ∀(w · t)   As
   | Show ∃(q · -s)
   | [Show ∀((s ≡ -w) ⊃ ∃(q · -s))]
   | [Show (s ≡ -w) ⊃ ∃(q · -s)]
   | 4. s ≡ -w   Tas
   | [Show ∃(q · -s)]
   | [Show q · -s)
   | [Show q]
   | 5. (p · q) · r   (∀E, 1)
   | 6. (p · q)   (&E, 5)
   | 7. q   (&E, 6)
   | [Show -s]
   | 8. w · t   (∀E, 3)
   | 9. w   (&E, 8)
   | 10. s ⊃ -w   (IffE, 4)
   | 11. -s   (DC, 9, 10)
   | 12. q · -s   (&I, 7, 11)
   | 13. ∃(q · -s)   (∃I, 12)
   | 14. (s ≡ -w) ⊃ ∃(q · -s)   (IfI, 4, 13)
   | 15. ∀((s ≡ -w) ⊃ ∃(q · -s)) (∀I, 14)
   | 16. ∃(q · -s)   (∃E, 2, 15)

10. | 1. ∃((s ≡ t) v r)   As
    | 2. ∀(-r · t)   As
    | 3. ∀(s ⊃ (p · q))   As
    | Show ∃(q v (p ≡ w))
    | [Show ∀(((s ≡ t) v r) ⊃ ∃(q v (p ≡ w)))]
    | [Show ((s ≡ t) v r) ⊃ ∃(q v (p ≡ w))]
    | 4. (s ≡ t) v r   Tas
    | [Show ∃(q v (p ≡ w))]
    | [Show q v(p ≡ w)]
    | [Show q]
    | 5. -r · t   (∀E, 2)
    | 6. -r   (&E, 5)
    | 7. (s ≡ t)   (DS, 4, 6)
    | 8. s ⊃ (p · q)   (∀E, 3)
    | 9. t ⊃ s   (IffE, 7)
    | 10. t ⊃ (p · q)   (HS, 8, 9)
    | 11. t   (&E, 5)
    | 12. (p · q)   (IfE, 10, 11)
    | 13. q   (&E, 12)
    | 14. q v (p ≡ w)   (OrI, 13)
    | 15. ∃(q v (p ≡ w))   (∃I, 14)
    | 16. ((s ≡ t) v r) ⊃ ∃(q v (p ≡ w))   (IfI, 4, 15)
    | 17. ∀((s ≡ t) v r) ⊃ ∃(q v (p ≡ w))) (∀I, 16)
    | 18. ∃(q v (p ≡ w))   (∃E, 1, 17)

EXERCISES 3.9

1. 1. There are no Unicorns, but there are Hobbits if you have read
      the Ring Trilogy.
   2. There are no U, but there are H if R by T Rule 17.
   3. ∀-U but there are H if R by T Rule 12.

4. ∀-U but ∃H if R by T Rule 11.
5. ∀-U but R ⊃ ∃H by T Rule 6.
6. ∀-U · (R ⊃ ∃H) by T Rule 1.

2. 1. If all bachelors are unmarried then none but married are not bachelors.
2. If all B are U then none but M are not B by T Rule 17.
3. If ∀(B ⊃ U) then none but M are not B by T Rule 8.
4. If ∀(B ⊃ U) then none but M are -B by T Rule 16.
5. If ∀(B ⊃ U) then ∀(-B ⊃ M) by T Rule 8.
6. ∀(B ⊃ U) ⊃ ∀(-B ⊃ M) by T Rule 6.

This sentence could also be translated another way. If we use the symbol -U for the word married the following translation is also correct: ∀(B ⊃ U) ⊃ ∀(-B ⊃ -U). This translation may seem strange to some because if we use this sentence as an argument, it turns out to be invalid. There are people, namely women, who are not married and not bachelors either.

3. 1. Either Jesse James is one of the guilty or he is not.
2. Either J is one of the G or he is not by T Rule 17.
3. Either ∃J · ∀(J ⊃ G) or he is not by T Rule 13.
4. (∃J · ∀(J ⊃ G)) v (-(∃J · ∀(J ⊃ G))) by T Rule 2.

EXERCISES 4.1

The following exercises can be done in more than one way.

1. 1. Washington is a constant by F Rule 2.
2. That city is a variable by F Rule 1.
3. Is near is a two-place relation symbol by F Rule 3.
4. Washington is near that city is a formula by lines 1, 2, and 3 and F Rule 4.
2. 1. That first city is a variable by F Rule 1.
2. That second city is a variable by F Rule 1.
3. Is near is a two-place relation symbol by F Rule 3.
4. That first city is near that second city is a formula by lines 1, 2, and 3 and F Rule 4.
3. 1. That second city is a variable by F Rule 1.
2. Is large is a one-place relation symbol by F Rule 3.
3. That second city is large is a formula by lines 1 and 2 and F Rule 4.
4. 1. That first city is a variable by F Rule 1.
2. Washington is a constant by F Rule 2.
3. Is near is a two-place relation symbol by F Rule 3.
4. That first city is near Washington is a formula by lines 1, 2, and 3 and F Rule 4.
5. For every first city that first city is near Washington is a formula by line 4 and F Rule 6.
5. 1. That first city is a variable by F Rule 1.
2. That second city is a variable by F Rule 1.
3. Is near is a two-place relation symbol by F Rule 3.
4. Washington is a constant by F Rule 2.
5. New York is a constant by F Rule 2.
6. That first city is near that second city is a formula by lines 1, 2, and 3 and F Rule 4.
7. Washington is near New York is a formula by lines 2, 4, and 5 and F Rule 4.

8. For every first city that first city is near that second city is a formula by line 6 and F Rule 6.
9. If for every first city that first city is near that second city, then Washington is near New York is a formula by lines 7 and 8 and F Rule 5.

6. 1. New York is a constant by F Rule 2.
   2. Washington is a constant by F Rule 2.
   3. That first city is a variable by F Rule 1.
   4. That second city is a variable by F Rule 1.
   5. Is near is a two-place relation symbol by F Rule 3.
   6. New York is near Washington is a formula by lines 1, 2, and 5 and F Rule 4.
   7. Washington is near that first city is a formula by lines 2, 3, and 5 and F Rule 4.
   8. New York is near that second city is a formula by lines 1, 4, and 5 and F Rule 4.
   9. Washington is near that first city or New York is near that second city is a formula by lines 7 and 8 and F Rule 5.
   10. New York is near Washington if and only if Washington is near that first city or New York is near that second city is a formula by lines 6 and 9 and F Rule 5.

7. 1. New York is a constant by F Rule 2.
   2. That first city is a variable by F Rule 1.
   3. Is near is a two-place relation symbol by F Rule 3.
   4. New York is near that first city is a formula by lines 1, 2, and 3 and F Rule 4.
   5. That second city is a variable by F Rule 1.
   6. That second city is near that first city is a formula by lines 2, 3, and 5 and F Rule 4.
   7. For some second city that second city is near that first city is a formula by line 6 and F Rule 6.
   8. If New York is near that first city, then for some second city that second city is near that first city is a formula by lines 4 and 7 and F Rule 5.
   9. It is not the case that if New York is near that first city, then for some second city that second city is near that first city is a formula by line 8 and F Rule 5.

EXERCISES 4.2

The following exercises can be done in more than one way.

1. 1. d is a constant by F Rule 2.
   2. c is a constant by F Rule 2.
   3. R is a one-place relation symbol by F Rule 3.
   4. P is a two-place relation symbol by F Rule 3.
   5. Pcd is a formula by lines 1, 2, and 4 and F Rule 4.
   6. Rd is a formula by lines 1 and 3 and F Rule 4.
   7. -Pcd is a formula by line 5 and F Rule 5.
   8. Rd ⊃ -Pcd is a formula by lines 6 and 7 and F Rule 5.

2. 1. d is a constant by F Rule 2.
   2. c is a constant by F Rule 2.
   3. R is a one-place relation symbol by F Rule 3.
   4. P is a two-place relation symbol by F Rule 3.
   5. x is a variable by F Rule 1.

6. Rx is a formula by lines 3 and 5 and F Rule 4.
7. Pxd is a formula by lines 1, 4, and 5 and F Rule 4.
8. Pdc is a formula by lines 1, 2, and 4 and F Rule 4.
9. Rx ⊃ Pxd is a formula by lines 6 and 7 and F Rule 5.
10. (x)(Rx ⊃ Pxd) is a formula by line 9 and F Rule 6.
11. Pdc ≡ (x)(Rx ⊃ Pxd) is a formula by line 11 and F Rule 5.
12. -(Pdc ≡ (x)(Rx ⊃ Pxd)) is a formula by line 11 and F Rule 5.

3. 1. d is a constant by F Rule 2.
   2. c is a constant by F Rule 2.
   3. R is a one-place relation symbol by F Rule 3.
   4. P is a two-place relation symbol by F Rule 3.
   5. x is a variable by F Rule 1.
   6. Rd is a formula by lines 1 and 3 and F Rule 4.
   7. -Rd is a formula by line 6 and F Rule 5.
   8. Rc is a formula by lines 2 and 3 and F Rule 4.
   9. -Rd v Rc is a formula by lines 8 and 8 and F Rule 5.
   10. Pdx is a formula by lines 1, 4, and 5 and F Rule 4.
   11. ∃xPdx is a formula by line 10 and F Rule 6.
   12. ∃xPdx ⊃ (-Rd v Rd) is a formula by lines 9 and 11 and F Rule 5.

4. 1. d is a constant by F Rule 2.
   2. c is a constant by F Rule 2.
   3. P is a two-place relation symbol by F Rule 3.
   4. x is a variable by F Rule 1.
   5. y is a variable by F Rule 1.
   6. Pdc is a formula by lines 1, 2, and 3 and F Rule 4.
   7. Pcd is a formula by lines 1, 2, and 3 and F Rule 4.
   8. Pxy is a formula by lines 3, 4, and 5 and F Rule 4.
   9. Pdc · Pcd is a formula by lines 6 and 7 and F Rule 5.
   10. Pxy ⊃ (Pdc · Pcd) is a formula by lines 8 and 9 and F Rule 5.
   11. (y)(Pxy ⊃ (Pdc · Pcd)) is a formula by line 10 and F Rule 6.
   12. (x)(y)(Pxy ⊃ (Pdc · Pcd)) is a formula by line 11 and F Rule 6.

5. 1. x is a variable by F Rule 1.
   2. y is a variable by F Rule 1.
   3. P is a two-place relation symbol by F Rule 3.
   4. R is a one-place relation symbol by F Rule 3.
   5. Rx is a formula by lines 1 and 4 and F Rule 4.
   6. Ry is a formula by lines 2 and 4 and F Rule 4.
   7. -Ry is a formula by line 6 and F Rule 5.
   8. Rx · -Ry is a formula by lines 5 and 6 and F Rule 5.
   9. Pxy is a formula by lines 1, 2, and 3 and F Rule 4.
   10. -Pxy is a formula by line 9 and F Rule 5.
   11. (Rx · -Ry) ≡ -Pxy is a formula by lines 8 and 10 and F Rule 5.
   12. (∃y)((Rx · -Ry) ≡ -Pxy) is a formula by line 11 and F Rule 6.
   13. (∃x)(∃y)((Rx · -Ry) ≡ -Pxy) is a formula by line 12 and F Rule 6.

EXERCISES 4.3

1. There are three occurrences of x in (x)∃yPxy ⊃ ((Rx ⊃ Ry) · (Rc · Rd)). The first occurrence is a quantifier, so we do not consider it. The next occurrence is bound, but the last occurrence is not. There are also three occurrences of y. The first occurrence is again a quantifier, so we do not consider it. The next occurrence is bound, but the last occurrence is not.

2. There are three occurrences of x in ∃xPxy ⊃ (x)Ry · Pcd. The first two occurrences are quantifiers, so we do not consider these. There are two occurrences of y. Neither occurrence is bound.

3. None of the variables in <u>Rx · Ry ≡ Pxy · -Pyx</u> are bound because there are no quantifiers.
4. There are five occurrences of <u>x</u> in <u>Pxy ⊃ (x)(Rx v ∃yRy) · -(x)Pxy</u>. The first occurrence is not bound. The second occurrence is a quantifier, so we do not consider it. The third occurrence of <u>x</u> is bound. The fourth occurrence of <u>x</u> is a quantifier, so we do not consider it. The last occurrence of <u>x</u> is bound. There are four occurrences of <u>y</u>. The first occurrence is not bound. The second occurrence is a quantifier, so we do not consider it. The third occurrence of <u>y</u> is bound. The last occurrence of <u>y</u> is not bound.
5. There are five occurrences of <u>x</u> in <u>(x)(Pdx ⊃ Ry) ≡ ∃x∃y(Pxy v Pyx)</u>. The first occurrence of <u>x</u> is a quantifier, so we do not consider it. The second occurrence of <u>x</u> is bound. The third occurrence of <u>x</u> is a quantifier, so we do not consider it. The fourth and fifth occurrences of <u>x</u> are bound. There are four occurrences of <u>y</u>. The first occurrence is not bound. The second occurrence of <u>y</u> is a quantifier, so we do not consider it. The third and fourth occurrences of <u>y</u> are bound.

EXERCISES 4.4

1. P x y ≡ -(R d ⊃ R c)
   <u>T</u> <u>0</u> <u>0</u> Ⓕ F F <u>0</u> T T <u>1</u>

2. - P x y · (P c d · P d c)
   F <u>T</u> <u>0</u> <u>0</u> Ⓕ F <u>1</u> <u>0</u> F F <u>0</u> <u>1</u>

3. R y ⊃ (R c ≡ (- P x y ⊃ P y d)
   F <u>0</u> Ⓣ T <u>1</u> T F <u>T</u> <u>0</u> <u>0</u> T <u>T</u> <u>0</u> <u>0</u>

4. (R d · P d c) ⊃ (P x y ⊃ R c)
   F <u>0</u> F F <u>0</u> <u>1</u> Ⓣ <u>T</u> <u>0</u> <u>0</u> T T <u>1</u>

5. P d x ⊃ (- R x · (P x d ⊃ R c))
   <u>T</u> <u>0</u> <u>0</u> Ⓣ T F <u>0</u> T <u>T</u> <u>0</u> <u>0</u> T T <u>1</u>

6. - - P x x ⊃ (P x x v (R d · R y))
   T F <u>T</u> <u>0</u> <u>0</u> Ⓣ <u>T</u> <u>0</u> <u>0</u> T F <u>0</u> F F <u>0</u>

7. ((P c d · P d c) v (P x y · P y x)) ≡ (R y · R x)
   F <u>1</u> <u>0</u> F F <u>0</u> <u>1</u> T <u>T</u> <u>0</u> <u>0</u> T T <u>0</u> <u>0</u> Ⓕ F <u>0</u> F F <u>0</u>

   Recall that the following exercises have a new possible situation:

8. (R y · R x) ⊃ -(R d v R c)
   <u>T</u> <u>1</u> T T <u>0</u> Ⓣ <u>T</u> <u>1</u> T T <u>0</u>

9. (- P x x v R d) ⊃ (· P x y · P d c)
   T F <u>0</u> <u>0</u> T T <u>1</u> Ⓣ T F <u>0</u> <u>1</u> T T <u>1</u> <u>0</u>

10. (P x d ⊃ R c) ≡ -((R d · R x) v (R y · R c))
    F <u>0</u> <u>1</u> T T <u>0</u> Ⓕ F T <u>1</u> T T <u>0</u> T T <u>1</u> T T <u>0</u>

11. (R c ⊃ - R x) ≡ -(P y x v P y y)
    <u>T</u> <u>0</u> F F T <u>0</u> Ⓣ F T <u>1</u> <u>0</u> T T <u>1</u> <u>1</u>

12. (- P c c · P d d) ⊃ -(- P x y v P y x)
    T F <u>0</u> <u>0</u> T T <u>1</u> <u>1</u> Ⓕ F T F <u>0</u> <u>1</u> T T <u>1</u> <u>0</u>

142

Part A

1. $(x)(y) P x y$
   $(y) P x_0 y \cdot (y) P x_1 y$
   $(P x_0 y_0 \cdot P x_0 y_1) \cdot (P x_1 y_0 \cdot P x_1 y_1)$

2. $\exists x\, R x \supset (y)\, P x y$
   $(R x_0 \lor R x_1) \supset (y)\, P x y$
   $(R x_0 \lor R x_1) \supset (P x y_0 \cdot P x y_1)$

3. $P x y \supset ((x)\, R x \lor \exists x\,(y)\, P x y)$
   $P x y \supset ((R x_0 \cdot R x_1) \lor x\,(y)\, P x y)$
   $P x y \supset (((R x_0 \cdot R x_1) \lor ((y)\, P x_0 y \lor (y)\, P x_1 y))$
   $P x y \supset ((R x_0 \cdot R x_1) \lor ((P x_0 y_0 \cdot P x_0 y_1) \lor (P x_1 y_0)$
   $ \lor (P x_1 y_0 \cdot P x_1 y_1)))$

4. $(y)\, \exists x\, P y x \equiv (R x \cdot \exists y\, R y)$
   $(\exists x\, P y_0 x \cdot \exists x\, P y_1 x) \equiv (R x \cdot \exists y\, R y)$
   $((P y_0 x_0 \lor P y_0 x_1) \cdot (P y_1 x_0 \lor P y_1 x_1)) \equiv (R x \cdot \exists y\, R y)$
   $((P y_0 x_0 \lor P y_0 x_1) \cdot (P y_1 x_0 \lor P y_1 x_1)) \equiv (R x \cdot (R y_0 \lor R y_1)$

5. $(x)(y)\, P x y \supset - P c d$
   $((y)\, P x y_0 \cdot (y)\, P x y_1) \supset - P c d$
   $((P x_0 y_0 \cdot P x_1 y_0) \cdot (P x_0 y_1 \cdot P x_1 y_1)) \supset - P c d$

6. $\exists x \exists y\, P x y \supset -\exists z(R z \lor P d c)$
   $(\exists y\, P x_0 y \lor \exists y\, P x_1 y) \supset -\exists z(R z \lor P d c)$
   $((P x_0 y_0 \lor P x_0 y_1) \lor (P x_1 y_0 \lor P x_1 y_1)) \supset -\exists z(R z \lor P d c)$
   $((P x_0 y_0 \lor P x_0 y_1) \lor (P x_1 y_0 \lor P x_1 y_1)) \supset -((R z_0 \lor R z_1) \lor P d c)$

7. $\exists z\,(y)\,(P z y \equiv (R y \supset P z y))$
   $(y)(P z_0 y \equiv (R y \supset P z_0 y)) \lor (y)(P z_1 y \equiv (R y \supset P z_1 y)$
   $((P z_0 y_0 \equiv (R y_0 \supset P z_0 y_0)) \cdot (P z_0 y_1 \equiv (R y_1 \supset P z_0 y_1)))$
   $\lor ((P z_1 y_0 \equiv (R y_0 \supset P z_1 y_0))) \cdot (P z_1 y_1 \equiv (R y_1 \supset P z_1 y_1)))$

Part B

The following solutions show the truth values for the expanded formulae:

1. $(P x_1 y_1 \cdot P x_0 y_1) \cdot (P x_1 y_0 \cdot P x_1 y_1)$
   F O O   F T O 1   Ⓕ   T 1 O   T T 1 1

2. $(R x_0 \lor R x_1) \supset (P x y_0 \cdot P x y_1)$
   T O   T T 1   Ⓣ   T 1 O   T T 1 1

3. $P x y \supset ((R x_0 \cdot R x_1) \lor ((P x_0 y_0 \cdot P x_0 y_1) \lor (P x_1 y_0 \cdot P x_1 y_1)))$
   T 1 O Ⓣ   T O   T T 1   T   F O O   F T O 1   T   T 1 O   T T 1 1

4. $((P y_0 x_0 \lor P y_0 x_1) \cdot (P y_1 x_0 \lor P y_1 x_1)) \equiv (R x \cdot (R y_0 \lor R x_1)$
   F O O   F T O 1   T   T 1 O   T T 1 1   Ⓣ   T 1 T   T O   T T 1

5. $((P x_0 y_0 \cdot P x_1 y_0) \cdot (P x_0 y_1 \cdot P x_1 y_1)) \supset - P c d$
   F O O   F T 1 O   F   T O 1   T T 1 1   Ⓣ T F O O

6. $((P x_0 y_0 \lor P x_0 y_1) \lor (P x_1 y_0 \lor P x_1 y_1)) \supset -((R z_0 \lor R z_1) \lor P d c)$
   F O O   T T O 1   T   T 1 O   T T 1 1   Ⓕ F   T O   T T 1   T F O O

7. $((P z_0y_0 \equiv (R y_0 \supset P z_0y_0)) \cdot (P z_0y_1 \equiv (R y_1 \supset P z_0y_1)))$
   F O O T T O F F O O   T T O 1 T T 1 T T O 1

   $\vee ((P z_1y_0 \equiv (R y_0 \supset P z_1y_0)) \cdot (P z_1y_1 \equiv (R y_1 \supset P z_1y_1)))$
   (T) T 1 O T T O T T 1 O   T T 1 1 T T 1 T T 1 1

EXERCISES 4.6

1. Universe of Discourse: $\{0, 1\}$; R: 0; B: 1; P: (0, 0), (1, 1)
   $(R x_0 \supset P x_0x_0) \cdot (R x_1 \supset P x_1x_1)$
   T O T T O O (T) F 1 T T 1 1

   $(P x_0x_0 \cdot B x_0) \vee (P x_1x_1 \cdot B x_1)$
   T O O F F O (T) T 1 1 T T 1

   So, $(R x_0 \cdot B x_0) \vee (R x_1 \cdot B x_1)$
   T O F F O (F) F 1 F T 1

2 Universe of Discourse: $\{0, 1\}$; D: 0, 1; C: ; E: 0, 1
   $((C x_0 \supset D y_0) \cdot (C x_0 \supset D y_1)) \cdot ((C x_1 \supset D y_0) \cdot (C x_1 \supset D y_1))$
   F O T T O T F O T T 1 (T) F 1 T T O T F 1 T T 1

   $(D y_0 \supset E y_0) \cdot (D y_1 \supset E y_1)$
   T O T T O (T) T 1 T T 1

   So, $((E y_0 \supset C x_0) \cdot (E y_0 \supset C x_1)) \cdot (E y_1 \supset C x_0) \cdot (E y_1 \supset C x_1))$
   T O F F O F T O F F 1 (F) T 1 F F O F T 1 F F 1

3. Because the argument has three quantifiers in both the assumption
   as well as the conclusion, we will need to expand both formulae
   three times. This means the expanded formulae will extend onto
   several lines as follows:

   Universe of Discourse: $\{0, 1\}$; E: 0; R: 0; D: 0, 1
   $((((R x_0 \cdot D y_0) \supset E z_0) \vee ((R x_0 \cdot D y_0) \supset E z_1))$
   T O T T O   T T O T T O T T O T F 1

   $\vee (((R x_0 \cdot D y_1) \supset E z_0) \vee ((R x_0 \cdot D y_1) \supset E z_1)))$
   T   T O T T 1 T T O T T O T T 1 T F 1

   $\vee ((((R x_1 \cdot D y_0) \supset E z_0) \vee ((R x_1 \cdot D y_0) \supset E z_1))$
   (T)   F 1 F T O T T O T F 1 F T O T F 1

   $\vee (((R x_1 \cdot D y_1) \supset E z_0) \vee ((R x_1 \cdot D y_1) \supset E z_1)))$
   T   F 1 F T 1 T T O T F 1 F T 1 T F 1

   So, $(- E z_0 \supset (R x_0 \cdot D y_0)) \cdot (- E z_0 \supset (R x_0 \cdot D y_1))$
   F T O T T O T T O   T F T O T T O T T 1

   $\cdot (- E z_0 \supset (R x_1 \cdot D y_0)) \cdot (- E z_0 \supset (R x_1 \cdot D y_1))$
   T F T O T F 1 F T O   T F T O T F 1 F T 1

   $\cdot (- E z_1 \supset (R x_0 \cdot D y_0)) \cdot (- E z_1 \supset (R x_0 \cdot D y_1))$
   (F) T F 1 T T O T T O   T T F 1 T T O T T 1

   $\cdot (- E z_1 \supset (R x_1 \cdot D y_0)) \cdot (- E z_1 \supset (R x_1 \cdot D y_1))$
   F T F 1 F F 1 F T O   F T F 1 F F 1 F T 1

4. Universe of Discourse: $\{0, 1\}$; P: (0, 1), (1, 1); c: 1; d: 1;
   R: 0, 1; D: 0, 1
   $P c d \supset ((R x_0 \supset D x_0) \cdot (R x_1 \supset D x_1))$
   T 1 1 (T) T O T T O T T 1 T T 1

144

((R x · P x d) · (R x · P x d)
 T O T T O 1   T T 1 T T 1 1

So, - D c
    F T 1

5. Universe of Discourse: {0, 1}; H: ; S:
   ((H x_0y_0 ≡ S x_0y_0) · (H x_0y_1 ≡ S x_0y_1)) · ((H x_1y_0 ≡ S x_1y_0)
    F O O T F O O   T F O 1 T F O 1   T   F 1 O T F 1 O

   · (H x_1y_1 ≡ S x_1y_1))
   T F 1 1 T F 1 1

   (- S x_0y_0 · - S x_0y_1) · (- S x_1y_0 · - S x_1y_1)
    T F O O T T F O 1   T T F 1 O T T F 1 1

So, (H x_0y_0 · H x_1y_0) · (H x_0y_1 · H x_1y_1)
     F O O F F 1 O   F F O 1 F F 1 1

EXERCISES 4.7

1. ∃xPdx
2. (x)Hxx ⊃ Pyy
3. (x)(y)(Pxy ≡ -Hyx)   (No change.)
4. ∃xHxx ∨ (x)Pcx
5. Pyy ∨ -Hyy
6. (x)(y)(Pxy ⊃ Hxz)   (No change.)
7. (x)(y)(∃z)(Hxz ∨ Pxx) ⊃ Tzz

EXERCISES 4.7

The following exercises can be done in more than one way:

1. | 1. (x)(Bx ⊃ Qx)   As
   | 2. (x)(Qx ⊃ Rx)   As
   | Show (x)(Bx ⊃ Rx)
   | [Show Bx ⊃ Rx]
   | 3. Bx ⊃ Qx   (∀E, 1, x/x)
   | 4. Qx ⊃ Rx   (∀E, 2, x/x)
   | 5. Bx   Tas
   | [Show Rx]
   | 6. Qx   (IfE, 3, 5)
   | 7. Rx   (IfE, 4, 6)
   | 8. Bx ⊃ Rx   (IfI, 5, 7)
   | 9. (x)(Bx ⊃ Rx)   (∀I, 8, x/x)

2. 1. (y)(x)Hxy   As
   Show (x)(y)Yxy
   [Show Hxy]
   2. (x)Hxy   (∀E, 1, y/y)
   3. Hxy   (∀E, 2, x/x)
   4. (y)Hxy   (∀I, 3, y/y)
   5. (x)(y)Hxy   (∀I, 4, x/x)

3. 1. (x)(y)Tyx   As
   Show (y)(x)Tyx
   [Show Tyx]
   2. (y)Tyx   (∀E, x/x)

145

```
         3. Tyx                                    (∀E, x/x)
         4. (x)Tyx                                 (∀I, x/x)
         5. (y)(x)Tyx                              (∀I, y/y)

4.  1. ∃x(y)Qxy                                    As
    Show (y)(∃x)Qxy
    [Show (x)((y)Qxy ⊃ ∃xQxy)]
    [Show ((y)Qxy ⊃ ∃xQxy)
         2. (y)Qxy                                 Tas
         [Show ∃xQxy]
         [Show Qxy]
         3. Qxy                                    (∀E, 2, y/y)
         4. ∃xQxy                                  (∃I, 3, x/x)
         5. (y)Qxy ⊃ ∃xQxy                         (IfE, 2, 4)
         6. (x)((y)Qxy ⊃ ∃xQxy)                    (∀I, 5)
         7. ∃xQxy                                  (∃E, 1, 6)
         8. (y)(∃x)Qxy                             (∀I, 7, y/y)

5.  1. (x)(Bx · Rx)                                As
    Show (x)Bx · (x)Rx
    [Show (x)Bx]
    [Show Bx]
         2. Bx · Rx                                (∀E, 1, x/x)
         3. Bx                                     (&E, 2)
         4. (x)Bx                                  (∀I, 3, x/x)
    [Show (x)Rx]
    [Show Rx
         5. Rx                                     (&E, 2)
         6. (x)Rx                                  (∀I, 5, x/x)
         7. (x)Bx · (x)Rx                          (&I, 4, 6)

6.  1. (x)Bx · (x)Rx                               As
    Show (x)(Bx · Rx)
    [Show Bx · Rx]
    [Show Bx]
         2. (x)Bx                                  (&E)
         3. Bx                                     (∀E, 2, x/x)
    [Show Rx]
         4. (x)Rx                                  (&E, 2)
         5. Rx                                     (∀E, 4, x/x)
         6. Bx · Rx                                (&I, 3, 5)
         7. (x)(Bx · Rx)                           (∀I, 6, x/x)

7.  1. (z)(Tz ⊃ Rz)                                As
    Show (z)Tz ⊃ (z)Rz
         2. (z)Tz                                  Tas
         [Show (z)Rz]
         [Show Rz]
         3. Tz ⊃ Rz                                (∀E, 1, z/z)
         4. Tz                                     (∀E, 2, z/z)
         5. Rz                                     (IfE, 3, 4)
         6. (z)Rz                                  (∀I, 5, z/z)
         7. (z)Rz ⊃ (z)Rz                          (IfI, 2, 6)

8.  1. ∃z(Bz · Tz)                                 As
    Show ∃zBx · ∃zTz
    [Show ∃zBz]
    [Show (z)((Bz · Tz) ⊃ ∃zBz)]
```

146

```
        [Show (Bz · Tz) ⊃ ∃zBz]
    ┌─2. Bz · Tz                        Tas
    │  [Show ∃zBz]
    │  [Show Bz]
    │  3. Bz                            (&E, 2)
    └─4. ∃zBz                           (∃I, 3, z/z)
    5. (Bz · Tz)⊃ ∃ zBz                (IfI, 2, 4)
    6. (z)((Bz · Tz) ⊃ ∃zBz)          (∀I, 5, z/z)
    7. ∃zBz                             (∃E, 1, 6)
       [Show ∃zTz]
       [Show (z)((Bz · Tz ⊃ ∃zTz))]
    ┌─ 8. Bz · Tz                       Tas
    │  9. Tz                            (&E, 8)
  ┌─└─10. ∃zTz                          (∃I, 9, z/z)
  │ 11. (Bz · Tz) ⊃ ∃zTz              (IfI, 8, 10)
  │ 12. (z)((Bz · Tz) ⊃ ∃zTz)        (∀I, 11, z/z)
  │ 13. ∃zTz                           (∃E, 1, 12)
  └ 14. ∃zBz · ∃zTz                    (&I, 7, 13)

9. │1. ∃x∃y∃zKxyz                                      As
   │Show ∃z∃y∃xKxyz
   │  [Show (x)(∃y∃zKxyz ⊃ ∃z∃y∃xKxyz)]
   │  [Show ∃y∃zKxyz ⊃ ∃z∃y∃xKxyz]
   │┌─2. ∃y∃zKxyz                                      Tas
   ││  [Show ∃z∃y∃xKxyz]
   ││  [Show (y)(∃zKxyz ⊃ ∃z∃y∃xKxyz)]
   ││  [Show ∃zKxyz ⊃ ∃z∃y∃xKxyz]
   ││┌─3. ∃zKxyz                                       Tas
   │││  [Show ∃z∃y∃xKxyz]
   │││  [Show (z)(Kxyz ⊃ ∃z∃y∃xKxyz)]
   │││  (Show Kxyz ⊃ ∃z∃y∃xKxyz]
   │││┌─4. Kxyz                                        Tas
   ││││  [Show ∃z∃y∃xKxyz]
   ││││  5. ∃xKxyz                                     (∃I, 4, x/x)
   ││││  6. ∃y∃xKxyz                                   (∃I, 5, y/y)
   │││└─7. ∃z∃y∃xKxyz                                  (∃I, 5, z/z)
   │││  8. Kxyz ⊃ ∃z∃y∃xKxyz                          (IfI, 4, 7)
   │││  9. (z)(Kxyz ⊃ ∃z∃y∃xKxyz)                     (∀I, 8, z/z)
   ││└─10. ∃z∃y∃xKxyz                                  (∃E, 3, 9)
   ││ 11. ∃xKxyz ⊃ ∃z∃y∃xKxyz                         (IfI, 3, 10)
   ││ 12. (y)(∃zKxyz ⊃ ∃z∃y∃xKxyz)                    (∀I, 11, y/y)
   │└─13. ∃z∃y∃xKxyz                                   (∃E, 2, 12)
   │ 14. ∃y∃zKxyz ⊃ ∃z∃y∃xKxyz                        (IfI, 2, 13)
   │ 15. (x)(∃y∃zKxyz ⊃ ∃z∃y∃xKxyz)                   (∀I, 14, x/x)
   │ 16. ∃z∃y∃xKxyz                                    (∃E, 1, 15)

10. │1. (z)Bz ∨ ∃yRy                   As
    │Show (z)∃y(Bz ∨ Ry))
    │  [Show (z)Bz ⊃ (z)∃y(Bz ∨ Ry)]
    │┌─2. (z)Bz                         Tas
    ││  [Show (z)∃y(Bz ∨ Ry)]
    ││  3. Bz                           (∀E, 2, z/z)
    ││  4. Bz ∨ Ry                      (OrI, 3)
    ││  5. ∃y(Bz ∨ Ry)                  (∃I, 4, y/y)
    │└─6. (z)∃y(Bz ∨ Ry)               (∀I, 5, z/z)
    │ 7. (z)Bz ⊃ (z)∃y(Bz ∨ Ry)        (IfI, 2, 6)
    │  [Show ∃yRy ⊃ (z)∃y(Bz ∨ Ry)]
```

```
8. ∃yRy                              Tas
  [Show (z)∃y(Bz v Ry)]
  [Show (y)(Ry ⊃ ∃y(Bz v Ry))]
  [Show Ry ⊃ ∃y(Bz v Ry)]
      9. Ry
      [Show ∃y(Bz v Ry)]
     10. Bz v Ry                    (OrI, 9)
    11. ∃y(Bz v Ry)                 (∃I, 10, y/y)
   12. Ry ⊃ ∃y(Bz v Ry)            (IfI, 9, 11)
   13. (y)(Ry ⊃ ∃y(Bz v Ry))       (∀I, 12, y/y)
   14. ∃y(Bz v Ry)                  (∃E, 8, 13)
   15. (z)∃y(Bz v Ry)              (∀I, 14, z/z)
16. ∃yRy ⊃ (z)∃y(Bz v Ry)         (IfI, 8, 15)
17. (z)∃y(Bz v Ry)                 (OrE, 1, 7, 16)
```

EXERCISES 4.9

1. 1. Some p̲ilots f̲ly some a̲irplanes that g̲lide.
   2. Some P F some A that G by T Rule 8.
   3. ∃x(Px · [F some A that G]x by T Rule 3.
   4. ∃x(Px · ∃y[A that G]y · Fxy) by T Rule 7.
   5. ∃x(Rx · ∃y(Gy · Ay) · Fxy) by T Rule 4.

2. 1. All d̲og catchers c̲atch all d̲ogs that s̲mell.
   2. All O̲ C̲ all D̲ that S̲ by T Rule 8.
   3. (z)(Ox ⊃ [C all D that S]x by T Rule 1.
   4. (x)(Ox ⊃ (y)([D that S]y ⊃ Cxy)) by T Rule 5.
   5. (x)(Ox ⊃ (y)((Dy · Sy) ⊃ Cxy)) by T Rule 4.

3. 1. Some w̲elders wo̲rk all j̲obs if and only if all f̲oremen p̲ay some
      w̲ages.
   2. Some E R all J if and only if all F P some W by T Rule 8.
   3. (Some E R all J) ≡ (all F P some W) by T Rule 5 from Chapter 2.
   4. ∃x(Ex · [R all J]x) ≡ (all FP some W) by T Rule 3.
   5. ∃x(Ex · [R all J]x ≡ (x)(Fx ⊃ [P some W]x by T Rule 1.
   6. ∃x(Ex · (y)(Jy ⊃ Rxy)) ≡ (x)(Fx ⊃ [P some W]x) by T Rule 5.
   7. ∃x(Ex · (y)(Jy ⊃ Rxy)) ≡ (x)(Fx ⊃ y(Wy · Pxy)) by T Rule 7.

4. 1. It is not the case that if some b̲ankers s̲ave all p̲ennies that
      s̲hine, then no c̲itizens spend all n̲ickels.
   2. It is not the case that if some B̲ A̲ all P̲ that S̲, then no C̲ E̲ all
      N̲ by T Rule 8.
   3. -(if some B̲ A̲ all P̲ that S̲, then no C̲ E̲ all N̲) by T Rule 3 from
      Chapter 2.
   4. -(if ∃x(Bx · [A all P that S]x, then no C E all N) by T Rule 3.
   5. -(if ∃x(Bx · (y)([P that S]y ⊃ Axy)), then no C E all N) by T
      Rule 5.
   6. -(if ∃x(Bx · (y)((Py · Sy) ⊃ Axy)), then no C E all N by T Rule
      4.
   7. -(if ∃x(Bx · (y)((Py · Sy) ⊃ Axy)), then (x)(Cd ⊃ -[E all N]x)
      by T Rule 2.
   8. -(if ∃x(Bx · (y)((Py · Sy) ∃ Axy)), then (x)(Cx)
      ⊃ -(y)(Ny ⊃ Exy))) by T Rule 5.
   9. -(∃x(Bx · (y)((Py · Sy) ⊃ Axy)) ⊃ (x)(Cx ⊃ -(y)(Ny ⊃ Exy)) by
      T Rule 6 from Chapter 2.

5. 1. If all b̲oys m̲ow all l̲awns that n̲eed no c̲are, then some neigh-
      bors y̲ell.
   2. If all B̲ M̲ all L̲ that N̲ no C̲, then some E̲ Y̲ by T Rule 8.

3. If $\underline{(x)(Bx \supset [M \text{ all } L \text{ that } N \text{ no } C]x)}$, then some E Y by T Rule 1.
4. If $\underline{(x)(Bx \supset (y)([L \text{ that } N \text{ no } C]y \supset Mxy))}$, then some E Y by T Rule 5.
5. If $\underline{(x)(Bx \supset (y)(Ly \cdot [N \text{ no } C]y \supset Mxy))}$, then some E Y by T Rule 4.
6. If $\underline{(x)(Bx \supset (y)(Ly \cdot (z)(Cz \supset -Nyz)) \supset Mxy}$, then some E Y by T Rule 6.
7. If $\underline{(z)(Bx \supset (y)(Ly \cdot (z)(Cz \supset -Nyz))) \supset Mxy}$, then $\exists w(Ew \cdot Yw)$ by T Rule 3.
8. $\underline{((x)(Bx \supset (y)(Ly \cdot (z)(Cz \supset -Nyz))) \supset Mxy \supset \exists w(Ew \cdot Yw)}$ by T Rule 6 from Chapter 2.

EXERCISES 5.1

The following exercises can be done in more than one way:

1. 1. <u>Great Britain</u> is a term by assumption.
   2. <u>France</u> is a term by assumption.
   3. <u>The ally of</u> is a one-place function symbol by assumption.
   4. <u>The ally of France</u> is a term by lines 2 and 3 and F Rule 9.
   5. <u>The ally of the ally of France</u> is a term by lines 3 and 4 and F Rule 9.
   6. <u>Great Britain is the ally of the ally of France</u> is a formula by lines 1 and 5 and F Rule 7.
2. This is not a formula according to the F rules because <u>France is the ally of Germany and Great Britain</u> is not a formula. To make it a formula, remove one of the terms <u>Germany</u> or <u>France</u>.
3. This is not a formula according to the F rules because <u>France and Great Britain</u> is not a term and <u>the nearest common ancestor of</u> must be connected to two terms rather than just one, namely <u>Germany</u>. To make it a formula, remove <u>France</u> from the beginning of the sentence and place it after <u>Germany</u> to obtain <u>Great Britain is the nearest common ancestor of Germany and France</u>.
4. This is not a formula according to the F rules because <u>the nearest common ancestor of</u> is connected to one term instead of two. To make this into a formula, insert a term in the correct place. If we add <u>Germany</u> in the appropriate place, we obtain the formula <u>Churchill is the ally of the nearest common ancestor of Germany and the ally of France</u>.
5. 1. <u>Hitler</u> is a term by assumption.
   2. <u>Germany</u> is a term by assumption.
   3. <u>Churchill</u> is a term by assumption.
   4. <u>DeGaulle</u> is a term by assumption.
   5. <u>Roosevelt</u> is a term by assumption.
   6. <u>The ally of</u> is a one-place function symbol by assumption.
   7. <u>The nearest common ancestor of</u> is a two-place function symbol by assumption.
   8. <u>The ally of Germany</u> is a term by lines 2 and 6 and F Rule 9.
   9. <u>The nearest common ancestor of DeGaulle and Roosevelt</u> is a term by lines 4, 5, and 7 and F Rule 9.
   10. <u>Churchill is the nearest common ancestor of DeGaulle and Roosevelt</u> is a formula by lines 3 and 9 and F Rule 7.
   11. <u>The ally of Germany</u> is a term by lines 2 and 6 and F Rule 9.
   12. <u>Hitler is the ally of Germany</u> is a formula by lines 1 and 11 and F Rule 7.

13. It is not the case that Churchill is the nearest common ances-tor of DeGaulle and Roosevelt is a formula by line 10 and T Rule 5.
14. Hitler is the ally of Germany or it is not the case that Church-ill is the nearest common ancestor of DeGaulle and Roosevelt is a formula by lines 12 and 13 and F Rule 5.

EXERCISES 5.2

The following exercises can be done in more than one way:

1. This is not a formula according to the F rules because $\exists y l y x$ is not a formula but only a term. To make this a formula, we could exchange the two-place function symbol l for the two-place rela-tion symbol P. This would give us the formula: $(x)((fx = gcc) \equiv \exists y P y x)$.
2. This is not a formula according to the F rules because lab is not a formula but only a term. To make it a formula, we could exchange the two-place function symbol l for the two-place relation symbol P. This would give us the formula: $Pab \equiv (x)(fx= gxx)$.
3. This is not a formula according to the F rules because $(x)(fx = gxx)$ is treated as a term in the entire expression $(x)(fx = gxx) = lab$. There are several methods for changing this expression into a formula. If we change the equals symbol (=) to an if and only if symbol ($\equiv$) and the two-place function symbol l to the two-place relation symbol P, we obtain the formula $(x)(fx = gxx) \equiv Pab$.
4. This is not a formula according to the F rules. $ffgce$ is simply a term and could be made into a formula by adding a one-place rela-tion symbol. If we add R then we obtain the formula $Rffgce$.
5. 1. e is a term by assumption.
   2. d is a term by assumption.
   3. f is a one-place function symbol by assumption.
   4. fd is a term by lines 2 and 3 and F Rule 9.
   5. ffd is a term by lines 3 and 4 and F Rule 9.
   6. $fffd$ is a term by lines 3 and 5 and F Rule 9.
   7. $fffd = e$ is a formula by lines 1 and 6 and F Rule 7.
   8. P is a two-place relation symbol by F Rule 3 of Chapter 4.
   9. x is a variable by F Rule 1 of Chapter 4.
   10. y is a variable by F Rule 1 of Chapter 4.
   11. Pxy is a formula by lines 9 and 10 and F Rule 4 of Chapter 4.
   12. R is a one-place relation symbol by F Rule 3 of Chapter 4.
   13. c is a term by assumption.
   14. Rc is a formula by lines 12 and 13 and F Rule 4 of Chapter 4.
   15. $Pxy \supset Rc$ is a formula by lines 11 and 14 and F Rule 5 of Chap-ter 4.
   16. $\exists y(Pxy \supset Rc)$ is a formula by line 15 and F Rule 6 of Chapter 4.
   17. $(x)(\exists y)(Pxy \supset Rc)$ is a formula by line 16 and F Rule 6 of Chap-ter 4.
   18. $(fffd = e) \equiv (x)(\exists y)(Pxy \supset Rc)$ is a formula by lines 7 and 17 and F Rule 5 of Chapter 4.

A. 1. f e
   (1) 1

2. f f e
  (1) 1 1

3. g c f d
  (1) 1 1 0

4. g f d g c d
  (1) 1 1 1 1 0

5. f g e b
  (1) 1 1 1

6. f f b
  (1) 1 1

7. f g f d c
  (1) 1 1 0 1

8. g f e f d
  (1) 1 1 1 0

9. f g f b g d c
  (1) 1 1 0 0 1

B. 1. R f d ≡ P f e f f e
    F 1 1 (F) T 1 1 1 1 1

2. - R g c f d ⊃ (P g e b d ∨ - P f f b c
    T F 1 1 1 0 (T) T 1 1 1 1 T F T 1 1 1 1

3. P g f e f d c ≡ R f g e b
    T 1 1 1 1 1 1 (F) F 1 1 1 1

4. f f f g f c f e = g f e f d
    1 1 1 1 1 1 1 (T) 1 1 1 1 0

5. (g f d g c d = f g f e d) ∨ R f g e b
    1 1 0 1 1 0 T 1 1 1 1 0 (T) F 1 1 1 1

C. 1. $(R g x_0 f c \vee R g x_1 f c) \equiv ((P g y_0 d \supset R y_0) \vee (P g y_1 d \supset R y_1)$
    T 0 0 1 1 T F 1 1 1 1 (T)   F 1 0 0 T T 0   T F 1 1 0 T F 1

2. $(P f x_0 y_0 \vee P g x_0 y_1) \cdot (P g x_1 y_0 \vee P g x_1 y_1)$
    F 1 0 0   T T 1 0 1   T   F 1 1 0   T T 1 1 1

    $\cdot (R g y_0 z_0 \cdot R g y_0 z_1) \vee (R g y_1 z_0 \cdot R g y_1 z_1)$
    (T) T 0 0 0   T T 0 0 1   T   F 1 1 1   F F 1 1 1

3. $((R z_0 \vee P x_0 d) \supset (P z_0 c \vee R f e)) \cdot ((R z_1 \vee P x_0 d)$
    T 0   T F 0 0   T   T 0 1 T F 1 1   T   F 1   F F 0 0

    $\supset (P z_1 c \vee R f e)) \cdot ((R z_0 \vee P x_1 d) \supset (P z_0 c \vee R f e))$
    T   T 1 1 T F 1 1   (T)   T 0   T F 1 0   T   T 0 1 T F 1 1

    $\cdot ((R z_1 \vee P x_1 d) \supset (P z_1 c \vee R f e))$
    T   F 1   F F 1 0   T   T 1 1 T F 1 1

4. $((P f e f d) \supset (R y_0 \cdot P x_0 f y_0) \vee ((P f e f d) \supset (R y_1 \cdot P x_0 f y_1))$
    T 1 1 1 0   T   T 0   T T 0 1 0   T   T 1 1 1 0   F   F 1   F T 0 1 1

    $\vee ((P f e f d) \supset (R y_0 \cdot P x_1 f y_0) \vee ((P f e f d) \supset (R y_1 \cdot P x_1 f y_1))$
    (T)   T 1 1 1 0   T   T 0   T T 1 1 0   T   T 1 1 1 0   F   F 1   F T 1 1 1

5. $(((P\ f\ x_0g\ y_0z_0 \supset -\ -\ R\ g\ x_0z_0) \cdot (P\ f\ x_0g\ y_0z_1 \supset -\ -\ R\ g\ x_0z_1))$

    <u>F</u> 1 0 0 0 0 <u>T T F T</u> 0 0 0   <u>T</u>   <u>F</u> 1 0 0 0 1 <u>T T F T</u> 0 0 1

v $((P\ f\ x_0g\ y_1z_0 \supset -\ -\ R\ g\ x_0z_0) \cdot (P\ f\ x_0g\ y_1z_1 \supset -\ -\ R\ g\ x_0z_1)))$

<u>T</u>   <u>T</u> 1 0 1 1 0 <u>T T F T</u> 0 0 0   <u>T</u>   <u>T</u> 1 0 1 1 1 <u>T T F T</u> 0 0 1

    $((P\ f\ x_1g\ y_0z_0 \supset -\ -\ R\ g\ x_1z_0) \cdot (P\ f\ x_1g\ y_0z_1 \supset -\ -\ R\ g\ x_1z_1))$

<u>T</u>   <u>F</u> 1 1 0 0 0 <u>T F T F</u> 1 1 0   <u>T</u>   <u>F</u> 1 1 0 0 1 <u>T F T F</u> 1 1 1

v $((P\ f\ x_1g\ y_1z_0 \supset -\ -\ R\ g\ x_1z_0) \cdot (P\ f\ x_1g\ y_1z_1 \supset -\ -\ R\ g\ x_1z_1)))$

<u>T</u>   <u>T</u> 1 1 1 1 0 <u>F F T F</u> 1 1 0   <u>F</u>   <u>T</u> 1 1 1 1 1 <u>F F T F</u> 1 1 1

EXERCISES 5.4

1. Universe of Discourse: $\{0, 1\}$; d: 1; R: 1; f: $(0, 1)$, $(1, 0)$; P: $(1, 1)$

$((R\ x_0 \supset P\ f\ f\ x_0d) \cdot (R\ x_1 \supset P\ f\ f\ x_1d))$

  <u>F</u> 0   <u>T F</u> 0 1 0 1   <u>T</u>   <u>T</u> 1   <u>T T</u> 1 0 1 1

$(R\ x_0 \lor R\ x_1)$

  <u>F</u> 0   <u>T T</u> 1

So, $(P\ f\ f\ x_0d \cdot P\ f\ f\ x_1d)$

  <u>F</u> 0 1 0 1 <u>F T</u> 1 0 1 1

2. Universe of Discourse: $\{0, 1\}$; R: 1; P: ; e: 0; d: 0; f: $(0, 1)$;

                                 g: $(0, 0, 0)$, $(1, 0, 0)$

$R\ f\ e\ \cdot\ -\ P\ f\ d\ e$

<u>T</u> 1 0 <u>T T</u> <u>f</u> 1 0 0

$P\ f\ d\ e \supset (R\ f\ g\ x_0d \lor R\ f\ g\ x_1d)$

<u>F</u> 1 0 0 <u>T</u>   <u>T</u> 1 0 0 0 <u>T T</u> 1 0 1 0

So, $-(R\ f\ g\ x\ d \lor R\ f\ g\ x_1d)$

  <u>F T</u> 1 0 0 0 <u>T T</u> 1 0 1 0

3. Universe of Discourse: $\{0, 1\}$; f: $(0, 1)$, $(1, 0)$; R: ; e: 0;

                                P: $(0, 0)$

$((P\ f\ y_0e \supset R\ f\ x_0) \lor (P\ f\ y_1e \supset R\ f\ x_0)) \cdot ((P\ f\ y_0e \supset R\ f\ x_1)$

  <u>F</u> 1 0 0 <u>T F</u> 0 0   <u>T</u>   <u>T</u> 0 1 0 <u>T F</u> 1 0   <u>T</u>   <u>F</u> 1 0 0 <u>T F</u> 0 1

                                       v $(P\ f\ y_1e \supset R\ f\ x_1))$

                                       <u>T</u>   <u>T</u> 0 1 0 <u>T F</u> 0 1

$-R\ f\ x_0\ \cdot\ -R\ f\ x_1$

<u>T F</u> 1 0   <u>T T F</u> 0 1

So, $-P\ f\ y_0e\ \cdot\ -P\ f\ y_1e$

  <u>T F</u> 1 0 0 <u>F F T</u> 0 1 0

EXERCISES 5.5

1. The term <u>gxfa</u> is bound in the formula $\exists xRgxfa$.

2. <u>Pgxdc</u> · <u>Rfgyc</u> has no bound terms. The terms in this formula could be bound in many different ways. If we added <u>for every x</u> to Pgxdc, we obtain <u>(x)</u>Pgxdc. Now, the term <u>gxdc</u> is bound. If we added <u>for every y</u> to Rfgyc, we obtain <u>(y)</u>Rfgyc. Now, the term <u>gyc</u> is bound.

3. <u>Pfgdx</u> $\supset \exists yRfx$ has no bound terms. To make both terms, <u>gdx</u> and <u>fx</u>, bound, we simply add either the quantifier <u>for some x</u> or <u>for every x</u> to the whole formula as follows: <u>(x)</u>(Pfgdx $\supset \exists yRfx$) or $\exists x$(Pfgdx $\supset \exists yRfx$).

4. (x)(Rgyd) $\equiv \exists y$(Pyx Rgxd) has no bound terms. To make <u>gyd</u> a bound term we could change <u>for every x</u> to <u>for every y</u> to obtain

(y)(gyd). To make gxd a bound term, we could change for some y to
for some x to obtain ∃x(Pyx ⊃ Rgxd).

5. (x)(y)(Pfz · Rfgcd) has no bound terms. If we change one of the
quantifiers, either for every x or for every y to for every z,
then the term fz would be bound as follows: (x)(z)(Pfz · Rfgcd)
or (z)(y)(Pfz · Rfgcd).

EXERCISES 5.6

1. 1. (x)(fx = gxx)   As
   2. Pfc   As
   Show Pgcc
   3. fc = gcc   (∀E, 1, x/c)
   4. Pgcc   (=E, 2, 3)

2. 1. (x)(Bx ⊃ ∃yHyfx)   As
   2. ∃xBx · ∃yHyc   As
   3. fx = d   As
   Show ∃yHyd
   4. ∃xBx   (&E, 2)
   5. ∃yHyfx   (∃E, 1, 4)
   6. ∃yHyd   (=E, 3, 5)

3. 1. (x)(Rx ⊃ Pfxfy)   As
   2. Rc   As
   3. fc = x   As
   Show ∃xPxfy
   4. Rc ⊃ Pfcfy   (∀E, 1, x/c)
   5. Pfcfy   (IfE, 2, 4)
   6. Pxfy   (=E, 3, 5)
   7. ∃xPxfy   (∃I, 6, x/x)

EXERCISES 5.7

1. 1. There is a building that is a fire trap.
   2. There is a B that is a I by T Rule 9.
   3. ∃y(y is a [B that is a I] by T Rule 5.
   4. ∃y([B that is a I]y by T Rule 2.
   5. ∃y(By · Iy) by T Rule 8.
2. 1. At most the son of General George Patton is a major.
   2. At most s q is a M by T Rule 9 (in which s is a one-place func-
      tion symbol).
   3. (x)(-(x = sg)) ⊃ -Mx by T Rule 3.
3. 1. If Lewis Carroll is Charles Lutwidge Dodgson, then it is not
      the case that there is one and only one logician.
   2. If l is c, then it is not the case that there is one and only
      one O by T Rule 9.
   3. If l is c, then it is not the case that ∃y(y is the one and
      only O) by T Rule 7.
   4. If l is c, then it is not the case that ∃y(x)((x = y) ≡ Ox)
      by T Rule 4.
   5. If (1 = c), then it is not the case that∃ y(x)((x = y) ≡ Ox)
      by T Rule 1.
   6. If (1 = c), then -(∃y(x)((x = y) ≡ Ox) by T Rule 3 from Chap-
      ter 2.
   7. (1 = c) ⊃ -(∃y(x)((x = y) ≡ Ox)) by T Rule 6 from Chapter 2.

4. 1. There is a $\underline{v}$acuum if and only if there is at most one vacuum and $\underline{s}$pace is the one and only vacuum.
   2. There is a $\underline{V}$ if and only if there is at most one $\underline{V}$ and $\underline{s}$ is the one and only $\underline{V}$ by T Rule 9.
   3. $\exists y(y$ is a V) if and only if there is at most one V and s is the one and only V by T Rule 5.
   4. $\exists y(y$ is a V) if and only if $\exists y($at most y is a V) and s is the one and only V by T Rule 6.
   5. $\exists y(y$ is a V) if and only if $\exists y($at most y is a V) and $(x)((x = s) \equiv Vx$ by T Rule 4.
   6. $\exists yVy$ if and only if $\exists y($at most y is a V) and $(x)((x = s) \equiv Vx)$ by T Rule 2.
   7. $\exists yVy$ if and only if $\exists y(x)(-(x = y) \supset -Vx)$ and $(x)((x = s) \equiv Vx)$ by T Rule 3.
   8. $\exists yVy$ if and only if $\exists y(x)(-(x = y) \supset -Vx) \cdot (x)((x = s) \equiv Vx)$ by T Rule 1 from Chapter 2.
   9. $\exists yVy \equiv (\ y(x)(-(x = y) \supset -Vx) \cdot (x)((x = s) \equiv Vx))$ by T Rule 5 from Chapter 2.

EXERCISES 6.1

The answer to Exercise 1 is given in the book.

The following exercises have more than one solution:

2. To make $(y)(Qyy \equiv Jy \cdot Ky)$ a correct defintion we must add a $\underline{for\ all}$ quantifier and change the variables in the formula in the appropriate places to match the new quantifier. If we add an $\underline{x}$ quantifier, we must also change one of the $\underline{y}$'s in $\underline{Qyy}$ to an $\underline{x}$ and change either $\underline{Jy}$ to $\underline{Jx}$ or $\underline{Ky}$ to $\underline{Kx}$. This will give the correct definition $(x)(y)(Qxy \equiv Jx \cdot Ky)$. $(z)(y)(Qyz \equiv Jy \cdot Kz)$ is also a correct definition.

3. To make $(x)(y)Qxy \equiv Jx \cdot Qyx)$ a correct definition we only need to change the two-place relation symbol in the definiendum to something other than $\underline{Q}$. If we change it to $\underline{P}$ we obtain the correctly formed definition $(x)(y)(Qxy \equiv Jx \cdot Pyx)$.

4. To make $j = gbj$ a correct definition we only need to change the constant $\underline{j}$ in the definiendum to some constant other than $\underline{j}$. If we change it to the constant $\underline{c}$ we obtain the correctly formed definition $j = gbc$.

5. To make $(y)(Qxy \equiv Jx \cdot Ky)$ a correct definition we only need to add a $\underline{for\ all\ x}$ quantifier. Thus, $(x)(y)(Qxy \equiv Jx \cdot Ky)$ is a correctly formed definition.

6. To make $(x)(y)(Qxyz \equiv (Jx \cdot Ky) \cdot Mz)$ a correct definition we need only add a $\underline{for\ all\ z}$ quantifier. Thus, $(x)(y)(z)(Qxyz \equiv (Jx \cdot Ky) \cdot Mz)$ is a correctly formed definition.

Index

NOTES

NOTES

NOTES